Managing Food Hygiene

FR & PERC

Related Macmillan titles

The New Catering Repertoire   H. L. Cracknell and G. Nobis
   Volume 1   Aide-Mémoire du Chef
   Volume 2   Aide-Mémoire du Restaurateur et Sommelier
Practical Professional Catering   H. L. Cracknell, G. Nobis and
                                   R. Kaufmann
Practical Professional Cookery   H. L. Cracknell and R. Kaufmann
Practical Professional Gastronomy   H. L. Cracknell and G. Nobis
Hospitality Management   Sally Messenger and Humphrey Shaw
Healthy Eating: a guide for chefs and caterers   Rob Silverstone

**In the Mastercraft series, published with the Hotel and Catering
Training Company:**

Customercraft: Keeping the Customer Satisfied   Roy Apps
Foodcraft 1: The Dry Processes
Foodcraft 2: The Wet Processes
Mastercraft 1: Working in the Hotel and
                 Catering Industry   Sally Messenger
Mastercraft 2: Health, Hygiene and Safety
                 in the Hotel and Catering Industry   Marion Kenber and
                                         William McCurrach

Professional Masters – all the professional student needs – in a single text:

Basic English Law   W. T. Major
Communication   Nicki Stanton
Company Accounting   Roger Oldcorn
Cost and Management Accounting   Roger Hussey
Employee Relations   Chris Brewster
Management   Roger Oldcorn
Marketing   Robert I. Maxwell
Personnel Management   Margaret Attwood
Study Skills   Kate Williams
Supervision   Mike Savedra and John Hawthorn

Please write to The Sales Department, Macmillan Education, Houndmills,
Basingstoke, Hants, for details of other Mastercraft titles, other Macmillan
textbooks and the current Further and Continuing Education catalogue.

Managing Food Hygiene

Nicholas Johns, BSc, PhD, Cert. Ed., Dip. FE, AMHCIMA
Reader in Hospitality Studies
City College, Norwich

MACMILLAN

First published 1991

Published by
MACMILLAN EDUCATION LTD
Houndmills, Basingstoke, Hampshire RG21 2XS
and London
Companies and representatives
throughout the world

Edited and typeset by Povey/Edmondson
Okehampton and Rochdale, England

Printed in Hong Kong

British Library Cataloguing in Publication Data
Johns, Nicholas
Manging food hygiene
1. Food. Hygiene
I. Title
363.192
ISBN 0–333–54134–0

To the memory of *Michael Allen*, FRCS, who gave me much help and encouragement for this book but sadly did not live to see its publication

Contents

3   Food Commodities, Food Processing and Cooking

6 Food Hygiene and the Management of Plant and Equipment

Introduction

Managing Food Hygiene is intended for management students and managers in the hospitality, catering and retail industries. It explains the problems of food hygiene and discusses how they may be tackled from an operational management point of view. It is designed to function as a textbook for coursework or self-study, as well as being a practical handbook for use at work. The content has been designed to meet the requirements of advanced certificate and diploma courses offered by the IEHO, RSH and RIPHH. The first three chapters are devoted to scientific and technical aspects of food hygiene and cover general hygiene, food microbiology, epidemiology and food technology. Chapter 4 is concerned with the law. Four principal areas of management concern are discussed, in Chapters 5–8 respectively: premises, plant/equipment, personnel and process. Chapter 9 describes how food hygiene is related to policy and strategy in operational management.

An important aim of such courses is to prepare managers to train their own staff. For this reason the section on training in Chapter 7: Food Hygiene and the Management of Personnel is especially detailed, making the book a useful reference source for those who wish to design and deliver hygiene courses.

Managing Food Hygiene will also be a valuable textbook for courses in hospitality, catering and retail management, i.e. degree and BTEC HND courses. The sections dealing with epidemiology, food technology and especially law have been brought up to date by means of an extensive literature search. The book deals with topical issues such as Listeria, BSE and machine recovered meat and explains their relevance to food hygiene management. The structure and influence of the 1990 Food Safety Act and its subsidiary legislation are also discussed.

In addition to this background knowledge, *Managing Food Hygiene* describes what must be done to maintain food safety within food production and sales operations. Uniquely it goes one stage further, illustrating the *management processes* which are required to support such action. Chapters 5–8 discuss in detail the operational management techniques which will undoubtedly be needed if systems such as HACCP (described in detail in Chapter 9) are to be widely adopted by the British hospitality industry.

The inclusion of management material in a book of this type will aid integration of the subject into management degree and Higher National Diploma courses. It may also point the way to curriculum development in this area. This integrated management material should also help to make

Managing Food Hygiene an indispensable handbook for practising managers in the industry.

Using This Book

Managing Food Hygiene is designed for self-study, reference, or for use as a textbook. The following points should be borne in mind.

In order to facilitate **self study** the book has been laid out in sections within chapters. Key words are presented in bold type to emphasize their importance and to aid learning. A glossary is provided at the end, to which the student is urged to refer. Throughout the book there are also short questions, to test comprehension. Students should keep a pencil and paper handy as they study, and should attempt to write down the answer to each question before proceeding through the section. The answer or explanation to each question is incorporated into the text immediately following it. In order to encourage the glossary habit, some of the questions ask the meaning of technical terms. The first two of these refer the student to the glossary.

Each chapter also contains three Study Examples, mostly located at or near the end of sections. Students should allow about 20–30 minutes for answering these examples and again it is a good idea to write the answers down clearly and to check them with the correct solutions. These are given at the back of the book.

Reference use is aided by a comprehensive index. Each section of the book is structured independently, to permit easy reference. However, some aspects require previous knowledge. For example, it may not be possible to fully understand Critical Control Points (Chapter 9) without previously learning about D and z values for bacterial destruction (Chapter 1). The text is cross-referenced to make this easier, but the reader should also make as much use as possible of the glossary and index.

Textbooks are often structured to match the syllabus with which they are intended to be used. This of course cannot be the case with *Managing Food Hygiene*, which is designed to meet the needs of several different syllabuses and teaching styles. Students who wish to use this book as a textbook should first draw up a list of the syllabus items they are required to learn. They should then look these up systematically, making notes as they go. It will frequently be necessary to transfer between chapters. For instance, details of insect and rodent pests are presented in Chapter 1, while the management of pest control is discussed in Chapter 5. Some syllabuses will require the student to put all this information together into one single package of notes. This may seem awkward at first, but it occurs to some extent in every book. The process of making and reorganizing notes is itself a very useful learning process.

Acknowledgements

All books are compilations of the work and experiences of others, and this is no exception. The list of references at the end bears witness to a heavy debt, and gratitude is owing to all those friends, colleagues and students who contributed ideas, read my work, and by discussion helped shape my ideas. Special mention should go to John Staples, Carolyn Owen, Philip Tyas and Jim Jones.

It is impossible to put together such a heterogeneous body of material without the help of librarians. I am deeply indebted to all the library staff at Norwich City College for their endless patience. Mention should also be made of the library staff of Colman Foods Ltd, the Institute of Food Research and the Norfolk and Norwich Hospital, who were kind and helpful whenever I needed them.

Thanks are due to the Computer Services Section at Norwich City College for their help and indulgence with keying in text and keeping the wheels rolling so that everything could be processed, copied and printed.

Finally and most importantly I must thank my wife Helen for tea, sympathy and space during the interminable working hours; my daughter Theresa for reading the typescript and compiling the glossary; and everyone else at home for their patience and forbearance.

NICHOLAS JOHNS

The author and publishers wish to thank the following who have kindly given permission for the use of copyright material:

Elsevier Science Publishers Ltd. for Fig. 8.4 from Milson & Kirk, 'The caterer as a process engineer', in *Advances in Catering Technology*, ed. G. Glew, Applied Science Publishers, 1979.

The Institution of Environmental Health Offices for an extract from R. A. E. North, 'Food contact surface disinfectants: additional criteria for selection', *Environmental Health*, 88(1), pp. 10–14; Fig. 2.5, 'Food epidemiology: gastro-intestinal infections, 1977–1985', *Environmental Health*, 94, 1986; Fig. 3.1, McDowell *et al.*, 'Bacterial microflora of chill-stored beef carcasses', *Environmental Health*, 94(3); Figs 5.2 and 5.3, Mendes, Lynch and Stanley, 'A bacteriological survey of kitchens', *Environmental Health*, 86(10), 1978; and Fig. 5.10, R. P. Robinson, 'Ridding NHS hospitals of serious infestations', *Environmental Health* 95(1), 1987.

Stanley Thornes (Publishers) Ltd. for Fig. 6.6, adapted from D. M. Allen, *Accommodation and Cleaning Services*, Vol. 1, Fig. 47(b), Hutchinson, 1983.

The Talbot Adair Press for Fig. 7.5, from J. Adair, *Training for Leadership*, 1988.

Every effort has been made to trace all the copyright-holders, but if any have been inadvertently overlooked the publishers will be pleased to make the necessary arrangement at the first opportunity.

1 Food Hygiene and General Hygiene

Objectives

To define the terms 'hygiene' and 'food hygiene'. To provide the food premises manager with technical information on food contamination and its prevention, on general hygiene and on pest control. These provide a firm basis for management action and control discussed elsewhere in the book.

Introduction

Hygiene is the science of preserving or promoting health. *Food hygiene* seeks to preserve or promote health by ensuring the safety and wholesomeness of food. An understanding of contamination and how it may be controlled is therefore fundamental to any study of food hygiene. Contamination, the main theme of this chapter, may be caused by physical, chemical or biological agencies. Most important of the biological contaminants are bacteria. They can be controlled by limiting their growth, or by destroying them.

Bacteria and other contaminants are present in dirt and are carried by pests. This chapter provides technical detail about cleaning and cleaning agents, and about pests and pest control agents. Subsequent sections of the book describe strategies for managing these operations in a food production environment.

Types of food contamination

Contamination is anything that threatens the wholesomeness of food. Food hygiene is therefore aimed at eliminating or minimizing contamination. Three main types can occur, all of which endanger human health. These are physical, chemical and biological contamination.

Physical contamination consists of detectable pieces of non-food material (so-called 'foreign bodies') which have found their way into food. They may come from machinery or the environment, from packaging, from personnel or from pests, see Table 1.1:

Table 1.1   Sources and agents of physical contamination

Source	Typical Agent(s)
Machinery/ the environment	Nuts, bolts,screws and metal fittings, paperclips, drawing pins, rust, glass shards, wood splinters, paper or card: old notices and memos, flaking paint, grease smudges and oil drops.
Personnel	Ear-rings and jewellery, buttons, plastic items, i.e. combs, pen tops, clips, chalk or wax crayons, finger nails, hairs, sweet wrappers, foil packages, cigarette ends.
Packaging	Cardboard, plastic wrapping, string, staples.
Pests	Insects, caterpillars and grubs, insect eggs, insect droppings, rat and mouse hairs, droppings and bodies, or body-parts.

Physical contamination is probably the least serious kind from the health point of view. However deaths can occur if consumers choke on large items. Sharp fragments of glass or metal may cause serious injury if they are swallowed. Certain items (particularly the plastic fasteners which are sometimes still used as polythene bag closures) may become lodged in the sphincter valves of the stomach. Such blockages usually have to be removed by surgery. However the general problem with 'foreign bodies' in food is that they are easily noticed by customers and can be traced.

They often become evidence for prosecution, and in any case they are a clear indication of problems with food hygiene management.

Question

What are the sphincter valves of the stomach? (Use the glossary.)

Sphincters are tight closures formed of muscle. The stomach has two sphincters: one by which food enters from the oesophagus, and another leading to the intestines, where the food passes for further digestion. These 'valves' are normally held tightly shut to close off the stomach, but they can be relaxed to allow food in or out.

Chemical contamination consists of poisons, i.e. substances which kill or cause physiological harm when they are ingested. Poisons get into food in two main ways. *Toxins* are biochemical poisons produced by living organisms. Certain species of plants fungi and shellfish naturally contain toxins. Most of these are well-known and can easily be avoided, but bacteria and moulds can also grow in stored or cooked food and produce toxins. This is a danger, because the contaminated food may seem quite wholesome. Natural toxins are dealt with in more detail in Chapters 2 and 3.

Other chemicals and poisons can find their way into food during production, transport or storage. They may come from the food production operation itself, from hygiene or pest control operations, from equipment or from the environment. Sources of natural and artificial chemical contamination are shown in Table 1.2.

Nitrates and nitrites are sometimes used in the kitchen to prepare salted or pickled meats. In small quantities they are regarded as harmless. Misreading the recipe, or mistaking sodium nitrate or nitrite for ordinary salt may result in dangerously high levels in food. Excessive use of other additives may also cause illness to some degree. For instance, mono-sodium glutamate can cause palpitations and hot flushes (the so-called 'Chinese restaurant syndrome').

Weedkillers and pesticides may be inadvertently added to food if they are stored in the kitchen, particularly in unlabelled containers similar to those used for food. All chemicals should be carefully stored and handled. Cleaning products may get into food if they are not rinsed off surfaces or equipment, or if instructions are not followed properly.

Poisoned baits intended for rats, mice or crawling insects may accidentally be added to food during careless handling or horseplay. Pest control baits should always be locked away from food and clearly marked.

Table 1.2   Sources and agents of chemical contamination

Source	Typical Agent(s)
Foods spoiled by bacteria or moulds	Toxins
Certain plants, fungi, fish and shellfish	Toxins
Cooking operations	Nitrates, nitrites
Hygiene operations	Cleaning agents, weedkillers, pesticides
Pest control operations	Rat and mouse poisons, insecticides
Cookware, pipes, equipment	Lead, antimony, copper, aluminium

Lead may be present in cooking water from old pipes, in paints and in white-metal engineering components in food equipment. The capsules of wine bottles are also made of lead. Zinc (from galvanized steel), copper and aluminium may be dissolved from metal buckets or saucepans by acid ingredients, e.g. lemon juice, tamarind or vinegar. Alternatively the tin lining of copper pans may react. Acid foods like rhubarb, apples or tomatoes can also dissolve enough of these metals to contaminate foods. Acids can also dissolve antimony from cheap enamelware. The only completely safe metal for cookware is stainless steel and this should always be used for handling acid foods. Poisonous chemicals may have acute or chronic effects. *Acute effects* are those caused by a few doses, or by one quite large one. The onset of symptoms is usually quite rapid and can easily be traced to the cause. *Chronic* effects are caused by many doses (usually very small ones) over a long period of time. Symptoms may take many years to develop and may seem unrelated to the poison. Thus foods heavily contaminated with heavy metal compounds may cause vomiting, but long-term ingestion of smaller doses may cause degeneration of the nerves and brain and, eventually, death. Aluminium is believed to be implicated in *Alzheimer's disease*, a kind of chronic poisoning which takes the form of premature senility (Prescott, 1989).

Biological contamination is caused by living things present in food. Some of these can invade (infect) the human body from the gut and cause disease when the food is eaten. Such disease-causing organisms are called *pathogens*. Some are so tiny that they cannot be seen except with powerful microscopes. They may be present in large numbers in food without there being any noticeable sign. Examples are *bacteria* and *viruses*. *Parasites*, capable of living in the human body, may also be present in food.

Question
Exactly what does the term pathogen refer to? (See glossary.)

Strictly speaking, a pathogen is anything which is capable of causing a disease. The term is used throughout this book to refer to pathogenic organisms i.e. harmful biological contaminants such as bacteria, viruses or parasites.

Types of pathogen

Bacteria (the word is plural – singular is bacteri*um*) are organisms so small that thousands can be transferred to food from the touch of a moist finger. They live mostly by breaking down dead organic material. Soil and excreted waste from humans and animals are rich in bacteria. It is estimated that about one-third of the dry weight of human faeces (solid excrement) consists of living and dead bacteria. Bacteria are also present in the intestines and on the skins of people and animals. The human stomach and intestines have natural protection against bacterial attack. Sometimes, however, the protection fails. Bacteria cause food poisoning symptoms by irritating the stomach or intestinal lining. In severe infections they may also invade the bodily organs or the bloodstream, causing severe illness. Some species of bacteria produce toxins inside the body. Several species are able to grow and multiply in our food (which is mostly made up of dead organic material). They may produce toxins or simply generate enough cells to overcome the body's defences when the contaminated food is eaten.

Viruses make up another class of pathogens. Those which produce vomiting and diarrhoea attack the cells lining the stomach and intestines, disrupting normal functions and causing illness. Viruses are even smaller than bacteria, and are also easily transferred to food by hands or equipment. But unlike bacteria, viruses cannot grow in food. Viruses may be present in materials touched by infected people or in foods such as shellfish, which have been in contact with sewage.

Parasites are creatures which live inside the bodies of animals or humans, relying on them for food, water and warmth. Human parasites are mostly flat- or round-bodied worms. Almost all are visible to the naked eye, and some are quite large. Parasite eggs are often very small and difficult to see in food. They are usually transferred to food from the skin or faeces of animals or humans. The eggs of several parasite species hatch into larvae, which burrow into the muscle of meat animals. When the meat is eaten the larvae change into the adult parasites in the human intestine.

Relative importance of bacterial food-borne illness

Figure 1.1 shows results from two studies of food-borne illness in the USA (Bryan, 1978) and the UK (Roberts, 1982). Statistics are gathered and processed differently in the two countries. This is why no figures are

Figure 1.1   Causes of food-borne illness in the USA and UK

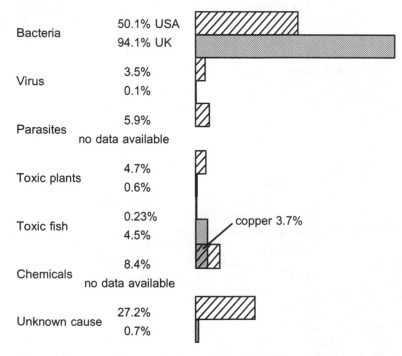

Sources: data from Bryan (1978) and Roberts (1982).

given for parasites or chemicals in the UK. The very different numbers of 'unknown cause' cases are due to differences in classification. By far the largest proportion of food-borne illness is caused by bacteria in both countries. All the types of contamination shown can be fatal, but the usual symptoms are mild to severe vomiting and diarrhoea. Some of the rarer forms of food contamination can cause high fatality rates. This makes it difficult to judge the 'relative importance' of different types of contamination.

Question

Why are bacteria the commonest cause of food-borne illness?

Bacteria multiply readily in food so that, given time, a mild level of contamination can spontaneously become a severe one. Harmful levels of contamination are therefore much more likely with bacteria than with viruses or parasites, which cannot use prepared food as a medium for growth.

Preventing food contamination

The vector/vehicle model

Food-borne illness occurs when a customer or employee eats contaminated food. Food for human consumption is usually processed in some way, by cooking, washing etc. Contaminated processed food is called the *vehicle*, because it carries the food poisoning agent to the customer. Food from a production process can become a vehicle for illness in three main ways:

- A contaminant (a toxin, bacterium, virus or parasite) present in the original uncooked/unwashed food survives the production process.
- Contamination (physical, chemical or biological) is added to the food during the production process.
- Bacteria multiply in the food, so that initially harmless numbers reach harmful levels.

Contamination does not arise spontaneously. Pathogenic bacteria enter the food production process on raw meat and vegetables and on the hands and bodies of employees. These contaminated inputs to the food production process are called **vectors**. Figure 1.2 is a systems diagram of food production from the food hygiene point of view. It shows the following:

Vectors: Materials, objects or living things which carry physical, chemical or biological contamination into the food production/service system.

System: The whole food production/service operation. It may be located all together on one site (restaurant and kitchen together) or it may involve several sites and transport between them, for example a centralized school meals operation.

Vehicle: A particular contaminated food output, responsible for causing disease.

   The objective of food hygiene management is to control the vectors and the production/service system so that contamination of the food output does not occur.

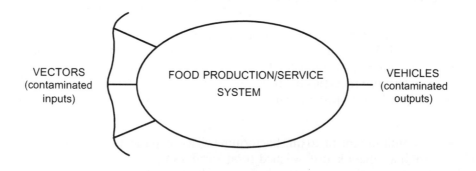

VECTORS
(contaminated
inputs)

FOOD PRODUCTION/SERVICE
SYSTEM

VEHICLES
(contaminated
outputs)

Figure 1.2   Systems model of food production and service

Study example 1.1

Sixty-one guests were ill after a banquet in a large restaurant. They mostly suffered from vomiting, diarrhoea and mild fever. All gave a positive stools analysis for *Salmonella* bacteria. The menu consisted of a starter containing Hollandaise sauce made with fresh eggs; this was followed by roast, stuffed turkey. Both food items were sampled and analyzed by the local Environmental Health Department. The starter contained five *Salmonella* cells per gram, the cooked turkey 1000 cells per gram.

1. What is meant by 'a positive stools analysis'?
2. Which vectors of contamination were involved?
3. Which is the most likely vehicle of food-borne illness here?
4. What probably went wrong to cause this incident?

Preventing Transfer of Contaminants

Physical contaminants usually find their way into food as a result of carelessness. If packaging materials are left about the kitchen, or machines are not regularly cleaned and serviced, particular patterns of contamination may arise. These may be recognized if customer complaints are systematically noted and logged. Occasionally employees may indulge a grudge by deliberately contaminating food with cigarette ends etc. Regular inspections of personnel can eliminate contamination by jewellery and cosmetics. Posters and signs should not be used in the kitchen unless they are robust, firmly fixed and unlikely to tear and fall into food.

Chemical contaminants can usually be controlled by proper use and labelling. For example if sodium nitrite must be used in food it should be kept in a clearly labelled container, away from salt or baking powder, with which it is easily confused. There should be clear, written instructions for its use and some sort of check or safeguard on the quantity used. There should also be clear, written instructions for using cleaning chemicals. Regular inspections should be made where these chemicals have been used, to ensure that any residue has been rinsed away. Copper and aluminium pans should not be used for cooking acid foods. Fruit, vinegar, or foods containing tamarind, tartaric or citric acid, should only be cooked and stored in stainless steel vessels. Waiters should wipe the tops of wine bottles with a moist cloth after removing the lead capsule and before drawing the cork. They should wash their hands between serving fine wines and handling food. Tin from tin cans may produce severe stomach irritation and other gastro-enteric symptoms at concentrations above 250 mg/kg. Tin poisoning can be avoided by rejecting dented or damaged cans and by removing food from the can as soon as it is opened.

Biological contaminants are present in most raw food-stuffs. They may also be transferred to food from humans, pests and pets. *Cross-contamination* means the transfer of bacteria from raw to cooked foods. It occurs when raw and cooked products touch, for example in the refrigerator or freezer. It may also occur when food handlers use the same equipment (for example slicers, mincers, chopping boards or knives) for both raw and cooked foods. Cross-contamination may occur if personnel do not wash between handling raw and cooked foods. It is best avoided by physically separating the handling of raw and cooked products as far as possible.

Humans, pests and pets carry bacteria on their skin and hair and in their mouth, nose and ears. Employees must wear protective clothing and hats and must wash after using the lavatory. A common food contamination route is the faecal–oral route. Bacteria are transferred to the hands when an individual goes to the lavatory and are not removed (due to inadequate washing). Eventually they will be transferred to food and contaminate it.

The human mouth, nose and ears are particularly rich in bacteria. Habits such as smoking, taking snuff or picking the nose or ears transfer bacteria to the hands and to anything that they touch. Individuals with coughs, colds, gastro-intestinal disease or boils may also contaminate food with pathogens. Animals are even more likely to carry bacteria, viruses or parasites. Pets should never be allowed into the kitchen. There should be a continuous programme of pest control.

Question

List the ways (physical, chemical, biological) in which personnel can contaminate cooked food.

Personnel can contaminate food physically, chemically or biologically in the following ways:

Physically: with jewellery, cigarette ends or other items.
Chemically: by carelessness with food additives or cleaning materials.
Biologically: by transferring bacteria from the hands, hair or clothing.

Preventing bacterial growth

Bacteria need certain conditions to grow. If these are not adequately present growth will be slowed or prevented. Controlling bacterial growth in foods means controlling the following growth conditions:

- Time available for growth.
- Temperature at which the food is stored or held.
- Acidity or pH of the food itself.
- Water activity or available water in the food.
- Oxygen in the atmosphere surrounding the food.
- Growth-regulating chemicals: preservatives, antibiotics or the toxins produced by other bacteria.

Time

Time is probably the most important factor in bacterial growth, because given time, most species can grow, even in unfavourable conditions. Bacteria which cause food-borne illness prefer a moist, bland, warm environment neither particularly acid nor alkaline, with the minimum of dissolved salt or sugar. They generally prefer foods rich in protein, such as meat, milk or egg. However, bacteria always need time to grow too. Figure 1.3 shows a typical growth curve for bacteria. The curve starts (at time = 0) with the initial bacterial contamination, from which the culture grows. These bacteria then need time to get used to the constituents of the broth. They need this even if the broth contains the ideal conditions for their growth. This period of adaptation appears as a level portion of the growth curve. It is called the *lag phase* of bacterial growth.

After the lag phase (at point A on the graph) the bacteria begin to grow rapidly. Their population doubles at regular intervals. In the example shown the number of cells doubles every 30 minutes. At this rate one single bacterium will produce two in 30 minutes, four in 1 hour, eight in 1.5 hours and sixteen in 2 hours. In seven hours the one original bacterium would have become 16,384. The 100 bacteria per gram which made up the original contamination would have become 1,638,400. The period during which this rapid doubling occurs is called the *exponential phase* of growth, or sometimes the *logarithmic* or *log phase*. After point B on the graph bacteria start to die until the death rate is as fast as the growth rate. The population curve flattens out and reaches what is called the *stationary phase* of growth. Point C on the graph represents the time when most of the food has been used up, or when waste products

Figure 1.3   Typical bacterial growth curve

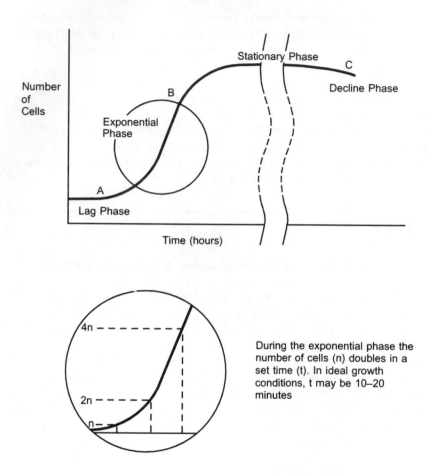

During the exponential phase the number of cells (n) doubles in a set time (t). In ideal growth conditions, t may be 10–20 minutes

produced by earlier growth start to overcome the bacteria. Numbers begin to decrease in what is called the *decline phase*.

Cooked food offers more or less ideal conditions for bacterial growth. It can easily become contaminated, from raw foods, from hands, or from the environment. If enough time is allowed bacteria will go through their lag phase, and exponential growth will begin to occur. Thus time is perhaps the most important control factor in food hygiene.

Study example 1.2

A can of meat is opened at 10.00 am using a wall can-opener. The can-opener is not washed and one day later at 10.00 am it is used to open another can of meat. This can is not used immediately. The contents are emptied out into a clean bowl, which is allowed to stand at the temperature of the kitchen until 6.00 pm. It is then made up into a salad. Guests eat the salad and become ill.

1. Where did the contaminating bacteria come from in the first place?
2. When did these bacteria have their first lag phase?
3. When did exponential growth most probably occur?
4. Why should canned food be transferred to a clean bowl?

Temperature

Temperature is another important factor for controlling bacterial growth and hence food hygiene. Most pathogenic bacteria prefer a temperature range of 20–40°C, i.e. close to that of the human body. However there are pathogen species which can grow anywhere in the range 5–63°C. This is known as the *temperature danger zone*. The ambient temperature of hot kitchens usually provides particularly good growth conditions. Above 63°C the cells are rapidly destroyed. Below 5°C they are not killed but they cannot feed or multiply and just lie dormant (This is a generalization. Some species can grow, slowly, at temperatures below 10°C.)

Bacteria which do best in this temperature range are called *mesophiles* (literally 'middle lovers'). There are also species of bacteria which can withstand high temperatures and grow best in the range 35–80°C. These are known as *thermophiles* (literally 'heat lovers'). None of these cause illness in humans, but they sometimes survive the heat treatment of foods and spoil canned or packaged products. Bacteria which prefer low temperatures are variously called *psychrophiles* ('cool lovers') *psychrotrophs* ('cool feeders') or occasionally *cryophiles* ('cold lovers'). These organisms can grow at temperatures between -8°C and +40°C. Most of the psychrophilic bacteria are harmless and the only damage they do is to slowly spoil foods held in the refrigerator. However in the last few years it has been discovered that some psychrophiles can grow to large numbers in chilled stored foods and will cause severe illness when the food is eaten. *Listeria monocytogenes* is a well-known example of this type.

All bacterial growth slows down in cold conditions. Even pathogenic psychrophiles such as *Listeria monocytogenes* grow only slowly. Therefore refrigeration is a very effective way of controlling bacterial growth in food. Some growth still occurs however, so storage times and stock rotation are very important.

Acidity and pH

Acids tend to inhibit bacterial growth, though they are not so effective against moulds and yeasts. Acids are present in sour-tasting foods: fruits, tomatoes, pickles, vinegar, yoghurt etc. Products containing these items tend to keep better and may be safer from contamination than neutral-tasting foods. The problem for the caterer is that of measuring and controlling acidity. Acidity is measured using a scale called the *pH scale*. The 'p' stands for 'power', because the digits of the pH scale are powers of ten. It is in lower case; the 'H' is a capital, standing for hydrogen. Acidity is caused by substances which release *hydrogen ions* into solution. The pH scale is a measure of the hydrogen ion concentration. For technical reasons the pH scale has 14 points: pH 7.0 is neutral, i.e. neither acid nor alkaline, pH values below 7.0 indicate the presence of acids, and those above 7.0 indicate alkalis. The acidity of foods can be measured using a special pH meter or with impregnated papers which change colour according to the pH.

Such methods are not suitable for kitchen use. The papers are small and it is easy to lose one into food during testing. The probes of pH meters contain glass, which will cause serious physical contamination if broken. However monitoring is not always essential. The use of sour flavourings: vinegar, lemon juice, tamarind or cream of tartar, e.g. in marinades, will help to preserve foods. Most pathogenic bacteria cannot grow at pH 4.5 (the pH of tomatoes and tomato sauces) and hardly any spoilage organisms can grow below pH 3.5 (the pH of wine). However, acidity only *inhibits* bacterial growth; it does not necessarily destroy the bacteria.

Question
A typical recipe for the German dish 'sauerbraten' involves marinading a 3lb piece of beef brisket in a seasoned 1:1 mixture of vinegar and water for up to a week. Is this safe?

Traditional recipes such as *sauerbraten* rely on acidity to check bacterial growth. In this case the vinegar mixture is well below pH 4.5 and penetrates to the centre of the meat. However bacteria may still be able to grow during the marinading period if conditions become warm enough. This can be prevented by keeping the meat refrigerated.

Water activity

Bacteria need moisture to grow. Digestion and breakdown of their food occurs outside the bacterial cells. Very concentrated solutions of salt or sugar draw water out of the cells by the process of *osmosis* and the bacteria may collapse and die. The water in such concentrated solutions is much less available to bacteria. The critical factor for bacterial growth is therefore not how much water is present but what fraction of that water is available. The availability of water is termed the *water activity* and is given the symbol A_w ('A' for activity; 'w' for water). Water activity of a food is defined as:

$$\frac{\text{The vapour pressure of water within the food}}{\text{The vapour pressure of pure water}}$$

This fraction varies from 0, when the food contains no water at all, to 1.00, when the 'food' is pure water. Vapour pressure is a measure of how readily water molecules can escape from the food. If they can vaporize into the atmosphere they must also be available to bacteria.

Pathogenic bacteria prefer A_w values of around 0.99. They cannot usually grow below A_w 0.95 although one species of skin bacteria (*Staphylococcus aureus* – see Chapter 2) can tolerate values down to 0.75. Table 1.3 gives some typical A_w values. It is not practicable to measure water activity in the kitchen. Laboratory facilities are required if it is to be used for controlling bacterial growth. Many preserved foods rely on reduced water activity for their keeping quality. A_w can be reduced by drying, or by adding salt or sugar (see Chapter 3). An understanding of water activity makes it easier to know which foods need special care.

Table 1.3   Typical A_w Values in Foods

Food	A_w value
Pure water	1.00
Fresh meat	0.95–0.99
Fresh bread	0.94–0.97
Cured meat	0.87–0.95
Jam	0.75–0.80
Saturated salt solution	0.75
Flour	0.67–0.87
Granulated sugar	0.19

Air and oxygen

Pathogenic bacteria come into three categories. Those which require oxygen for growth are called *aerobes*. Those which are unable to grow when oxygen is present are named *obligate anaerobes*. A third class, called *facultative anaerobes* are not affected by oxygen one way or the other. Growth of bacteria cannot be prevented simply by excluding air from foods. This would merely encourage the anaerobic species. However vacuum-packing, or packing in an atmosphere rich in oxygen are used to increase the holding time of certain chilled products. These techniques are able to discourage the bacteria species which do the most immediate harm.

Preservatives

Sodium nitrite, *potassium nitrate*, *sulphites*, *sorbates* and *propionates* all inhibit microbial growth when added to food. However bacteria will generally grow eventually, given adequate time, warmth and moisture. Bacteria, fungi and other microorganisms also produce substances which inhibit the growth of other species. Toxins are produced by several species during the decline phase of growth. Some foods produced using bacterial cultures contain natural antibiotics. An example is cheese, which contains a substance called *nisin*, produced by the souring bacteria.

Destroying bacteria

Bacteria are not effectively destroyed by acids, low A_w, or exclusion of air. The only sure way to kill them is with heat. Large numbers are destroyed when the heat is first applied, but the death rate quickly drops. For example, Salmonella requires about 4 minutes at 60°C to reduce its numbers to one tenth (Genigeorgis and Riemann, 1979). If there were originally 1,000,000 *Salmonella* cells per gram of food, there would be 100,000 after 4 minutes at 60°C, 10,000 after 8 minutes and 1,000 after 12 minutes. After a further 12 minutes we would expect 1 bacterium per gram of food to remain. This pattern of bacterial destruction is shown in Figure 1.4. Four minutes at 60°C is the *decimal destruction time* or *D value* for *Salmonella*. The D value is defined as: *the time required, in minutes, for bacterial numbers to fall to a tenth of their value*; or else as *the time, in minutes, for bacterial numbers to fall by 90%*.

Figure 1.4   Thermal destruction of bacterial cells

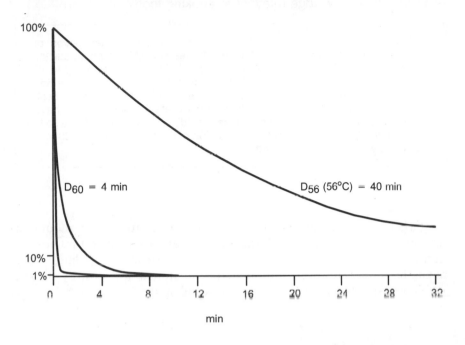

Question
What use is this knowledge for the food production process?

It is as important to destroy bacteria as to prevent their growth. Therefore it is important to know how they can be destroyed. D values permit the numbers of surviving bacteria, and hence the risk of contamination, to be estimated. Decimal destruction times are important in hazard and risk analysis, discussed in Chapter 9.

As the temperature rises, the D value decreases because bacteria are killed more rapidly. But at lower temperatures D values quickly increase. Another measure of bacterial destruction, the *z value*, is defined as: *the temperature rise, in degrees centigrade, which will reduce the D value to one tenth its former value*. Most *Salmonella* species have a z value of 4–5°C . This means that if it takes 4 minutes to destroy 90% of the bacteria at 60°C, it will take 40 minutes if the temperature drops to 56°C (i.e. 4°C; one z value lower). One z value higher, i.e. 64°C it will only take 0.4 minutes to kill 90% of the *Salmonella* organisms. Destruction curves for *Salmonella* at these different temperatures are shown in Figure 1.4.

Question
How is this knowledge relevant to cooking food?

> A few degrees difference in temperature may mean the destruction of virtually all the bacteria or only a few. Heat does not kill bacteria as quickly in fatty or sugary foods. In chocolate or egg yolk, D values may be up to 10 times greater than in plain water. Moderate temperatures, in the range 55–65°C may not be enough to kill bacteria in these foods. This can be critical, because chocolate, egg and other fatty and sweet emulsions usually have to be heated very carefully to prevent them curdling. On the other hand salty and acid foods tend to hasten the destruction of bacteria and may reduce D values; z values are not affected.

Bacteria in food are only effectively destroyed by heating throughout to a temperature of at least 65°C and holding at this temperature for 30 minutes or more. This will usually reduce any bacterial population to a negligible level. However, although this treatment will destroy all the viable growing bacterial cells it does not kill spores.

Spores

Several species of bacteria react to adverse conditions by encapsulating some of their cell contents within a hard, resistant shell to form *spores* These remain dormant until conditions become suitable for further growth. Then they germinate and form normal bacterial cells again. Bacterial spores, also called *endospores* ('inside spores', because they form inside the bacterial cell), are very heat resistant. They may have D values of several minutes even at 100°C. Complete destruction of spores is only achieved by pressure-cooking for 20–30 minutes i.e. in moist heat temperatures of up to 120°C. Spores are stimulated by the shock of being heated. Those that do not die during cooking germinate quickly as soon as their environment has cooled enough. In theory heating to boiling, allowing to cool and then boiling again will often kill spore-forming bacteria. However this is not practically applicable in the kitchen. Spores are protected by oils and fats, which stop the moist heat getting to them. Fatty or oily foods should be shaken or agitated during heat processing so that all the spores come into contact with water and are destroyed.

Summary – Food Hygiene

Food hygiene consists of preventing bacterial contamination and growth in food. Contamination is carried into the production system by vectors. Bacteria may produce toxins or infect customers. The most effective way to prevent contamination is to control times and temperatures of food storage. However the acidity, water activity, oxygen environment and preservative content of foods also plays a part. Food hygiene also involves ensuring that foods are thoroughly cooked. Bacteria can generally be destroyed quite quickly at temperatures above 60°C but some food constituents protect them and some species form resistant spores.

General hygiene

An important part of food hygiene is general hygiene, the basis of which is the process of *cleaning*. Cleaning is important because even microscopic particles of dirt can harbour bacteria. Systematic cleaning is necessary to remove all dirt and contaminating bacteria. Food hygiene is concerned with the cleaning of hands, utensils, equipment, protective clothing, plant and the food production/service environment.

Types of dirt and soiling

The cleaning process aims to remove dirt and soiling from objects, surfaces etc. The main categories of dirt and soiling are:

- Waste food residues.
- Fats, oils and grease.
- Litter, packaging, paper.
- Dust, grit.
- Corrosion and tarnish.

Waste food residues provide opportunities for food poisoning bacteria to multiply. They may already be contaminated from raw foodstuffs or from the mouths and hands of employees or customers. If waste comes into contact with cooked food or with the hands of food handlers, contamination will result.

Fats, oils and grease may be spilt on floors, equipment or clothing. They bind dust, dirt and bacteria. Grease from machinery can be transferred to food directly, or via clothes and equipment, causing physical contamination.

Litter, packaging and paper can also physically contaminate food. If items must be unwrapped near food production or service, this should be done without tearing or scattering the packaging materials. Litter should be rapidly and efficiently removed from kitchens, stores etc.

Dust is made up of fine particles in the range 0.5–20 micrometres across. The composition of dust is roughly as shown in Table 1.4.

Table 1.4 Composition of dust

Constituent	Typical % composition by weight
Silica and other minerals	50
Human/animal hair and sputum	12
Cellulose (from paper and fabric)	12
Resins, gums, starches	10
Fats, oils grease etc.	6
Gypsum (particles of plaster)	5
Moisture	3
Protein, bacteria, spores	2

Source: Allen (1983).

Dust is always present in the air and therefore continually contaminates uncovered food, utensils, plant and clothing.

Grit consists of particles larger than 20 micrometres across. It enters buildings on clothing or footwear and tends to contain more mineral matter: sand, metallic granules etc. than dust. Like dust it generally contains bacteria.

Corrosion and tarnish are produced when oxygen or sulphur compounds in the atmosphere react with metals. Neither silver nor copper react directly with acids, but tarnish from both these metals will dissolve in acids, producing poisonous solutions. Aluminium and the zinc from galvanized items both oxidize in air. These metals also react directly with acid foods.

The cleaning process

Cleaning processes for equipment, premises, utensils, clothing etc. all have five basic stages. These are:

- Preparation or pre-cleaning.
- Cleaning operation.
- Rinsing.
- Disinfection.
- Drying.

The five stages vary in relative importance depending upon what is being cleaned. Sometimes two stages may be accomplished at the same time. To understand any cleaning operation it is necessary to identify all five.

Preparation and pre-cleaning may involve dismantling equipment ready for cleaning. Removal of loose dirt such as plate waste (prior to dishwashing) or litter (prior to cleaning a floor) also comes under this heading. Soaking heavily-soiled garments in water or a 'biological', protein-digesting prewash agent is another example of a pre-clean.

Question
When might a pre-clean not be strictly necessary?

When items are not heavily soiled a preclean may not be absolutely necessary. For example, chefs' whites may not need soaking if they are not stained or badly soiled. Plates may not always need to be scraped clean of waste. However pre-cleaning should be allowed for, as there is always a possibility that it may be needed.

The cleaning operation removes dirt, usually with water and a detergent. Most dirt and soiling consists of particles of food, dust etc. which have become attached to a surface by dried starch, grease or oil. Hot water will soften and remove starch-bound dirt. Water alone will only remove grease-bound dirt if the temperature is above about 80°C. This is too hot for handling and not very efficient. Soap or detergents are used to help the removal of grease. For example, sanitizers and liquid cleaners are used for cleaning kitchen surfaces, and soap for hand washing. It is always best to use hot water, even when detergents are used, but temperatures of 50–60°C are adequate and are not too hot to handle. Dirt that is bound by resinous material such as burned-on residues of cooking oil, may need to be cleaned with an abrasive detergent such as scouring powder. Some dirt is bound by proteins rather than by grease and this can be removed by protein-digesting enzymes. 'Biological' washing powders and pre-wash formulations contain these enzymes.

Rinsing aims to remove the traces left after cleaning. The cleaning operation should loosen all dirt that is bound by starch, grease, resins or protein. This dirt then remains suspended in the cleaning water, together with detergent and other residues. Rinsing with clean water removes these residues so that they are not re-deposited on the cleaned article. The most efficient way to rinse is to use several small batches of water or running water. A single, large batch of rinse water becomes contaminated with dirt and detergent so the articles never become completely clean. Cleaning temperatures generally have to be low enough for hand contact. Temperatures for removing protein-bound dirt are even lower, as enzymes are destroyed by heating above 40°C. Thus although cleaning removes the dirt it does not kill bacteria.

Disinfection is required in order to destroy bacteria which survive the cleaning process. Disinfection is usually carried out by heating or by using chemicals such as bleach. Heat disinfection is often employed in dishwashers, for instance, which spray utensils with water at 85°C after the main wash. Thus they disinfect at the same time as they rinse. *Chemical disinfectants* are often used in lavatories and in the dirty areas in kitchens. Chemicals, like heat, do not kill bacteria immediately. They need time to act, called the *contact time*. Disinfectants may be inactivated by waste food materials, by the fabric of cleaning cloths and by the materials of some surfaces. Bleach attacks cloths, some plastics, and metal fittings. Many disinfectants will taint food and sometimes a second rinse is necessary to remove traces.

Drying is required because wet objects tend to attract bacteria. Dust also adheres to them and water acts as a medium for bacterial transfer and growth. Drying may be by evaporation or with a towel. Hot, recently sterilized objects can be allowed to dry by evaporation. Some dish-washing systems use a stream of warm air. However articles which are left uncovered for any length of time will pick up bacteria and dust. Towel-drying is quick and efficient. It allows the minimum opportunity for re-contamination but the towel itself must be very clean. Disposable paper towels are very effective but care must be taken that torn pieces of paper do not become a source of physical contamination.

Detergents

Detergents have two main properties. They lower the surface tension of water and they suspend or emulsify grease and dirt. Molecules of water attract one another strongly so that water behaves as if there were a tight, elastic skin over its surface. This effect is known as *surface tension*. Surface tension prevents water from removing blobs of grease from dirty objects. The water is simply unable to get under the grease and lift it off. If the grease does come loose, by physical agitation for instance, the water is unable to hold it in suspension. The surface tension of the water tends to push the particles of grease together again so they recombine into blobs.

Detergents contain substances called *surfactants* or *surface active agents*. At one end of each surfactant molecule is a group of atoms which are attracted to water. This is called the *hydrophilic* (water seeking) group. The remainder of the molecule is repelled by water, but attracted by oil, grease or fat. This is the *hydrophobic* (water hating) part of the molecule. Figure 1.5 shows surfactant molecules as 'tadpoles' with hydrophilic 'heads' and hydrophobic 'tails'. When the surfactant is mixed with water the molecules cover the surface. The hydrophilic 'heads' remain in the water and the tails project into the air. This interferes with the mutual attraction of water molecules at the surface and lowers the surface tension. Surfactant molecules also cover the boundary between water and blobs of grease. Agitation and scrubbing further breaks up the grease, and each new grease/water interface becomes covered with surfactant. Tiny grease droplets are formed which do not coalesce into blobs again because of mutual repulsion of the hydrophilic groups in their surfaces. Hydrophilic groups may contain a negative electrical charge, a positive electrical charge, no electrical charge, or both positive and negative. Surfactants containing these different types of hydrophilic group are referred to respectively as *anionic*, *cationic*, *non-ionic* and *amphoteric surfactants*.

Anionic surfactants contain a negatively-charged hydrophilic group. They have powerful detergent action but may be affected by hard water. Examples are soap, soapflakes, detergent washing powders and dish-washing powder formulations.

Cationic surfactants contain a positively-charged hydrophilic group. They are unaffected by hard water but are only weak detergents. Unlike anionic surfactants, cationics have disinfectant properties. They are used as skin disinfectants (e.g. antiseptics such as 'Savlon') and occasionally as sanitizers. Fabric softeners such 'Comfort' are also based on cationic surfactants.

Figure 1.5   Surface active agents – mechanism

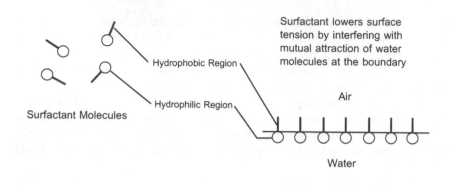

Surfactant lowers surface tension by interfering with mutual attraction of water molecules at the boundary

Hydrophobic Region

Hydrophilic Region

Surfactant Molecules

Air

Water

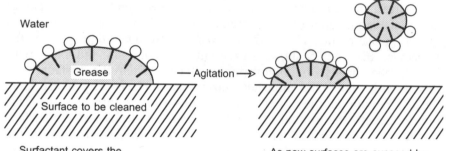

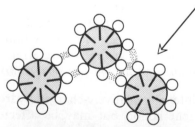

Water

Grease

— Agitation →

Surface to be cleaned

Surfactant covers the grease/water boundary

As new surfaces are exposed by agitation the surfactant covers them

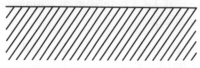

Grease droplets are formed which do not coalesce, because repulsion of the hydrophilic groups holds them apart

Non-ionic surfactants contain no electrical charge. Instead the hyrophilic group contains oxygen or nitrogen atoms which attract water. Non-ionics have quite strong detergent power and are used in washing-up liquids such as 'Fairy Liquid'. 'Solvent' washing powders such as 'Drive' contain both anionic and non-ionic surfactants in the same formulation.

Amphoteric surfactants contain both a positive and a negative charge. They combine good cleaning power with disinfectant action and are used in clear-liquid sanitizer formulations such as 'Tego 51'.

Detergent formulations

Commercial cleaning products usually contain several other constituents in addition to surfactants. Formulations usually vary widely, depending on their end use. The following are typical constituents.

Abrasives are added to formulations for scrubbing or polishing surfaces. Pumice, fly ash, Fuller's earth or chalk may be used depending on how harsh a cleaning action is required. Scouring powders may also contain chlorine compounds to kill bacteria.

Disinfectants are incorporated into some liquid soaps for washing hands. Sanitizers are formulations for cleaning and disinfecting surfaces, and they always contain a disinfectant as well as their surfactant properties.

Sequestering/chelating agents such as phosphates are added to washing powders (e.g. 'Daz') to bind the calcium ions present in hard water. This allows the anionic surfactant to be more effective.

Builders or *fillers* are added to bulk out some cheaper powders.

A bleaching agent, in the form of **Sodium perborate** is added to most washing products such as 'Daz' and 'Persil'. It reacts with water at temperatures above 80°C to produce hydrogen peroxide, which does the actual bleaching.

Enzymes are added to break down protein that binds dirt to clothing. They are commonly used as prewashes, such as 'Bio-Tex'. Enzymes are inactivated by temperatures grater than 40°C. The enzymes in 'biological washing powders' are in fact destroyed by most washing conditions before they can have any effect. However, since 1984, 'New Persil Automatic' has contained a special **catalyst** which enables the production of hydrogen peroxide from perborate at temperature below 60°C.

The enzyme and bleach may then work in the same wash, but it is doubtful whether bacteria are killed at these low temperatures.

Alkalis are frequently used in formulations for cleaning dirty areas in the kitchen. Alkalis react with fats and grease in a process called *saponification*. This produces soap-like materials which actually assist the cleaning process. Alkalis are powerful poisons and skin irritants. They should never be used near food or on food utensils as they are generally poisonous and also taint.

Question

Name the alkalis commonly used for cleaning kitchens.

> Alkalis are common domestic chemicals as well as ingredients in cleaning agents. The commonest ones are **caustic soda** (sodium hydroxide), used for cleaning drains and blocked sinks. **Washing soda** (sodium carbonate) is present in many cleaning formulations, as is **ammonia**.

Disinfectants

Heat is not a convenient way to disinfect bulky objects, heat-sensitive articles, or items which cannot be heated completely through. Thorough cleaning, followed by treatment with chemical disinfectant is usually the most effective procedure and should be carried out regularly. **Sanitizers**, which combine the two operations in one, can be used to 'clean-as-you go' during food production/service. Chemical disinfectants should conform to British Standard 2462:1961. The most commonly used chemical disinfectants are as follows.

Chlorine and chlorine compounds react vigorously with organic matter. They destroy bacteria rapidly but are themselves rapidly destroyed if there is much waste food, blood, excreta, soap or other organic material about. Chlorine compounds react with water to produce 'available' chlorine which is the active disinfectant. Chlorine may damage metals, fabrics and some plastics. It kills all types of bacteria, viruses and moulds. Examples of chlorine disinfectants are bleach, 'Milton' and the **chloramines**. The latter are used in low temperature dishwashing formulations to ensure sterilization. 'Chlorine bleach' (**sodium hypochlorite**) is highly poisonous and can react with foods, causing taints. Solid chlorine compounds (chloramines and **dichloroisocyanurates**) are more suitable for disinfecting food handling equipment.

Iodophors are compounds of a non-ionic surfactant plus iodine. They destroy a wide spectrum of bacteria, viruses and moulds and act rapidly, like chlorine. Chlorine compounds, particularly bleach, are alkaline but iodophors are moderately acid. The latter are therefore milder and less poisonous, although they are more expensive. Iodophors are inactivated by organic waste and by some plastics. They taint food if they come in contact with it and if not well rinsed they may leave a brown stain.

Question
For which applications are iodophors particularly suitable?

Iodophors are most appropriate for use in dairies and similar operations. It must be possible to rinse down everything well after disinfection, to prevent staining and tainting.

Cationic surfactants include **quaternary ammonium compounds** (**QACs**), *diguanides*, and mixtures of the two. QACs are available as odourless, colourless solutions. This makes them attractive for where food is being prepared. QACs have a limited spectrum of activity. Several species of food spoilage bacteria can actually grow in the disinfectant, and most spores survive. Cationic detergents may be inactivated by anionic detergents such as soap or washing powder. They are very easily inactivated by organic materials; wood and cellulose sponges render them ineffective and so does any kind of food or organic waste.

Diguanides such as **chlorhexidine** are only used as skin disinfectants. They have a slightly wider spectrum of activity than QACs but some bacteria can still grow in their presence. Mixtures of diguanides and QACs are also used for skin disinfection. It has been claimed that the two are *synergistic*, i.e. the mixture is more potent than either of the single constituents. Both diguanides and QACs are expensive.

Amphoteric surfactants (sometimes also called **amphotensides**) are used in clear liquid products such as 'Tego 51'. They combine beneficial properties of both cationic and anionic surfactants. Amphotensides are strong surfactants but also have a wide spectrum of activity against bacteria, moulds and viruses. This makes them particularly suitable for use as sanitizers. Amphotensides leave a colourless, odourless disinfectant residue on surfaces after use, which continues to work for days after application (Edelmeyer, 1982). Amphoteric surfactants are almost as easily inactivated by organic matter, fabric etc. as cationic surfactants. They are also relatively expensive. Despite these drawbacks they are a very attractive class of disinfectants for food use.

Phenol derivatives such as *'Jeyes' Fluid'*, *'Lysol'*, *'Dettol'*, *pine fluids* etc. have a good spectrum of activity. However all are liable to taint food by contact. Food may even become tainted from the vapour through being in the same room. For this reason phenolic disinfectants should never be used near food production, storage or service.

Study example 1.3

'In the worst case, from deciding that a surface needs disinfection, a further 23 decisions may have to be correctly made before disinfection can be guaranteed.
[a] Using a plain white powder, one must first decide whether or not the particular powder is a sanitizer and not something else.
[b] Secondly, decisions have to be made as to which dosage rate must be employed, as this varies with the soil load of the surface
[c] then the actual dose relative to the container volume used must be decided. Decisions must follow on [d] the type and the cleanliness of the container, [e] the type and soil loading of the cloth used and whether the water temperature is sufficient, both initially and while in use.' (North, 1980, p.12)

1. (i)   What are the alternatives to using a 'plain white powder' [a] ?
   (ii) How can the employee be helped to make this decision [a]?
2. How can the responsibility of decisions [b] and [c] be lifted from the cleaning operative?
3. The point [d] in the passage refers to the fact that sometimes sanitizer batches might be mixed up in saucepans, even dirty saucepans. What are the problems with this?
4. Why, at [e], is cloth type and soil loading important?

Summary – cleaning

Do

- Clean in five stages: pre-clean, main clean, rinse, disinfect, dry.
- Select detergents carefully, as they are formulated to specific needs.
- Use hot water, at the highest temperature the situation will allow.

- Rinse in several separate stages or with running water.
- Select disinfectants carefully.
- Disinfect in a separate step as far as possible.

Do not

- Use phenolic disinfectants in food premises.
- Use sanitizers (mixed detergent/disinfectant formulations) for the only regular disinfection. They *are* suitable for 'clean as you go' routine during the working period.

Pests and pest control

Pests are unwanted animals or insects which depend wholly or in part on human food for their nutrition. When they take food they often leave behind hairs, body parts, bodies, droppings, urine or saliva. Some insect species actually live *in* the food, contaminating it with eggs, larvae, larval webs etc. Pests are responsible for the spread of food-borne illness. In addition, their physical presence may be discovered by customers, leading to legal action. Pests also damage buildings, furniture and fittings in various ways. There are four main pest classes:

- Rodents: rats and mice.
- Crawling insects: cockroaches, ants, silverfish.
- Flying insects: houseflies, wasps, fruit flies.
- Commodity insects: booklice, mites, plus various moths, beetles and weevils.

Rodents

Rats

Two species of rat are found in Great Britain. The **brown rat** (*Rattus norvegicus*) is by far the most common. It has a blunt nose and small ears and the tail is shorter than the head plus body combined (see Figure 1.6). It grows quite large; up to 500 grams if the food supply is adequate. It is a good swimmer and frequents sewers, streams and canals as well as buildings. Brown rats burrow and nest in the ground, often beneath the

30

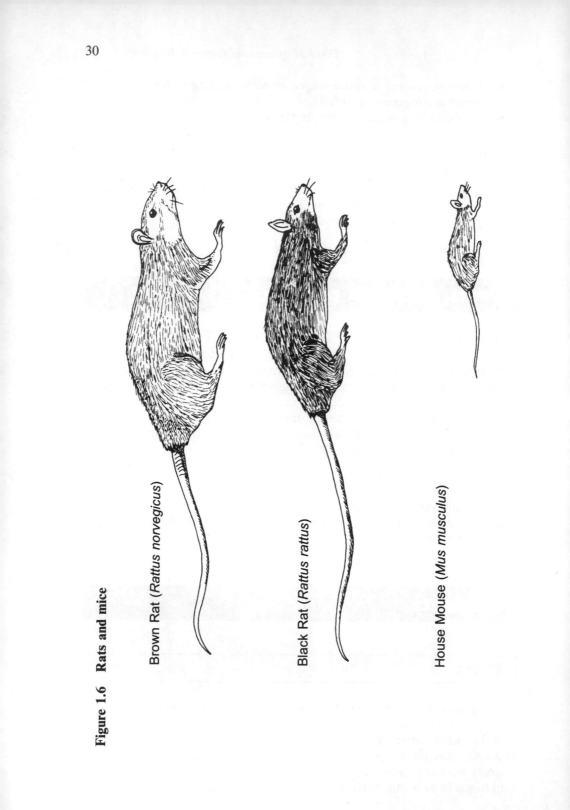

Figure 1.6 Rats and mice

Brown Rat (*Rattus norvegicus*)

Black Rat (*Rattus rattus*)

House Mouse (*Mus musculus*)

suspended floors of buildings. From this area they forage, usually returning again and again to one single food store. They will eat most foods but prefer grain and cereals.

The **black rat** (*Rattus rattus*) is virtually only found in seaport towns. It has a darker back and lighter underbody than the brown rat. Its nose is more pointed and its ears larger (see Figure 1.6). The tail is usually longer than the combined head and body. The black rat is slightly smaller than the brown; about 300 grams is the maximum body weight. It is a good climber and tends to live and nest in roof spaces and the upper floors of buildings. Black rats tend to roam more widely than brown rats and may obtain their food from several widespread locations. Their preference is for vegetables and fruit.

Both species of rat require sources of food and water. They visit rubbish tips as well as stores of human food, transferring contamination from one to the other. Rat populations act as a reservoir for many serious diseases, the best known being **bubonic plague**. The blood, urine and other liquid secretions of rats carry the *Leptospirae* bacteria which cause **Weil's disease**. This can be contracted by touching rats or rat runs with bare hands, or from water where rats have been. It is fatal if not diagnosed early. Like other rodents rats have a need to gnaw. Their front teeth grow continuously and cause them problems unless steadily worn away. Rats will gnaw woodwork, electrical fittings and even lead water pipes. Considerable damage may result through fires and floods.

Question

How can specialists detect which species of rat is present?

It is easier to control rat infestations if the species is known. Specialists identify rat species by the way they forage and nest and by their foot and tail prints. Brown rats can often be detected by the presence of well-frequented runs.

Mice

The **house mouse** (*Mus musculus*) is the species commonest in buildings, though the **long-tailed field mouse** (*Apodemus sylvaticus*) occasionally comes into buildings during cold weather. House mice have a pointed nose and large ears. The tail is much longer than the head and body (see Figure 1.6). House mice are generally grey with a lighter coloured underbody. Field mice are pale, reddish-brown above, also with a whitish underbody. Mice are much smaller than rats, and seldom attain a body weight more than 20 grams. They do not roam far in search of food. They make their nests in warm, dry places using gnawed scraps of paper, fabric, leather or other soft materials. Stored books, linen, feathers etc. may be badly damaged. Mice do not need a supply of water as long as moisture is present in their food. They nibble at and spoil many different types of food while foraging, but they do most damage to grain and cereals.

Recognition and treatment

Rodents leave droppings, gnaw-marks and nests. Brown rats tend to frequent the same run for a long time. Eventually they leave greasy smudges as they brush against obstacles along the way. Foods eaten by rats and mice are unmistakable; packaging is gnawed away and food and droppings scattered about. Tracking powder such as talc, chalk or flour may be used to identify types of rodents from tail and foot prints. This will also show foraging patterns. Rodents are usually controlled with baits, traps or contact dust.

Baits combine a **rodenticide** (rodent poison) with some attractive food. Only scheduled, 'humane' poisons may be used. Baits are often placed in enclosed boxes so that they offer less danger to personnel or domestic animals. Boxes also make rats and mice feel more secure and more likely to take the bait.

Traps are used to identify pest species, or to catch individual survivors from a baiting programme. They may be boxes which imprison the live animal, spring-loaded devices which kill when triggered or sticky boards which catch the animals' fur.

Contact dust containing a rodenticide is sprinkled along runs so that rats pick it up on their feet and fur. The animals ingest it when they hold food in their paws or groom themselves. Contact dust should not be used near food handling processes.

Rodenticides

Three main types of poison are currently permitted as rodenticides: **anticoagulants**, **calciferol** and **anaesthetics**.

Anticoagulants prevent the blood of mammals from clotting. They cause rodents to bleed from the nose, mouth and joints, or from the slightest wound. Anticoagulants are derived from the chemical **dicoumarin**.

Warfarin was the first such derivative, but most mice and several rat populations are now resistant to it. Currently *difenocoum* is used instead, and others may need to be developed.

Calciferol (vitamin D) is poisonous to mammals in excess, because it disrupts calcium metabolism. In rodents it causes functional disruption of the nervous system, liver, kidneys and bones. There are no calciferol-tolerant rat populations.

Anaesthetics such as *alphachloralose* cause rats and mice to fall asleep away from their nests. In this condition their small bodies rapidly lose heat and they die of hypothermia. Anaesthetics are more effective against mice and the smaller individuals among a rat population.

All these classes of rodenticide are poisonous to humans. Great care should be taken not to let them come into contact with food. However, humans would normally survive moderate doses. Illness and inconvenience are more likely to result from accidental poisoning, than fatality.

Crawling insects

Cockroaches

There are hundreds of cockroach species worldwide. Only two of these, the Oriental cockroach and the German cockroach, are widespread in the UK. Certain of the other species have been observed in ports and occasional specimens may escape from laboratories. Cockroaches prefer a constant temperature of 25–30°C. Buildings which are allowed to get cold in winter are seldom infested. However the eggs and possibly some dormant adults may survive cold conditions.

The *oriental cockroach* (*Blatta orientalis*) resembles a large (about 25 mm), black or dark brown beetle, with a flattish body and stubby, vestigial wings (see Figure 1.7). It cannot fly but will crawl through extremely small gaps and up vertical surfaces, provided they are not glossy. It requires moisture and frequently congregates near patches of condensation or near drains. The eggs are laid in a capsule, called the *ootheca* which the female attaches to some solid object. Cockroaches usually enter buildings in unhatched oothecae attached to packing cases or furniture. From these hatch tiny, transparent *nymphs*, replicas of the adult. These shed successive shells as they grow into adults. There is no larval or caterpillar stage.

The *German cockroach* (*Blattella germanica*) is smaller than the oriental cockroach and only grows to about 15 mm long. It too is flat-

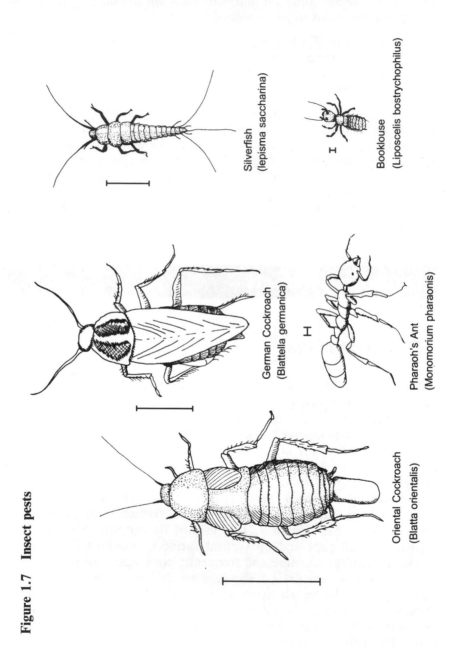

Figure 1.7 Insect pests

bodied and is pale brown in colour, with two distinguishing dark bands on the front part of the thorax (the *promotum*) (see Figure 1.7). The German cockroach has quite large, clear wings and can fly, or at least glide away when threatened. It can climb up very smooth surfaces, and may be found clustered around drops of condensation on painted walls. Like the oriental cockroach it needs moisture and warmth and it feeds on any waste food or rubbish which is left about.

Recognition and treatment

Cockroaches hide away in crevices and behind equipment during the day. They can be seen scuttling away if the light is suddenly switched on at night or if they are disturbed during the day e.g. by something being moved. They leave faecal pellets and fragments of moulted shell about. Established groups of cockroaches have a characteristic unpleasant, rancid smell.

Cockroaches may carry bacteria, parasite eggs etc. straight to human food. Therefore they should be destroyed. Traps can be used to monitor infestation. These usually consist of small cardboard boxes containing an attractive food and lined with a sticky substance to catch the insects. Modern types of trap may be impregnated with substances called *pheromones*. These are powerful sex attractants produced by the female insects. Such traps can detect very low infestation levels. Under certain circumstances they may also be able to remove all the males or all females so that the pest population dies out completely. Baits containing an attractive food plus *sodium fluoride* or *boric acid* can also be used against cockroaches. Other procedures include spraying with phosphate ester insecticides such as *fenitrothion*. Alternatively, infested areas may be painted with a lacquer containing a long-term insecticide. *Lindane* or *diazinon* are commonly used.

Ants

The *black (or garden) ant* (*Lasius niger*) is a small ant, about 2 mm in length. It nests outside buildings but trails of ants often enter and raid food supplies. They prefer fruit and sweet, sugary foods. They are normally controlled with a solution of boric acid in sugar syrup. The ants take this back to the nest to feed their larvae, which then die. Insecticidal sprays, powders or lacquer may also be used but should be kept well away from foods.

Pharaoh's ant (*Monomorium pharaonis*) is a pale golden colour, also about 2 mm in size (see Figure 1.7). It needs a constant, warm temperature and only survives in buildings with permanent central heating. It may make quite long journeys from the nest to its food source. Pharaoh's ant prefers sweet syrups and high protein foods such as meat or liver. The most effective means of control is by baiting with small pieces of food containing **methoprene**. This is an insect growth regulator which prevents the brood developing. Eventually the whole nest dies. Methoprene is harmless to humans and pets.

Silverfish (*Lepisma saccharina* or *L. domestica*) are insects with flexible, silver-coloured bodies tapering off toward the tail. The head bears long antennae and the tail, bristles (see Figure 1.7). They require access to moisture and often live in washrooms or in moist parts of the kitchen. Silverfish do not usually contaminate cooked food. They tend to live on the minute scraps that get swept into corners etc. They can be controlled with insecticidal sprays or lacquers.

Flying insects

'Blow-flies'

Four species of flies commonly lay their eggs in prepared and waste food. They are:

Common housefly	(*Musca domestica*)
Bluebottle flies	(*Calliphora erythrocephala* or *vomitoria*)
Greenbottle flies	(*Lucilia sericata* and *Dasyphora cyanella*)
Lesser housefly	(*Fannia canicularis*)

These flies have no jaws. They all feed by vomiting digestive enzymes on to solid food, trampling the food to soften it, and then sucking up the digested material through a special mouth tube or proboscis. When blow-flies feed on rubbish they pick up bacteria, parasite eggs etc. Thus their feet become highly contaminated and pathogens may survive in their digestive tract. The flies then contaminate anything on which they subsequently walk or feed. Blow-flies lay clusters of small, white elongated eggs on raw or cooked food, especially on meat. The eggs hatch into **maggots** (**larvae**) which eat the food and grow to almost 10 mm in length. When fully grown the maggots encase themselves in a reddish brown **pupa** case. During this dormant phase the larvae change into adult flies which eventually emerge from the pupa cases. The life cycle takes about three weeks in warm weather but eggs, pupae and dormant adult flies can survive right through the winter too.

Question
Why are 'blow-flies' so called?

The eggs of these six fly species are visible as tiny white specks. In the past they were thought to be dust particles 'blown' on to the meat by the beating of the flies' wings. Food bearing the little clumps of eggs is still referred to as 'fly-blown' and the flies as 'blow flies'.

Fruit flies

Drosophila species are small flies 2–3 mm in length. Their life cycle is similar to that of blow-flies but they prefer liquid foods such as syrups, fruit juices and wine. These products do not commonly contain pathogenic bacteria. Fruit flies do carry spoilage bacteria and yeasts, but they are not a serious hazard to human health.

Wasps

The wasp (*Vespa vulgaris*) is attracted to human foods and to rubbish during summer and autumn. It will eat most types of food but especially sweet things. Wasps have jaws so do not need to vomit over food. However, they can pick up pathogens on their feet as they crawl over rubbish. Contamination is not as serious as that from blow-flies.

Control of flying insects

The best means of control is the *electronic fly-killer*. An ultraviolet light attracts the insects without producing excessive glare for the human eye. Flies and wasps are electrocuted as they pass between high voltage bars to get to the light (see Figure 1.8). Electronic fly killers should be positioned fairly high in rooms, and away from the glare of direct sunlight. They must be accessible so the dead insects can regularly be emptied. *Sticky fly papers* are recommended for storage areas, but they rapidly attract dust and fluff if positioned near a radiator or fan. *Fly-sprays*, *thermal vaporizers* or *plastic strips* impregnated with *dichlorvos* should not be used near stored or open food.

Figure 1.8 Electronic insect killer

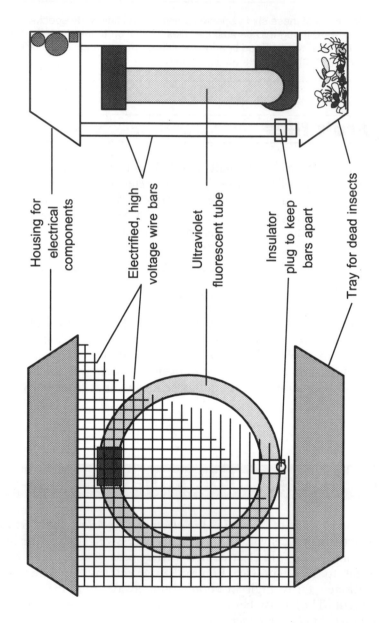

Housing for electrical components

Electrified, high voltage wire bars

Ultraviolet fluorescent tube

Insulator plug to keep bars apart

Tray for dead insects

Stored product insects

Several insect species infest stored foods, some are omnivorous, others found only in specific foods. They may spread spoilage organisms but they do not usually carry food-poisoning bacteria. The main danger is physical contamination of food with bodies, larvae, eggs or droppings. The commonest stored product insects are booklice and mites.

Many species of **Booklice (*Psocids*)** are known, but the African species *Liposcelis bostrychophilus Badonel* has been a growing problem since the early 1960s (Turner, 1987). It has a seasonal growth pattern, which peaks in the autumn. Its preferred food is flour but it also grows in sugar, rice, cake mixes and related products. It is a small (1–2 mm), light-brown, ant-like insect (see Figure 1.7).

Mites (*Acaridae*) are tiny (less than 1 mm), eight-legged spider-like creatures. They are difficult to see until they move. Commonest is the **cheese mite** (*Tyroglyphus domesticus*), which may infest flour and salami as well as cheese. Mites require a moisture content above 15% and tend to infest damp, inadequately ventilated areas.

Recognition and treatment

Only very close inspection of foods will detect booklice and mites. The less common beetles, weevils, moths and their larvae are larger and leave more obvious signs. These may include live and dead adults and larvae, larval web (like thick spiders' web), droppings and tunnels. Noticeably infested food should be thrown away and other foods should be checked. Food suppliers and manufacturers have hitherto fumigated certain products with poisonous gases: **ethylene oxide** or **bromomethane**. This practice will be discontinued from 1990, except for the fumigation of spices.

Ecological control

Pest control is not only a matter of killing things. The most sound approach is to deny them access, shelter, food and moisture (Phillips, 1986). For example, concreting the whole site beneath suspended floors prevents rodents entering and burrowing. Screens at windows exclude flying insects. Efficient removal of humidity/condensation and of food waste denies pests water and food. Elimination of cracks in walls and inaccessible spaces behind and below equipment removes hiding places. Pest-proof containers can be used for storing foods. These aspects of pest control are examined in greater detail in Chapters 5 and 6.

Question

What does the food premises manager need to know about pests, and why?

Food premises managers must be able to recognize infestation swiftly and assess approximately what treatment is needed. However destruction of pests requires a high level of expertise and should be carried out by a recognized, reliable specialist firm. Much pest control is also possible at the kitchen design stage. A knowledge of pests' habits and needs is very helpful in ecological control.

Summary – Pest Control

Do

- Regularly inspect premises, stored foods and incoming raw materials for infestation.
- Use fly electrocutors wherever there is open food about.
- Store foods in pest-proof containers.
- Arrange for treatment at the first sign of infestation.
- Use a recognized, reliable pest control specialist.
- Ensure that waste is regularly removed.
- Ensure adequate cleaning.
- Ventilate food production and storage areas

Do not

- Leave unmarked poisoned baits about.
- Use insecticide sprays, vaporizers, dusts or lacquers in food production or storage areas.

2 Food-borne Illness, Microorganisms and Parasites

Objectives

To define the term 'food-borne illness'. To provide the food premises manager with background information about epidemiology and to identify the principal sources of biological contamination.

Introduction

The term 'food-borne illness' was used in Chapter 1 to describe any illness caused by the physical, chemical or biological contamination of food. It is quite difficult to obtain general statistics about the incidence of food-borne illness. Types of illness are classified differently in different countries, so, for instance, authorities in the USA include parasites and chemicals under causes of food-borne illness. UK statistics omit both, and refer to food poisoning and food-borne illness separately, defining them as follows.

Food poisoning is a rather mild, short-lived type of illness, i.e. vomiting, diarrhoea, sometimes with other symptoms. Food poisoning is usually caused by bacteria, viruses or the toxins naturally present in fish or plants. Usually a relatively large quantity of organisms or toxin is regarded as necessary to cause illness, but this is not always the case.

Food-borne diseases are severe, frequently fatal diseases such as typhoid fever, which are transmitted by contaminated food. Because the organisms tend to be very virulent, tiny numbers of microorganisms may be enough to cause the symptoms.

Though these definitions are useful for recording patterns of disease, they are of little help to the food premises manager, who must use the same hygiene techniques to deal with both. Certain types of 'food poisoning' (e.g. botulism) have a considerable fatality rate. Some bacterial species (for instance *Salmonella*) cause both categories of food-borne illness. For these reasons the term 'food-borne illness' is used throughout this book to cover all types of illness and all forms of contamination.

Epidemiology

Epidemiology is the study of disease outbreaks (epidemics). It involves collecting and analyzing statistics in order to provide information about the nature, sources, means of spread and control of illness. The main sources of these statistics in the UK are the Office of Population Censuses and Surveys (OPCS) and the Communicable Disease Surveillance Centre (CDSC). Both these institutions produce annual statistics of food poisoning and food-borne disease. They prepare their statistics at different times and therefore produce somewhat different estimates, as shown in Table 2.1 (adapted from Anon., 1986).

Table 2.1   Estimates of food poisoning cases in England and Wales, 1982–84

Year		OPCS	CDSC
1982	Officially notified	9962	12684
	Otherwise ascertained	4228	
	Total	14190	
1983	Offically notified	12265	15168
	Otherwise ascertained	5461	
	Total	17726	
1984	Offically notified	13247	not yet
	Otherwise ascertained	7455	available
	Total	20702	

Source: Anon. (1986).

Investigating an outbreak

First signs of an outbreak of food-borne illness are usually staff sickness or customer complaints. Although there is no general requirement to report food poisoning outbreaks, managers are legally obliged to notify certain illnesses to the District Medical Officer of Health. The list of notifiable illnesses includes *Salmonella* infections and dysentery. Managers are also required by law to assist local authority officers who may wish to carry out medical or bacteriological screening of food or personnel. The usual procedure is as follows.

1.   Identify and contact all sufferers. It is important to stop the spread of illness. Some infections may be passed from victims of the original food (primary contacts) to their friends or family (secondary contacts). Sufferers will also provide information about their symptoms and what they have eaten. Faecal samples are obtained in special sterile bottles and sent for analysis.

2.   Identify the food vehicle. Ideally investigating officers would like to sample all foods eaten. Often these have been discarded by the time sufferers' symptoms develop. It is generally possible to trace how particular foods were cooked and stored. Sometimes samples of the original raw materials are available for analysis (e.g. frozen foods such as chicken). It may be necessary to produce a flow chart of events in order to pinpoint likely vehicles.

3.   Identify the contaminant. That is, the organism or toxin in the vehicle which caused the illness. The same contaminant should be present in the original food and in the faeces of victims if it to be pinpointed as the cause. Physical and chemical contaminants may be particularly difficult to identify in faeces. They may become lodged in the gut or changed by digestive processes. Often the only evidence of parasites is their eggs, present in faeces. Bacteria are relatively easy to identify in food and faeces, and are responsible for most outbreaks.

Bacteria

Structure

Bacteria are primitive, single-celled organisms about 1 micrometre in size, that is 1/1000 of a millimetre. A generalized bacterial cell is shown in Figure 2.1. It has the following features.

Protective outer layers: **slime capsule** – some bacteria continuously produce an outer coating of jelly-like material. This may protect them from drying out or from being digested as they pass through the human

44

Figure 2.1 Typical bacterial cell structure

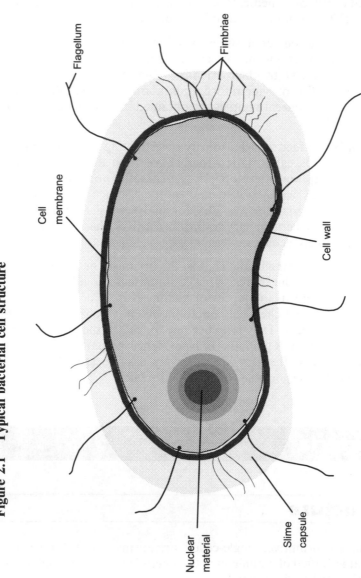

Flagellum

Fimbriae

Cell
membrane

Cell wall

Nuclear
material

Slime
capsule

gut. **Cell wall**: this is a rigid structure; bacteria cannot change shape and this property can be used to recognize them. **Cell membrane**: a thin, flexible, permeable 'skin' which controls the passage of food, water and waste in and out of the cell.

Cell contents: **Cytoplasm** – a jelly-like material which carries out all the life processes of the bacterial cell. **Nuclear material**: bacteria do not have a distinct **nucleus** enclosed in its own membrane. This means that sometimes portions of nuclear material, called **plasmids**, can pass from one cell to another. Populations of bacteria may acquire characteristics from one another in this way such as antibiotic resistance, or the ability to cause particular disease symptoms.

External features: **Flagella** (singular flagell**um**) are long, whip-like threads. They are used for mobility, but are only present in a few species. **Fimbriae** (singular fimbri**a**) are very fine, short threads. Bacteria use them to anchor to the insides of human intestines, to kitchen surfaces etc.

Spores

Certain bacterial species protect themselves by forming **endospores** ('inside spores'). When conditions become unsuitable for growth, a hard, spherical or egg-shaped shell develops around the nuclear material and some of the cytoplasm (see Figure 2.2). In several species toxins are produced in the cell as the spore forms. Eventually the original cell wall breaks away releasing the toxin, which causes food poisoning.

Spores are extremely resistant to chemicals, dryness and heat. They germinate again when conditions are right for growth; germination is encouraged if the spores are heated and then cooled.

Question
Look back at Figure 1.3 (Chapter 1). In which phases of the bacterial growth curve would you expect spore formation to occur?

Bacteria form spores in response to worsening conditions. These are most likely to be present during the stationary and decline phases of growth when food and moisture may be running low and waste products are building up.

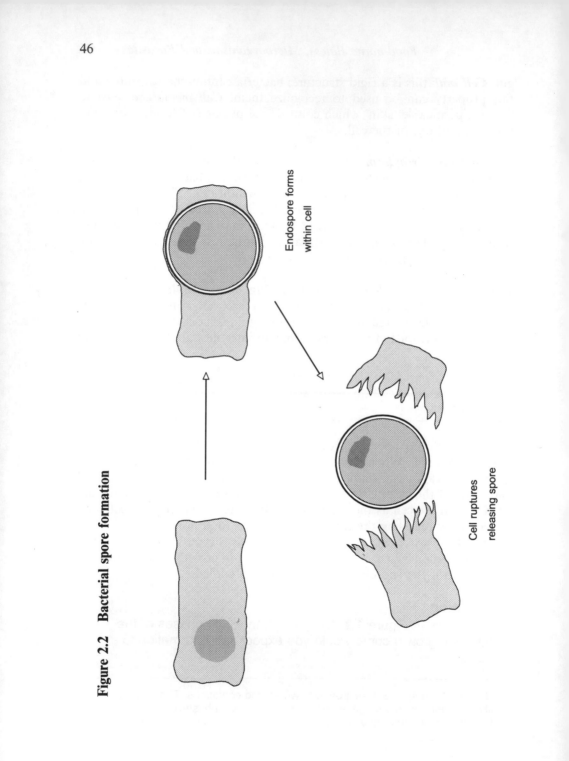

Figure 2.2 Bacterial spore formation

Endospore forms
within cell

Cell ruptures
releasing spore

Bacterial reproduction

Bacterial cells split into two to reproduce; the process is called **binary fission**. Often the two new cells remain attached for a time so that chains or clumps are formed. The two daughter cells are alike so there are no parent and daughter generations.

Bacteria therefore do not die of old age. They must be destroyed by heat or chemicals. Unfavourable conditions such as dryness or lack of nutrients cannot be relied upon to kill them.

Question

During the exponential growth phase the bacterial population doubles in set time. How does this relate to binary fission?

In theory the doubling time of a whole bacterial population is the same as the time it takes for each bacterial cell to split into two. However some cells also die due to local adverse conditions, so the doubling time is usually a little longer than the binary fission time. The two come closest together during the exponential phase, when the growth rate is optimum.

Identification of bacteria

In epidemiology it is important to identify *causes* of illness. The following techniques are used by public health laboratories to identify species and strains of pathogenic bacteria:

- Culture.
- Staining.
- Microscopy.
- Biochemical reactions.
- Serotyping.
- Phage typing.

Culture

Bacteria are usually grown on a jelly-like medium made of broth plus **agar**, an inert thickener obtained from seaweed. The hot agar mixture is poured into shallow petri dishes and allowed to set. A growth medium containing hydrolyzed protein, sugars and minerals will support most species of bacteria. It is called *general* or *nutrient agar*. Single bacteria multiply and produce *colonies* on the agar surface. The number of these colonies is called the *total viable count* (*TVC*). The first phase of identification is to observe the shape and appearance of the colonies. These may be round or irregular, coloured, transparent, glistening and so on.

Agar media can be prepared in such a way that only one species or group of species can grow on them. These are called *specific media* and usually contain added chemicals or antibiotics to limit the range of growth. Use of specific media can narrow down the identification of bacteria considerably. It is also possible to keep agar plates in selective atmospheres, with no oxygen, or with a controlled amount. This technique can be used to identify aerobes and obligate anaerobes. Bacterial culture using general and selective techniques can narrow down the field of identification considerably. It is also used to isolate a pure culture of the organism on which further techniques can be used.

Staining and microscopy

Bacteria are visible under the microscope. However they are so small that very high magnification is needed. This usually involves special techniques and oil-immersion microscope lenses. Different types of bacteria can be recognized by the shapes of their cells and by the way they group together. Figure 2.3 shows the distinctive shapes and groupings of some common types of bacteria. Features such as flagella and spores may also help the identification.

Bacterial cells are almost transparent and must usually be *stained* to be seen. The staining process itself also helps to identify bacteria, because different species absorb different stains. One of the most common procedures is *Gram's stain*. A smear of the sample is 'fixed' on to the microscope slide by drying it over a flame. After this the dried smear is washed carefully with crystal violet, iodine solution, methylated spirit and another dye called safranin. *Gram positive* bacteria appear purple and *gram negative* cells pink after this treatment. All spore-forming bacteria are gram positive, while gram negative cells are often the more resistant to antibodies and disinfectants.

Biochemical reactions

Besides restricting growth to one species or group, selective media can be used to monitor biochemical reactions. Media containing blood indicate the presence of haemoglobin-destroying bacteria by changing colour.

Figure 2.3 Shapes and clusters of bacterial cells

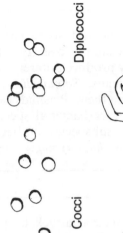
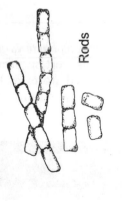

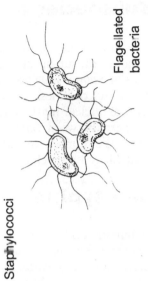

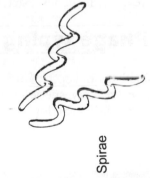

Diplococci

Vibrios

Flagellated bacteria

Cocci

Staphylococci

Rods

Streptococci

Spirae

Salmonellae convert bismuth sulphite to shiny, metallic bismuth sulphide. A large number of identification media have been developed based on biochemical reactions of growing colonies.

Subspecies and strains

There are thousands of species of bacteria and some species have thousands of sub-species or **strains**. For example over two thousand strains of *Salmonellae* are known. Each may produce different symptoms and severity of illness. Mutation is rapid because *Salmonella* strains can exchange nuclear material (plasmids) between them. Plasmids can also be exchanged between *Salmonellae* and the other bacterial species which inhabit the human intestine. Strains and subspecies of bacteria are identified by two techniques: **serotyping** and **phage typing**.

Serotyping

The human body protects itself against bacterial attack by producing special proteins called **antibodies**. These bind to the outer surface of bacteria and inactivate them. Antibodies are highly specific and can 'recognize' even slightly mutated cells of the original strain. Serotyping involves isolating the antibody from laboratory animals and allowing it to react with the test bacteria.

Phage typing

Some bacterial species are attacked by viruses known as **bacterio-phages**. These are very species-specific and can only attack certain strains of bacteria. Microbiological laboratories keep catalogued stores of bacteriophages, which are used to identify particular bacterial strains.

Bacteria which cause food-borne illness

Salmonella species

Common vectors for *Salmonella* species are raw meats, particularly raw chicken. The bacteria are frequently transferred to cooked foods by cross-contamination, or survive cooking due to previous inadequate thawing or poor time/temperature control. *Salmonellae* (plural) may be transferred from raw to cooked food on the hands of personnel. Some individuals are carriers, i.e. *Salmonellae* live amongst their other intestinal bacteria without causing harm. Carriers can also infect cooked food. There are numerous species and strains of *Salmonella*. The most virulent cause typhoid and paratyphoid fevers, which are often fatal. Much more common are the milder *Salmonella* species, which usually cause vomiting, diarrhoea and fever. All the *Salmonellae* are infective organisms which invade the human body. Even the mildest strains may cause death in very young or very old individuals. The infective dose varies between 10 and 100,000 cells, depending upon the susceptibility of the victim and the virulence of the strain. Strains causing typhoid and paratyphoid fevers are highly infective and only a few cells may be needed to cause the disease. Milder strains generally need a time/temperature opportunity in order to grow to infective numbers. The commonly regarded safe limit for *Salmonella* is less than one cell per 25 grams of food

Salmonella species are gram-negative, kidney-shaped, flagellated bacteria (see Figure 2.3). They are closely related to, and similar in appearance to the other human intestinal bacteria. They grow best between 10–45°C, i.e. in food that is left unrefrigerated. *Salmonellae* are facultative anaerobes, independent of oxygen for their growth. They do not form spores and are quite easily killed as long as cooking is adequate.

Question

How can outbreaks of illness caused by *Salmonella* be prevented?

Particular care should be taken with the thawing and cooking of poultry and meats. Potential cross-contamination should be scrupulously avoided. All cooked foods, especially meats, should be kept in the refrigerator. Personnel should be screened to ensure that they are not *Salmonella* carriers.

Clostridium perfringens

This organism is very common in soil and faeces. Raw meats and unwashed vegetables are common vectors. *C. perfringens* forms spores, which are virtually certain to be present in all raw and many cooked foods. Bacteria and spores are transferred by cross-contamination; the spores also survive short periods of boiling and germinate at temperatures as high as 55°C. The organism causes quite mild food poisoning. Symptoms are diarrhoea and abdominal cramps; vomiting is rare.

Clostridium perfringens grows in the human intestine, producing a toxin, which in turn causes the symptoms. Food must contain a large number of bacteria (1,000,000 or more cells per gram) in order to cause illness. One hundred cells or spores per gram of prepared food is regarded as a safe upper limit for *Clostridium perfringens*. Like other spore-formers this organism is gram positive. It has rod-shaped cells (see Figure 2.3) and is an obligate anaerobe. Growth occurs between 15–55°C. At the higher temperature the population may double every 10 minutes. Typical vehicles are meat pies, stews and large stuffed meat items. Growth occurs rapidly in the oxygen-free interior while these items are being held hot.

Question

How can outbreaks of illness caused by *Clostridium perfringens* best be avoided?

Food items which contain meat should be kept adequately hot before serving (i.e. > 65°C). It is important that cool spots do not develop. Hot-holding times should be limited and operating temperatures of hot-holding equipment checked. Large pots of stew and large stuffed meat items should be cooled as quickly as possible and stored in the refrigerator to prevent bacterial growth.

Campylobacter jejuni and Campylobacter coli

These closely related species were originally discovered in Czechoslovakia and have only been reported in the UK since the early 1970s. They are common in poultry carcasses but not in other meats. Milk is a reported vector and vehicle (Blaser, 1982). Cases are not well documented but the organism is certainly transferred by cross-contamination. Available data suggests that only a small dose is necessary to cause the infection. *Campylobacter* is killed rapidly above 60°C. Food poisoning sufferers have flu-like symptoms: headache and fever, as well as nausea, diarrhoea and abdominal pain. The symptoms may take up to 11 days to appear and can last up to 3 weeks. Affected individuals may continue to excrete live *Campylobacter* organisms for several weeks after the symptoms have passed. During this time they can be regarded as vectors. Campylobacter infection is spread readily between humans and from animals (Holt, 1981). At least one outbreak has been recorded where the organism was transmitted by puppies (Miller *et al.*, 1986)

Campylobacter organisms have short, spiral cells similar to vibrios (see Figure 2.3). They grow best in low concentrations of oxygen (**micro-aerobic**) between 5–40°C. Growth is likely to occur in inadequately chilled units such as display cabinets, as well as in unrefrigerated foods.

Question
Which are the most likely vehicles of *Campylobacter* infection?

> Outbreaks of *Campylobacter* illness frequently involve inadequately cooked chicken and cross-contaminated cooked meats. However, foods touched by human or animal carriers may also transmit the organism.

Staphylococcus aureus

Human skin and hair are common vectors of this organism. Large numbers may also be present in moist areas of the body such as the mouth, nose and ears. Spots, boils, whitlows and wounds are also heavily infected. Pus is a mixture of living and dead bacteria and white blood cells. *Staphylococcus aureus* is usually transferred to cooked food from personnel, but also occasionally from pets or pests. The cells secrete a toxin as they grow in food. This is resistant to heat and is only destroyed by boiling for well over 30 minutes (Denny *et al.*, 1971). Symptoms of illness are vomiting and stomach cramps, occasionally followed by diarrhoea. Onset is often rapid. It may be as little as one hour and customers or guests may actually fall ill while on the premises. Fatalities are very rare. Bacterial numbers found in food at incidents are always very large, usually in excess of 1,000,000 cells per gram. *Staphylococcus aureus* is a gram-positive, facultative anaerobe. It is salt-tolerant and can grow at A_w 0.70 or less. Thus it grows in such products as cured meats and dressed crab. The cells are spherical (i.e. typical cocci) and form clumps (see Figure 2.3). A large number of strains are found inhabiting the human body. Only about half of these produce the toxin.

Question
How can the manager ensure that food handlers do not transfer *Staphylocci* to food?

> Staff with spots, boils, whitlows, nose or throat infections must not be allowed to handle food. Hand-to-mouth habits such as smoking must not be permitted. Staff must wear protective head coverings and clothing. Staff must be trained to wash adequately and to handle foods no more than is necessary.

Bacillus species

Three *bacillus* species have been identified as causes of food-borne illness. *Bacillus cereus* is the best-documented. Certain strains of the food spoilage organisms *Bacillus subtilis* and *Bacillus licheniformis* are also reported to cause problems. All three species are common in soil and can easily enter food premises.

Cereal products and spices are the usual vector for *Bacillus cereus*. The organism grows well in agricultural soil. It forms spores which find their way into harvested grain and can survive milling and other processing. The spores germinate readily in cereal foods which have been boiled briefly and are then stored in the temperature danger zone, between 10–65°C. Boiled rice from oriental take-aways is a common problem. It is often held hot for long periods, because oriental cooks dislike refrigerating cooked rice, claiming that this makes the grains sticky. Other vehicles of *Bacillus cereus* poisoning are cornflour products, custards and occasionally curries. The organism reportedly causes two types of illness. In boiled rice it produces a toxin which can cause vomiting and stomach cramps after an incubation time of 2–7 hours. When cornflour items or highly spiced products are the vehicle, symptoms generally consist of abdominal pain and diarrhoea. In this case the onset time is usually 12 hours or more (Gilbert and Taylor, 1976). *Bacillus cereus* illness tends to be mild and there is no fever. The bacteria can apparently produce an emetic (vomit inducing) toxin when they grow in boiled rice (Melling and Capel, 1978). In the other cases *B. cereus* apparently grows and produces its toxin inside the human intestine. In all reported cases the infective dose was greater than 100,000 organisms per gram of food.

Bacillus subtilis and *B. licheniformis* are spore formers like *B. cereus*. They are common food spoilage organisms and vectors are more likely to be dust, rubbish and spoiled foods rather than specifically ceral products. The most likely transfer route is cross-contamination, directly or through food handlers. Usual symptoms are vomiting and stomach cramps, indicating a toxin produced before consumption. Very large numbers of bacteria (1,000,000 per gram or more) must be present to cause illness. The bacilli ('Little rods' in Latin) are all gram-positive, aerobic, spore-forming, rod-shaped organisms. They can grow in the range 10–45°C. Illness incidents mostly involve rice, cornflour or highly spiced products which have been kept inadequately hot or inadequately cold for several hours.

Question
How can the manager help staff ensure that rice and custard are kept adequately hot or cold?

> Digital thermometers should be issued and staff required to check and record temperatures of cooked rice, custard and other cereal products kept in the refrigerator or *bain-marie*.

Vibrio parahaemolyticus

Seafoods are common vectors of this organism, particularly imported shellfish. The bacteria are common in shallow coastal waters in the East, but have also been isolated from marine mud samples taken around the UK. They can survive below 10°C but are inactive at those temperatures. *Vibrio parahaemolyticus* is well documented as a cause of food-borne illness in Japan. It usually enters the UK in raw seafoods such as frozen king prawns. Cross-contamination to cooked, peeled prawns may also occur during production or in transit. The bacteria grow best in cooked prawn meat (Barrow and Miller, 1976). Symptoms of infection are diarrhoea, sometimes with vomiting, severe abdominal cramps and frequently fever. Incubation is usually 12–24 hours but may take as little as 2 hours depending on the infecting dose. Bacteria are excreted during the illness but this stops rapidly with recovery.

Vibrio parahaemolyticus is a gram negative, facultative anaerobe. Cells are shaped like twisted rods with a single flagellum. The temperature range for growth is 10–44°C. Typical outbreaks involve thawed frozen prawns in salads and risottos which have not been adequately refrigerated. The bacteria are easily destroyed by cooking.

Question

What precautions should be taken with frozen, raw king prawns?

> Raw, frozen seafood products should be stored wrapped. They should be defrosted before cooking and cooked thoroughly. Kitchen staff should wash carefully after handling such foods.

Coliforms

Several species of bacteria inhabit the human intestine. Most of these are grouped together as *coliforms*. They all have the ability to ferment lactose and this biochemical reaction is used to identify them. Coliforms are present in vast numbers in faeces and sewage and provide a very sensitive way of showing that faecal contamination has occurred. They are called *indicator organisms*, because they indicate likely contamination by pathogenic bacteria. Most coliforms are harmless, although a few strains can cause food-borne illness.

Escherichia coli

This is a common coliform, but different human populations have different strains. Travellers may acquire a strain to which they are not accustomed. Usually this is passed on by food handlers who do not adequately wash their hands after using the lavatory (the so-called *faecal–oral route*). Illness is much more likely to occur if foods are stored at room temperature after handling, as large numbers of bacteria (100,000 or more per gram of food) are generally needed to cause illness. Symptoms of infection are diarrhoea, abdominal cramps, depression and fever. In adults the symptoms often linger and recur for up to three weeks from onset. *E. coli* can also cause severe diarrhoea in babies, which may be fatal due to dehydration. In adults a kind of haemorrhagic colitis is caused by a newly-reported strain of *E. coli*. Symptoms are severe abdominal cramps and bloody diarrhoea, with little or no fever (Galbraith *et al.*, 1987).

Escherichia coli is a gram-negative, kidney-shaped, flagellated organism. A wide growth range: 4–44°C has been reported (Olsvik and Kapperud, 1982). However, outbreaks are usually traced to foods that have been stored warm for some time after handling.

Question
What is the faecal–oral route?

> As its name suggests, the faecal–oral route involves transfer of bacteria from the faeces to the mouth. It is a route for food-borne illness and also for reinfection of carriers and sufferer. Bacteria are transferred to the hands when individuals go to the lavatory. If personal hygiene is poor the bacteria are not removed by washing. They may be transferred to foods during preparation.

Streptococcus species

Faecal **streptococci** are another common group of intestinal bacteria, more resistant to heat and chemicals than the coliforms. They are used as indicator organisms to check critical stages in food processing and packaging. Faecal *streptococci* have been identified in foods investigated after incidents of food-borne illness. It is possible that they were the cause, but this is not proven.

Streptococcus zooepidemicus causes mastitis in cows. If humans drink unpasteurized milk from infected cows they may contract the organism. The illness is very severe: flu-like symptoms of fever and headache may develop into meningitis and septicaemia and fatalities are common.

Streptococci are gram-positive, spherical cells which group together in characteristic chains (see Figure 2.3). Faecal *streptococci* require warm conditions i.e. 10–44°C to grow. *S. zooepidemicus* is not known to multiply in milk; foods are only the medium of transfer.

Shigella infections

Shigella species cause **dysentery**. The organisms do not grow in stored food and food handlers are the usual vector. The bacteria are also known to survive for hours on toilet seats, tap handles, nail brushes etc. They are easily transferred from unwashed hands to cooked foods (i.e. the faecal–oral route). Shigellae are highly infectious and just a few organisms can cause illness. Tropical species frequently cause fatalities. The species found in the UK is **Shigella sonnei**. Symptoms are mild to severe diarrhoea, often with blood and mucus. Fever and cramps are common. *Shigella sonnei* dysentery is not usually fatal, but patients can be debilitated for several weeks.

Shigella species are related to the *Salmonellae* and *Coliforms*. They are gram-negative, flagellated, kidney-shaped facultative anaerobes. They grow best at 37°C and are destroyed above 55°C.

Question
What can be done to prevent the spread of *Shigella* dysentery?

Staff suffering from dysentery must not be allowed to work with food. Lavatories and wash rooms should be thoroughly cleaned and disinfected; particular attention should be paid to lavatory seats, wash basins and tap handles. Nail brushes should be soaked in sterilant. The need for personal hygiene should be emphasized to staff.

Clostridium botulinum

This organism is fairly common in soil, in rotting vegetables and in marine mud. *Clostridium botulinum* forms very resistant spores which can survive hours of boiling and can grow in canned and vacuum packed foods, from which the air is excluded. Canneries therefore have to control the timing and temperature of the cooking process very carefully. However, the bacterium is unable to grow below pH 4.5 or in the presence of nitrites. For this reason sodium nitrite is commonly added to high pH canned items, such as meats. *Clostridium botulinum* produces a toxin called **botulin** which affects the human nervous system. A tiny quantity of toxin, i.e. just one mouthful of apparently unconta-minated food, is sufficient to cause the illness known as **botulism**. Onset is quite slow: 24 hours or more. The first symptom is usually blurred or double vision. Victims then have difficulty swallowing or speaking and may become confused. Paralysis gradually ensues, death being caused by respiratory failure. The fatality rate is high. Antitoxin can be admin-istered, but recovery may take months or even years.

Clostridium botulinum* is a gram-positive, rod-shaped obligate anaer-obe. At least six distinct strains are known, most of which grow best around 30°C. However **type E**, which is found in the gut of many fish is psychrotrophic and can grow at temperatures as low as 3°C. There are several distinct botulin toxins, all lethal, but all quite quickly destroyed at temperatures above 85°C. Until recently, *Clostridium botulinum* was almost exclusively a problem of the canning industry. However it is also a potential danger in cook–chill catering systems such as **sous vide** and **Capkold**, which use vacuum packing to prolong product life. Chilled, vacuum-packed foods are high quality products in which additives such as nitrite would be considered out of place. Unless pH is carefully adjusted below 4.5 *Clostridium botulinum* may grow in the anaerobic, refrigerated conditions. Food manufacturers using the sous vide process have to be offically registered in the UK and USA.

Listeria monocytogenes

This bacterium is a common organism of soil, manure, food waste and other decaying organic matter. Typical food vectors are cheeses, raw and processed meats and raw vegetables. *Listeria monocytogenes* is remark-ably resistant to heat. It is known to survive 15-second pasteurization at 72°C, and dairies now often pasteurize at 76°C. Little is known about contamination routes, but foods held in chilled storage are the typical vehicles. *Listeria* illness is an infection. It begins as a flu-like illness, with general aches and fever, but in pregnant women it may cause abortion. As the illness progresses meningitis and septicaemia can develop, with a fatality rate of 30%, particularly in the very young and very old. The onset period of listeriosis varies with different individuals and may be several months. This makes the detection and study of outbreaks very difficult. The infective dose is not known but the recommended safety limit in food is less than one organism per 25g. Unfortunately present culture techniques are unable to detect the presence of *Listeria* at this level (Lacey and Kerr, 1988).

Listeria monocytogenes* is a gram-positive, aerobic coccus. It is psychrotrophic, growing well in the range 3-35°C. In cold conditions it therefore competes very successfully with food-borne mesophiles, which require higher temperatures for growth. It is estimated that 10 organisms can increase to 1,000,000 during 10 days' chilled storage at 5°C. A recent study of chilled school meals (Armstrong *et al.*, 1989) identified *Listeria* in several chilled, cooked chicken and meat dishes. Contamination routes involved the chilling water, the dicing machine and the hands of personnel.

Question

How can the *Listeria* problem be minimized in a cook–chill operation?

Cook–chill systems are particularly at risk from psychrotrophs such as *Listeria*. Precautions against such pathogens include standardizing time/ temperature conditions for cooking and storage. Handling between cooking and chilling should be minimized and stock rotation of chilled items meticulously observed.

Yersinia enterocolitica

Yersinia is another organism able to grow under refrigeration. Vectors are raw milk and meat, particularly pork, but the organism is also found in shellfish and other foods. Transfer routes are not proven but probably involve cross-contamination and undercooking. Only one case was reported in the UK in 1975; by 1985 the number had risen to 411. Symptoms are diarrhoea, abdominal pain, sore throat and flu-like symptoms i.e. fever and general aches. Infected individuals are probably capable of transferring the organism to foods. *Yersinia enterocolitica* is a gram-negative, facultative anaerobe related to the *Salmonellae* and *Coliforms*. It grows well in the range 3–35°C. Contamination of food vehicles probably occurs much the same as with *Listeria*.

Aeromonas hydrophila

Aeromonas is a pathogen of fish and frogs. It is also capable of multiplying in protein-rich media at low temperatures. The bacterium has been isolated in several outbreaks of food-borne illness, mostly in the USA. Symptoms consist of vomiting and diarrhoea followed by fever and pneumonia-like illness.

Aeromonas hydrophila is a gram-negative, facultative anaerobe capable of growth as low as 1°C. So far there is no evidence linking the bacterium to any outbreak involving chilled food, although this is always a possibility with psychrophilic pathogens.

Brucella and Mycobacterium species

Brucella abortus and *Brucella melitensis* are pathogens of cattle, causing abortion and general illness in cows. The organisms can be transferred to humans by direct contact with infected animals or from raw milk. Symptoms are intermittent fever, depression, headache, weakness and aching limbs. The illness may last several months. *Mycobacterium tuberculosis* and *Mycobacterium bovis* are also pathogens of cattle and other animals. They can be transmitted through raw milk. The bacteria cause characteristic tuberculosis of the kidneys and other organs. Illness develops slowly and often goes unnoticed for several years. The Ministry of Agriculture, Fisheries and Food has succeeded in virtually eradicating both brucellosis and tuberculosis in cattle, by a concerted programme of veterinary inspection and treatment.

Question

What should the food premises manager do to avoid spreading these animal diseases?

Meat and milk should only be bought from reputable suppliers and should have undergone the proper inspection and treatment. The sale of raw milk for human consumption is strictly controlled under EC Regulations. Cheese made from unpasteurized milk is currently being investigated within the EC, although the danger of disease transmission from this source is quite small.

Study example 2.1

Study the graph in Figure 2.4. It is derived from the Annual Abstract of Statistics and shows reported cases of food-borne illness in the UK between 1976–86.

1. Which illnesses are classified as food-borne diseases by the Office of Statistics?
2. Which organisms cause these food-borne diseases in the UK?
3. In which group of statistics would you expect botulism and listeriosis to be included?

Figure 2.4   Cases of foodborne disease and food poisoning – 1976–86

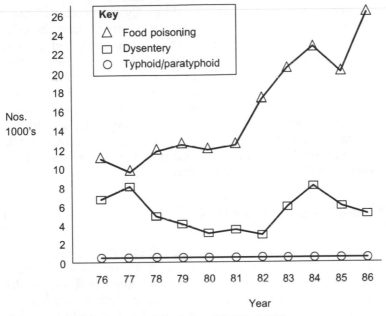

Source: Annual Abstract of Statistics, HMSO (1988)

Viruses

Structure

Viruses are not organisms at all in the strict sense. A 'virus' is made up of particles called ***virions***. Each particle consists of a tiny piece of genetic material wrapped in a protein shell. Virions are around 30 nanometres in size, that is only 0.03 (three hundredths) the size of most bacteria. Virions cannot be seen through an ordinary microscope. However, most of them can be observed with an electron microscope and recognized by their characteristic shapes. Virus particles cannot move about by themselves, or adhere to inorganic surfaces as bacteria can. They multiply only by infecting living cells. A virion first 'recognizes' a particular type of cell and locks on to it.

Genetic material from inside the virion is then injected into the cell. It jams the messages by which the cell nucleus controls the biochemical processes of the cell. Instead of its normal function, the cell is instructed to make more viruses. When the cell is full of virus particles it bursts and releases them. Various toxic by-products of the virus manufacture are also released. The new virions then infect other cells.

Viruses are very specific. They usually infect only one species of host, and attack only one type of cell within the host. For instance the cold virus only attacks the epithelial cells of the human nose and throat. Viruses cannot multiply in food, cooked or raw. Animal viruses cannot usually invade a human host. Unlike bacteria, viruses cannot be isolated or identified by culturing on agar, which is non-living material. Virions are destroyed by heat and chemical disinfectants as bacteria are, but do not form resistant spores. Viruses can however survive dry conditions much better than bacterial cells. They are highly infectious and only a few virions are needed to cause illness. Food-borne viral illnesses include *gastro-enteritis*, *hepatitis A* and *poliomyelitis*.

Viral gastro-enteritis

The two main forms of viral gastro-enteritis are infantile diarrhoea and winter vomiting disease. *Infantile diarrhoea* is a severe illness of young children, involving protracted diarrhoea, dehydration and fever. Adults are unaffected, but are thought to transfer the disease by inadequate washing between changing nappies and handling food or feeding bottles. Infantile diarrhoea is caused by a group of viruses called *rotaviruses*. It may sometimes reach serious epidemic levels in hospital wards.

Winter vomiting disease affects all age groups. The symptoms are nausea, vomiting and abdominal pain. Sometimes there is also mild diarrhoea. Incubation is 24–48 hours and the illness itself usually only lasts about 48 hours. Winter vomiting disease is transferred by infected food handlers via the faecal–oral route. It can also be spread by raw or uncooked shellfish, particularly oysters, cockles and mussels. These animals pick up the virus from water-borne sewage. The cause of the illness was first identified in Norwalk, Ohio. The viruses are referred to as *Norwalk-like viruses* (*NLV*). There appears to have been some mutation of the virus, because virions isolated from outbreaks in the UK are similar, but not identical under the electron microscope to those discovered in the USA. These gastro-enteritis viruses belong to one family, collectively called the *caliciviruses* (Riordan, 1988).

Hepatitis A

This is also called *infective hepatitis*, to distinguish it from hepatitis B. The latter can only be passed from blood to blood, like AIDS. Hepatitis A begins with fever, nausea and abdominal pain, after which jaundice develops. Incubation is 15–50 days and the illness lasts from a week up to several months. It may be very debilitating and even fatal. Transfer routes are exactly the same as for winter vomiting disease. The faecal–oral route, from infected individuals and the shellfish route, from seaborne sewage, have both been implicated. Hepatitis A is much commoner in the Near and Far East than in the UK. It may be brought back by food handlers who have visited India or Malaysia.

Poliomyelitis

Polio is a severe disease which begins with fever and muscular cramps. Paralysis may develop, causing death by respiratory failure. Incubation and development of the disease may last weeks or months. Polio has largely disappeared in the UK as a result of inoculation. The disease is spread through infected water or raw milk. Inoculation is also given by mouth, on a sugar lump.

Question
How can the food premises manager help to avoid outbreaks of food-borne viral illness?

Staff should be screened daily for signs of illness. The highest standards of personal hygiene should be encouraged. Lavatories and washrooms should be regularly cleaned and disinfected. Shellfish and milk should be purchased from reputable suppliers.

Distribution of bacterial and viral food-borne illness

Official figures (Annual Abstract of Statistics, 1988) for food poisoning and the common food-borne disease are shown in Table 2.2. Food poisoning reports doubled during the period 1976–86, while the more serious illnesses remained constant or declined slightly. Roberts (1982) analyzed the origins of foods incriminated in 1044 outbreaks of illness. She found that commercial catering accounted for 41.6% and public sector catering for 38.6%, a total of 80.2%. Family homes were responsible for 19.8%. The proportion of meals eaten outside the home has grown steadily over the last two decades. Commercial and institutional catering are almost certainly responsible for the recent rise in food poisoning statistics. Comparative statistics of organisms causing food-borne illness in the UK are quite rare and do not necessarily agree with one another. Roberts (1982) found the breakdown shown in Table 2.3.

Table 2.2   Reported food-borne illness in the UK – 1976–86

Year	Food poisoning	Dysentery	Typhoid/ paratyphoid
1976	11276	7354	294
1977	9639	8332	327
1978	12167	5486	353
1979	13128	4037	313
1980	12021	3595	307
1981	12994	3674	277
1982	17478	3256	253
1983	20486	6039	269
1984	23237	8734	219
1985	20242	6111	262
1986	26645	5096	260

Source: Annual Abstract of Statistics, HMSO (1988)

Table 2.3   Analysis of 1044 food poisoning outbreaks by cause

Causal agent	No. of outbreaks	%
Salmonella spp.	396	37.9
C. perfringens	387	37.1
S. aureus	133	12.7
Bacillus spp.	53	5.1
V. parahaemolyticus	8	0.8
E. coli	3	0.3
C. botulinum	1	0.1
Y. enterocolitica	1	0.1
Viruses	1	0.1
Toxic fish	47	4.5
Toxic plant foods	7	0.7
Not known	7	0.7

Source: Adapted from Roberts (1982).

Bacteria caused 94.1% of all these cases, 37.9% of which were due to *Salmonella* species. However, patterns of food-borne illness are changing. Figure 2.5 (Anon., 1986) shows a fall in *Salmonella* cases in 1986, with a steep rise in *Campylobacter* incidences.

Figure 2.5   Causes of gastrointestinal infections – 1977–85

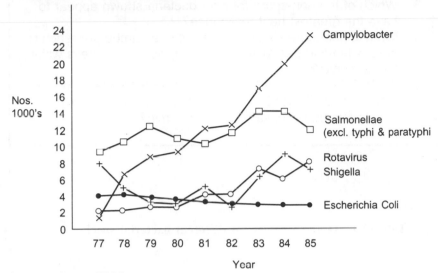

Source: Anon. (1986).

Summary – bacterial food-borne illness

Incidence of food-borne illness is rapidly increasing in the UK. Bacteria are overwhelmingly the cause and the majority of cases involve catered foods. *Salmonella*, *Campylobacter*, *Clostridium perfringens* and *Staphylococcus aureus* are the commonest organisms.

Study example 2.2

Thermal destruction data for several species of bacteria and viruses are shown in Table 2.4 below (source: Genigeorgis and Riemann, 1979). The figures are approximate because they depend partly on the food medium in which the organisms are heated.

1. Look back at the section on D and z values in Chapter 1 (pp. 16–18), and make a note of the definitions.
2. Which foods tend to protect bacteria from destruction by heat?

3. Which of the non-spore-forming bacteria shown appear to have the greatest heat-resistance?
4. What temperature should the centre of a hamburger reach to ensure ten-fold destruction of *Staphylococcus aureus* within half a minute?
5. The US Public Health Service recommend pasteurizing ice-cream at 68.3°C for 30 minutes to destroy viruses. Why should this be necessary if D_{60} = 1 min?

Table 2.4   D and z values for different bacterial species

Species	approx. D	approx. z
Non spore formers:		
Salmonella spp.	4 min (D_{60})	4°C
S. aureus	5 min (D_{60})	10°C
V. parahaemolyticus	3 min (D_{55})	–
E. coli	5 min (D_{60})	–
S. faecalis	10 min (D_{60})	–
B. abortus	5 min ($D_{62.8}$)	–
Spores:		
C. botulinum	2 min (D_{100})	10°C
C. botulinum: E type	3 min (D_{80})	10°C
C. perfringens	2 min (D_{100})	10°C
B. cereus	3 min (D_{100})	8°C
Viruses:		
Poliomyelitis	1 min (D_{60})	–

Source: Genigeorgis and Riemann (1979)

Parasites

Parasites are organisms which rely on a host for their food, moisture, warmth and shelter. Without the host the adult parasite would often die.

Parasites always harm the host in some way, by taking available food, by producing harmful waste or by burrowing into living tissue and damaging it. Three types of parasite are found in humans in the UK: protozoa, roundworms and flatworms.

Protozoa

These are single-celled organisms, but larger and more complex than bacteria. Protozoa are comparatively easy to see under the microscope. Several species of protozoa cause illness in the tropics, but only two are regularly found in the UK. These are *Giardia lamblia* and *Cryptosporidium*.

Giardia lamblia

This organism is usually contracted abroad. Returning sufferers then transmit the illness (known as *giardiasis*) via the faecal–oral route, or it may arise in foods and drinking water contaminated with sewage. Symptoms of giardiasis are watery diarrhoea, flatulence and abdominal pain. Children are more severely affected than adults. Incidence of the illness more than doubled in the period 1975–85 (Galbraith *et al.*, 1987). Currently more than 5000 are reported per year. *Giardia* is easily killed by cooking food and by boiling or chlorinating water.

Cryptosporidium species

These organisms are usually found in water contaminated with sewage. They form egg-shaped cysts called *oocysts*, which pass out with the faeces and can survive for long periods. Oocysts have been found in drinking water and may survive some water-treatment processes. However heating to 55°C for 30 minutes or to 100°C for 5 minutes is reported to kill them effectively. It is not certain whether infected individuals or animals can transfer the disease to food, but this is likely. Symptoms of the illness (*cryptosporidiosis*) are vomiting, diarrhoea and abdominal pain. In the UK, 61 cases were reported in 1983, 1900 in 1985 and 3614 in 1986. Most of these are thought to have been acquired abroad. *Cryptosporidium* is also a problem in the USA, where it has been the subject of much public health research (Rose, 1988)

Roundworms

Oxyuris vermicularis (threadworm)

Threadworms are small, white or colourless worms usually less than 1 cm and pointed at the ends. They are a common parasite, particularly of children and pets. The worms migrate to the anus, nose and mouth to lay eggs. Some of these reinfect the individual, but they may also be transferred to food and passed to other people. Threadworm eggs are commonly found on unwashed vegetables and fruit. A threadworm infection is not usually serious, and symptoms normally consist of itching around the mouth, nose and anus. The tiny, colourless worms can be seen moving about in fresh faeces. Treatment of threadworms consists of two doses of *piperazine phosphate*, a drug which paralyzes the worms so that they are flushed from the gut by the digestive process. The first dose destroys the adult worms and the second, administered two weeks later, eliminates the next generation of hatched eggs. Threadworms are highly infectious and it is recommended that sufferers should be excluded from normal food handling duties until they have been medically treated (PHLS, 1983).

Ascaris species

Several other species of intestinal roundworms are found in man, all members of the genus Ascaridae. They are similar to threadworms but larger; between 5–25 cm in length. They are less infectious and less common than *Oxyuris*, but may do more damage. Occasionally they leave the gut and invade other parts of the body. *Ascaris* worms are transferred in a similar way to threadwoms.

Trichinella spiralis

This microscopic worm (about 1 mm long) is a parasite of pigs and also of rats. Trichinella larvae burrow into the muscles of pigs and form tiny egg-shaped cysts. When the infected meat is eaten the larvae become adult worms, which lay eggs in the human intestine. The eggs hatch into larvae which burrow through the gut wall, enter the bloodstream and are carried to the muscles. They burrow into the muscle tissue and form cysts, so completing the cycle. This causes the human host much pain and fever and may be fatal.

Roundworms and their eggs and larvae are killed by freezing, salting and smoking. Meats are only harmful if fresh, and raw or inadequately cooked. Parasitic worms, eggs and cysts are effectively killed above 60°C.

Flatworms

Tapeworms

Adult tapeworms are long, whitish, tape-like organisms. They anchor themselves in the intestine of their host. Tapeworm eggs are produced in great numbers and pass out with the faeces. They can be transmitted via the faecal–oral route or by direct contact of animal or human hosts with food. Ingested tapeworm eggs hatch into larvae. These find their way into flesh in much the same way as those of *Trichinella*. Tapeworm cysts are much larger than those of *Trichinella*, and easily visible in raw meat. They develop into adults when the meat is eaten. Adult tapeworms do little damage and can be treated relatively easily. Larvae may cause blindness and other damage by burrowing into eyes or other organs. The five common species of tapeworms are listed in Table 2.5.

Table 2.5   Species of tapeworm found in humans

Species	Larval host can be man	Adult host can be man
(a) *Taenia solium* (pork tapeworm)	yes	yes
(b) *Echinococcus granulosus*	yes	no
(c) *Taenia hydatigena* (dog tapeworm)	yes	no
(d) *Taenia saginata* (beef tapeworm)	no	yes
(c) *Diphyllobothrium latum* (fish tapeworm)	no	yes

Question

How are species (a), (b) and (c) transmitted?

The tapeworm species (a), (b) and (c) are potentially the most harmful, as it is the larval stage of the life-cycle which does the most harm to the (human) host. *Taenia solium* (a) may be contracted from foods (usually meat) contaminated with the faeces of farm animals. Species (b) and (c) are associated with dogs. The eggs are transmitted through being licked by dogs, or by eating food contaminated by dogs or dog faeces.

The only species which can infect humans both in the larval and adult stage is *Taenia solium*. It is recommended that individuals who have contracted the adult worm are excluded from food handling work until they have been medically treated. (PHLS, 1983). Tapeworms, their eggs and larvae are destroyed by freezing and by adequate cooking. Only raw or partly cooked fresh meats are at risk.

Fasciola hepatica (liver fluke)

The liver fluke is a parasite of sheep. Adults live in the bile duct of the animal and eat liver cells. Eggs pass out with the host's faeces and those that are carried into streams and ponds infect water snails. The larvae develop in the snails and then burrow out of these primary hosts. They climb to the top of water plants and are eaten by sheep, thus completing the cycle. Humans contract the parasite by eating carelessly cultivated, unwashed salad plants, particularly watercress. Symptoms are lethargy and jaundice, but the condition can be treated medically. Liver fluke is severe, but rare.

Moulds and yeasts

Moulds are microscopic fungi, which live by breaking down dead organic matter. Since most human food consist of dead organic material, moulds are an important cause of food spoilage. Numerous techniques are used to deter them. As with bacteria there are a great many different species, and each of these may have many subspecies. Although moulds do most damage by spoiling human food, a few subspecies produce harmful toxins, which can cause food-borne illness. These are termed *mycotoxins* (meaning 'fungal toxins').

Moulds generally need less moisture than bacteria for their growth and can cope with A_w values of 0.85 and below. However an A_w value

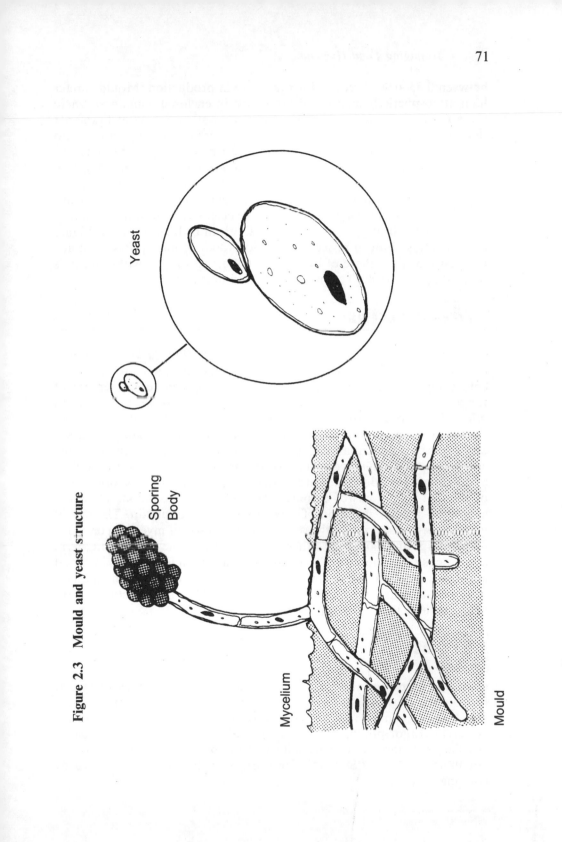

Figure 2.3 Mould and yeast structure

Yeast

Sporing Body

Mycelium

Mould

between 0.85–0.90 is required for mycotoxin production. Moulds prefer high atmospheric humidity and grow best in enclosed containers where the air cannot circulate. They need oxygen but can grow at lower pH than most bacteria. Many species can also tolerate low temperatures and they are a common cause of spoilage in refrigerated foods. Moulds and other fungi grow by a process called *filamentous extension*. Long thin cylindrical cells (called *hyphae*) form buds at the ends. The growing cells digest their way through the food, eventually forming a felt-like network (collectively called the *mycelium*). Hairlike cells also grow upwards out of the food, each bearing a cluster of black, green or brown spores (Figure 2.6). It is this that can be seen on mouldy food. Mould spores are much less resistant than those of bacteria. They are destroyed within seconds by heating above 90°C or by chemical disinfectants.

Mycotoxins

Aflatoxin is produced by certain strains of *Aspergillus flavus*. This mould is quite common, particularly in the tropics. Peanuts are the most commonly affected food, although there have been recent reports of the toxin in dried fruits, particularly figs. Aflatoxin poisoning (known as *aflatoxicosis*) occurs from time to time among farm animals in the UK. There are no reports of acute poisoning among the human population any country. Acute aflatoxicosis symptoms are internal haemorrhaging and a yellowish, jaundiced skin colour and there is damage to the liver and kidneys. In Indonesia, where fermented peanut products form a part of the diet, symptoms of chronic aflatoxicosis are common. These are caused by regular ingestion of tiny quantities of aflatoxin. The mould growth needed to produce this amount may consist of mycelium only, i.e. with no sporing bodies or other visible signs in the food. Long-term aflatoxicosis may result in liver damage, cancers and changes in blood and bone function. Aflatoxin is not destroyed by cooking. Indonesian-style products are growing in demand in the UK, but no studies have been made of their aflatoxin content.

Ergot

Claviceps purpurea (also called *ergot*), is a parasitic fungus of rye. It forms dark brown, spur-like growths on the rye grains in the growing ear. It is not common in the UK except as a parasite of wild, roadside rye-grass. Ergot produces toxins which affect the brain and the blood circulation. Symptoms include hallucination, pins and needles and loss of circulation to limbs ('St John's fire'). Ergot toxins are not destroyed by cooking.

Other mycotoxins

Several species of *Aspergillus* and *Penicillium* moulds are known to produce substances toxic to man and animals. These substances have been detected in very small quantities in a wide variety of foods (Jarvis, 1976). However there are no confirmed cases of food poisoning in the UK by these substances or by mouldy food.

Yeasts

Yeasts are not known to produce mycotoxins or to cause severe food-borne illness. However several yeast species are known to cause food spoilage. Most prefer to grow in fruit juices, syrups or jam. A few will also cause spoilage of cheeses and cured meats. Yeasts are single-celled fungi, and like fungi they tolerate lower pH (i.e. *higher* acidity) and lower temperatures than most bacteria. Most yeast species ferment sugars to alcohol. Occasionally, spoiled products cause mild intestinal discomfort when eaten. However yeasts are not regarded as causes of food-borne illness and do not produce toxins.

Study example 2.3

Food-borne illness may be caused by infection or intoxication.

Infection is caused by a living organism establishing itself in the human body and living there parasitically, harming the host in some way. *Intoxication* is caused by a chemical or biochemical substance which is toxic (poisonous) to the human body.

Use the information presented in this chapter to draw up a table of the following organisms, indicating whether they cause infective or toxic food-borne illness:

Salmonella spp., *Clostridium perfringens*, *Campylobacter* spp., *Staphylococcus aureus*, *Bacillus* spp., *Vibrio parahaemolyticus*, *Escherichia coli*, *Streptococcus zooepidemicus*, *Shigella sonnei*, *Clostridium botulinum*, *Listeria monocytogenes*, *Yersinia enterocolitica*, *Aeromonas hydrophila*, *Brucella* spp., Viruses, Protozoa, Roundworms, Flatworms, Moulds.

Summary

Biological contaminants, particularly bacteria, are the cause of most cases of food-borne illness. The evidence suggests that catering practices are the cause of most outbreaks. The following list gives some general examples of good practice:

Do

- Store food above 65°C or below 5°C.
- Check stored food temperatures at regular intervals.
- Rotate stocks regularly – particularly of chilled, cooked items.
- Inspect staff daily for illness or infection.
- Observe and correct staff hygiene practices, particularly hand washing after using the toilet and between handling raw and cooked items.
- Buy from reputable suppliers and check incoming foodstuffs.
- Discard mouldy foods.

Do not

- Prepare foods too far in advance.
- Allow cooked food to stand at room temperature for more than one hour.
- Store raw and cooked foods in the same refrigerator.
- Handle raw and cooked foods in close proximity.
- Allow staff suffering from boils, whitlows, sores, nose/throat infections, diarrhoea or parasitic worms to handle food.
- Permit any suspect infected or mouldy commodities to be used.
- Allow pets or other animals near open food.

3 Food Commodities, Food Processing and Cooking

Objectives

To assess the natural contamination of food commodities. To outline the industrial treatment of raw and processed foods. To examine common cooking and food-holding methods used in quantity food production and to assess their effectiveness in controlling contamination and growth.

Introduction

Contamination is present in most raw foods, because most commodities are derived from living plants and animals. All such living things are associated with bacteria, viruses and parasites of one sort or another throughout their life before harvesting. Of the vast number of different species of bacteria, moulds and parasitic animals which live in association with animals and plants, only a few cause food-borne illness. However the number of known harmful organisms is growing and raw food commodities should generally be regarded as contaminated.

Besides biological contamination, some commodities also contain natural, harmful substances. Certain plants synthesize toxic substances as a part of their biological defence mechanism. On the other hand, fish and shellfish can accumulate poisons from their food. This means that some quite common foods may become harmful under certain circumstances. Those who handle food should know how and when these poisons are likely to occur, and whether they are destroyed during cooking and processing.

Processed foods are commonly thought to be sterile and harmless. Sometimes this view is justified, but processing is not always able to destroy bacteria, toxins, chemicals or spores. The storage both of raw and processed food has an important influence on quality and hygiene.

Cooking, hot- and cold-holding of food are the last lines of defence against biological contamination in the food chain. Cooking processes differ in their impact on bacterial populations in food. Some destroy bacteria completely, others only partially. Hot- and cold-holding techniques also vary in effectiveness. This chapter examines the inherent contamination of food commodities and how this may be controlled by processing storage and cooking.

Food commodities

Meat and poultry

Raw meat and poultry are very important sources of biological contamination. Conditions of temperature, moisture, pH and nutrient availability in the bodies of meat animals and birds are similar to those within the human body. Bacteria and parasites may therefore easily infect the human body and cause illness. Meat also provides a good environment for bacteria to multiply and this increases the chance of contamination. Farming practice is one source of meat carcass contamination. Animals are often confined to overcrowded sheds for intensive rearing so that pathogens such as *Salmonella* can easily spread through the population. Poultry rearing sheds are particularly noted for crowding and for poor construction. Cleaning is often inadequate and disinfection impossible. Contaminated feed is regarded as an important source of *Salmonella* bacteria, but rats and wild birds probably also play a part in spreading them. Salmonellae readily become part of the natural intestinal flora of poultry and may be passed down from generation to generation. The bacteria have also been discovered in eggs. The *Protein Processing Order, 1981* demands that animal protein destined for animal feed should be heat-sterilized. However this legislation seems to have had little impact on the spread of *Salmonella* in chickens.

Question
How does chicken feed become contaminated with *Salmonella*?

> Despite the Order it seems that waste chicken flesh and other meats may still be incorporated into feed, without adequate heat sterilization.

Salmonella is less common in red meat than in poultry, but there are many documented instances in beef, pork and lamb. Reptiles and amphibians are generally infected with *Salmonellae*. Turtles and frogs' legs are known sources of contamination (Hobbs, 1976). Poultry also commonly carry *Campylobacter*. Frogs may be infected with *Aeromonas hydrophila*. Intestinal and soil bacteria are common in all types of meat and poultry. These include coliforms (e.g. *Escherichia coli*), faecal *Streptococci, Clostridium perfringens, Clostridium botulinum, Listeria monocytogenes, Yersinia enterolitica* and *Bacillus* species. Various non-pathogenic food spoilage bacteria are also present. Red meat may also contain cysts of tapeworm larvae and the eggs of *Ascaris* worms. *Trichinella* cysts may be present in pork.

Preparation of meat carcasses

Animals transported to slaughterhouses are generally allowed to rest before slaughter. Fatigue, excitement or stress may be produced by overcrowding in lorries and pens. These factors increase the excretion of faecal bacteria. They also decrease the glycogen content of the muscles. This produces meat of poorer quality, more susceptible to bacterial spoilage. At the same time, contamination by faecal bacteria is rendered more likely. The rested animals are stunned electrically and then drained of blood. Hides and **viscera** (intestines and offal) are removed and the carcass is suspended by the rear legs to extend the leg muscles. Raising the animal's anal region also increases the chance of faecal bacteria dripping on to the meat. It is thus impossible to avoid some contamination during the processing of carcasses. Faecal bacteria are transferred to the meat from the intestines and soil bacteria from the hide. Bacteria from the hands of slaughterhouse workers or from the floor may also contaminate the meat. Scalding tanks are used to soften pigs' bristles and to make chickens easier to pluck. They will transfer bacteria if they operate below 60°C.

After slaughter the carcasses go into *rigor mortis*. Muscles continue to respire anaerobically and contract in an uncontrolled way, so that the carcass stiffens and becomes warm. Stores of muscle glycogen are converted into lactic acid and the pH of the meat drops to around 5.6. Meat is then 'ripened' by cold storage (0–2°C) for about 14 days. The rigor passes off and the flesh softens again. Bacteria are present in much larger numbers on the surface of a carcass than within the flesh itself. The interior is not contaminated during slaughter and in any case is partly protected by the lactic acid and low pH. However, bruises on animal or poultry carcasses may also contain bacteria, which can contaminate the surrounding meat. Any cutting or chopping tends to spread contamination from the surface throughout the meat.

Machine recovered meat (MRM)

This term refers to meat which is mechanically gleaned from bones after the normally usable flesh has been removed by hand. In one process the bones are scoured with toothed wheels. Alternatively they can be fed into a machine which scrapes them with sharp blades in water under high pressure. The product is a fine purée, with no remaining meat texture. Machine recovered meat is incorporated into pies, hamburgers and other products. Concern has been expressed that MRM is microbiologically inferior to other chopped meats, particularly as organ meats are often incorporated into it. There is also a fear that the use of brain, spinal cord and certain glands from cattle may spread the disease *bovine spongiform encephalopathy* ('mad cow disease') to man. Since Autumn 1989 the use of these organ meats from cattle has been banned, but organs from other meat animals are still permitted.

Question

What other precautions could be taken with machine recovered meat to make it safer?

> There is some consumer pressure for products containing MRM to be labelled as such. MRM is both more likely to be contaminated and more susceptible to bacterial growth. Therefore there are grounds for urging that specific instructions for cooking and storage be provided on packaging.

During ripening and chilled storage the numbers of mesophilic bacteria in carcasses fall. Psychrophile numbers increase as shown in Figure 3.1 (McDowell *et al.*, 1986). Raw meat and poultry should be stored as cold as possible, as long as they do not actually freeze. A temperature of about 2°C is usually used. *Listeria monocytogenes* and *Yersinia enterolitica* only grow slowly at this temperature. Raw meat and poultry should be stored separately from other foods. If it is necessary for some reason to store them in the same refrigerator, raw foods should always be placed below cooked ones. This minimizes the chance of blood or pieces of meat falling down and contaminating cooked products.

Slaughterhouse controls

The *Slaughterhouse (Hygiene) Regulations, 1977* and the *Poultry Meat (Hygiene) Regulations, 1976* bring slaughterhouse hygiene in England

Figure 3.1   Changes in brisket microflora during chilled storage

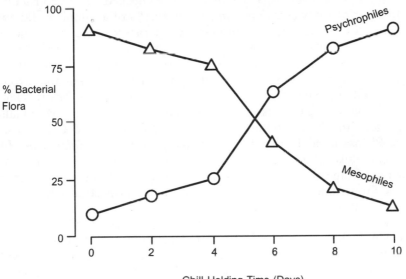

Source: McDowell *et al*., (1986) p. 65.

and Wales to the standard required by the European Community. Parallel Scottish Regulations were passed in 1978 and 1987 respectively. They aim to ensure good hygiene of slaughterhouse premises, equipment and personnel. In addition, under the *Meat Inspection Regulations, 1963*, all meat carcasses and offal leaving slaughterhouses must be inspected using a specified procedure. Acceptable meat is stamped as fit for consumption. Unfit meat must be stained black, stored and transported in locked containers, and heat sterilized before use in animal feed.

Game

Use of game is on the increase in catering, particularly in the commercial sector. Increased farming of game has meant greater supplies to satisfy the demand. Slaughter of game animals and birds is not controlled by law. When game is shot in the wild, quick, efficient evisceration and dressing of carcasses (e.g. of deer) is impossible. Even the slaughter and preparation of farmed deer is much less hygienic than normal slaughter-house practice. Historically there has been less statutory control, and only a small percentage of game carcasses are checked before consumption. In a recent study (Beynon *et al.*, 1988) 16.5% of a sample of fallow deer carcasses showed serious diseases or parasitic infections. Game animals are almost always frightened or stressed when they are shot or slaughtered, and they are not immediately bled. This means that the flesh always has a higher moisture content and higher pH than that from domesticated animals. Bacteria can invade it relatively easily. The practice of hanging game also increases the bacterial content. Mammals such as deer and hares undoubtedly contain coliforms and *Clostridium* species. Pheasants and other birds are likely to contain *Salmonella*. In 1980 tuberculosis (*Mycobacterium bovis*) was identified in deer, presumably spread from cattle via badgers and other wild animals. In December 1989 the Government launched a new veterinary inspection scheme for tuberculosis in farmed deer herds.

Dressed carcasses of deer and hares should be stored at 2°C with other meats. Unplucked birds should be stored below 5°C, but must not be kept with dressed carcasses or cut meats as cross-contamination will occur. Diseased or injured carcasses should be returned to the licensed game dealer.

Question

What precautions should the caterer or food handler take with game?

> Game should automatically be regarded as contaminated. Particular care should be taken to prevent cross-contamination during storage and handling. It should be cooked thoroughly; i.e. stewing and pot-roasting are preferable to roasting or grilling because heat transfer is better.

Raw vegetables and fruit

Fruit and vegetables are an important source of contamination. They commonly carry bacteria from soil, from manure and from the hands of pickers. Fresh fruit and vegetables are still living at the time of use, so bacteria on the surface are unable to multiply or to invade the interior. However bacteria from these raw foods may be transferred to hands, and equipment such as knives, and contaminate cooked products. Vegetables such as green peppers are often used raw or only partly cooked in order to preserve their texture. This can introduce harmful bacteria into cooked products intended for chilled storage. Salad vegetables are generally safe when well washed. It is also possible to use a mild chlorine disinfectant such as **sodium dichloroisocyanurate** in the washing water. Highly infective organisms such as *Shigella* and parasite eggs may be transferred to salads by handlers. Beansprouts are often contaminated with *Escherichia coli* and other intestinal bacteria during culture (Reid, 1986). They need very careful washing, preferably with a mild disinfectant, if they are to be eaten raw. Watercress should be carefully washed as it occasionally carries liver fluke larvae.

Few poisonous plants are likely to cause foodborne illness through catering operations. **Oxalic acid** in mature rhubarb stems and leaves is very bitter and astringent at toxic concentrations. Plants such as deadly nightshade do not find their way into commercial salad vegetables. However certain strains of potatoes contain the alkaloid **solanin** in harmful quantities, particularly in the skins of green tubers. Solanin may cause dizziness, palpitations and sickness if the dose is large enough. It is only likely to be fatal in small children. Incidents are extremely rare.

Bacteria found on fungi are similar to those on other vegetable foods. Contamination may be considerable in wild fungi, but cultivated ones are grown on sterilized manure. Cultured spawn is very pure, so there is no danger of buying cultivated mushrooms which might contain poisonous fungi. Nor is this a significant danger with commercially picked wild species. However the use of oyster mushroom, jew's ear, cep and other wild varieties is increasing. Any fungi in a batch which appear different in shape, structure or colour from the others should be rejected.

Fruit, vegetables and fungi should be stored in cool (10–15°C), dry conditions in the dark. Ideally items should be stored separately on racks, so that air can circulate and inhibit mould growth. Particular care should be taken with soft fruits and vegetables, which must be used quickly and discarded if spoiled.

Cereals and pulse foods

Cereal products frequently contain *Bacillus cereus* spores. Rice and cornflour are reported sources. It seems likely that cereals grown in hot regions are most at risk. However other sources of the organism will probably be identified in time. Cereals are prone to attack by moulds. **Ergot** may be present in imported rye or rye flour. **Aflatoxin-** and **patulin-** producing moulds have been reported on spaghetti and wheat.

The growing trend toward vegetarianism and healthy eating has led to increased use of beans, nuts and other pulse foods. Nuts are an important source of aflatoxin, particularly peanuts. Certain dried beans, particularly red kidney beans, contain poisons called *haemagglutinins* (Noah *et al.*, 1980). These substances act rapidly to cause vomiting and severe abdominal cramps, with an onset time of one to four hours. Haemagglutinins are destroyed by cooking at 100°C for ten minutes. Most of the reported cases have been caused by inadequate cooking of beans. Electrical slow cookers, which often operate around 90°C, have been responsible for several domestic incidents. If beans are inadequately cooked during the preparation of vegetarian versions of burgers, lasagne etc, food poisoning may result.

Milling processes do not reduce the bacterial or toxic content of cereals and pulses. In fact they may distribute contamination through the product. After milling, white wheat flour is bleached with chemical additives. These probably help to reduce populations of bacteria, weevils and other pests. Untreated products, such as unbleached and wholemeal flours tend to have a higher bacterial population.

Wholegrain and milled cereals and pulses should be stored in sealed, rodent-proof containers on shelves off the floor. The store area should be well ventilated and maintained at low humidity. Cereals and pulses are *hygroscopic*, i.e. they pick up moisture from moist air. When this happens, insect eggs may hatch or mould may begin to grow. Spilt cereal products should be swept up immediately. Otherwise they will attract pests and moulds to the food store.

Dairy products

Despite strict dairy hygiene regulations, raw milk may contain bacteria from faeces (*E. coli*, *Salmonella*, *Campylobacter*), from soil (*Clostridium perfringens*, *Listeria monocytogenes*) and from human and animal skin (*Staphylococcus aureus*). In addition a number of diseases of cattle can also be passed to man. *Zoonoses* (singular: *Zoonosis*) is the term used for animal diseases of this type. Examples are tuberculosis, brucellosis and *Streptococcus zooepidemicus* infection. The sale of raw milk is now very strictly controlled. Almost all retail milk is heat-treated to destroy pathogenic bacteria. Three techniques are commonly used: pasteurization, UHT treatment and sterilization.

Pasteurization involves heating the milk at 72°C for 15 seconds, then rapidly cooling to below 10°C. The process kills *Salmonella* efficiently.

Question
How does this relate to the information about thermal death time, D and z values, given in Chapters 1 and 2?

D_{60} for *Salmonella* is about 4 minutes and z is about 4°C. So for every rise of 4°C we achieve another 10-fold reduction in numbers. D_{72} ought to be 1/10 x 1/10 x 1/10 x 4 minutes, or 240 thousandths of a second (about a quarter of a second). Therefore 15 sec would result in a 1060-fold reduction. But milk contains sugar and fat which help to protect the bacteria.

However *Listeria monocytogenes* has been shown to survive pasteurization at 72°C in viable numbers. In the USA, the temperature for flash pasteurization (i.e. the 15-second process) has been raised to 76°C. Whichever process is used, the milk still contains spoilage bacteria, which limit its usable life to about five days.

Ultra-high-temperature (UHT) treatment involves heating the milk to 132°C for one second. This is a continuous process like flash pasteurization, in which the milk is heated and cooled by passing through heat exchangers. The milk is aseptically packed (see below under food processing) and will keep for six months or more at room temperature. UHT gives milk a more noticeably 'cooked' taste than pasteurization.

Sterilized milk has an even more 'cooked' flavour. The batch process involves heating the milk in sealed bottles at 112°C under pressure for 15 minutes. The bottles are rapidly cooled to 80°C and then allowed to reach ambient temperature. All bacteria and almost all spores are destroyed and the product has a usable life of years.

Cream is made by continuously centrifuging raw milk so that the natural butterfat globules separate out. It is pasteurized at 74°C for 15 seconds or UHT-treated, like milk. Cream is a good medium for bacterial growth, and is easily contaminated during whipping, piping and filling. Cream cakes and desserts may therefore contain high counts of coliforms, *Staphylococci* and even *Salmonella* unless handled very carefully (Clacherty *et al.*, 1988). These bacteria mostly originate from food handlers, not from the cream itself.

Butter is made by churning pasteurized cream mechanically at a temperature of about 7°C. Granules of solidified butter form, which are skimmed off, salted, and pressed into blocks. The water content of butter is lower than that of milk or cream, and bacterial growth is inhibited by the added salt. However although butter has a comparatively low bacterial count, its fat content is likely to protect bacteria and spores during subsequent cooking.

Cheese-making involves curdling pasteurized milk using *rennet*, an enzyme extracted from the stomachs of calves. A bacterial culture is also added, to sour the curdling milk. Protein and milk fat separate together as curds which are salted and packed in cheesecloth. Hard cheeses are also squeezed at this stage to remove more of the watery 'whey'. Most types are then ripened by long storage, which gives each type of cheese its character. Cheeses contain natural antibiotic-like substances, such as *nisin*, which tend to protect them from bacterial spoilage. However *Listeria monocytogenes* can multiply in refrigerated cheeses, particularly soft varieties with a pH greater than 4.5. Cheeses may also be contaminated with *Salmonella*, *E. coli* or *Staphylococcus aureus* during handling. Bacterial contamination may be invisible to inspection at first. Growth eventually produces sliminess or an off-flavour. Yeasts may grow on cheese as slimy, whitish patches, and moulds as green, grey, black or brown areas. Blue cheeses are produced by deliberately inoculating with strains of *Penicillium* mould. Some of these are known to produce the mycotoxins penicillic acid and patulin but no cases of food poisoning from this source have been reported.

Yoghurt is made by culturing a mixture of milk and milk solids with bacteria: *Streptococcus thermophilus* and *Lactobacillus bulgaricus* are commonly used, although some producers use other species. *Lactose* in the milk is converted to *lactic acid* which acts as a natural preservative. Protein is precipitated at the lowered pH and the mixture thickens. Yoghurt may be pasteurized or sold 'live'. Bacteria in the latter go on working and acidification continues until the product is too sour to eat. Refrigerated yoghurts have a shelf life of about 10 days. Most spoilage is due to moulds or yeasts, but a few bacteria may also grow in yoghurt. For instance, *Pseudomonas* bacteria taint yoghurt with an off-flavour resembling overripe strawberries.

Dairy foods should be stored under refrigeration at about 4°C. Stock rotation should be strict and rapid. Dairy-packed, pasteurized milk and cream should be used within 2 days. Once cream has been whipped and piped it should not be held for more than 12 hours. For safety's sake, yoghurt should be used within 7 days. Hard cheeses such as Cheddar or Parmesan may be held chilled for several weeks but soft cheeses like Brie, Camembert or Limburger should be used within 10 days. Dairy products are easily tainted by odours from solvents, chemicals or other foods, and should always be wrapped or covered before storage.

Dairy controls

The *Milk and Dairies (General) Regulations, 1959* require milk producers and distributors to register with local authorities and specify the hygiene of cows, milkers and dairy premises. The *Milk (Special Designations) Regulations, 1986* set out process times and temperatures for pasteurization, sterilization and UHT processing of raw milk and cream. Standards and tests for the fat content, non-fat solids, blood albumin and bacterial content of milk are also specified. These regulations also stipulate the labelling and colour-coding of heat-treated milk. The dairy regulations have been amended several times to bring them into line with technological advances and with EC directives.

Ice-cream is traditionally made from cream, sugar and eggs plus a thickener such as cornflour or gelatine. A few high quality products still use these classic ingredients. However most ice-cream today is prepared from hydrogenated vegetable oil, powdered dried milk, sugar, gelatine, emulsifiers and water. These are mixed together, pasteurized or sterilized, mixed again and frozen. The second mixing step suspends (*emulsifies*) the fat in the finely-divided form necessary for freezing. Commercial ice-cream must by law be pasteurized or sterilized. For pasteurization any of the following time/temperature treatments may be used:

80°C	for 15 seconds
71°C	for 10 minutes
65.5°C	for 30 minutes

Question
Why are these temperature/time treatments higher than for milk?

Ice-cream is rich in sugar and fat, both of which increase bacterial resistance, so the pasteurization conditions need to be harsher than those for milk. Commercial sterilization involves heating to 149°C for two seconds followed by cooling to below 7°C within 1.5 hours.

Ice-cream must be kept below −2.2°C at all times after freezing. Soft ice-cream is made by reconstituting powdered ice-cream solids with water and then freezing in a special machine. Great care must be taken with personal hygiene and with the cleaning of machines. Factory-wrapped ice-cream usually contains very low bacterial numbers.

Fish

Fish contain very few pathogenic bacteria when they are caught. Some oriental species may contain *Vibrio parahaemolyticus*, derived from water-borne sewage. *Clostridium botulinum* (type E) is also found in fish intestines. Otherwise most harmful bacteria are introduced from the hands of food handlers, from dirty equipment, from contaminated tables or from floors. Fish flesh is more watery and has a higher pH than meat. This makes it very prone to bacterial growth, particularly by salt-tolerant organisms such as *Staphylococcus aureus* or *Vibrio parahaemolyticus*.

Fish sometimes contain cysts of the tapeworm *Diphyllobothrium latum*. These may develop into the adult worm in the human intestine, but the worm is relatively easily diagnosed and treated. Farmed fishes may carry *Aeromonas hydrophila* bacteria (Roberts, 1976). Mackerel, tuna and sprats are rich in the amino acid **histidine**. Spoilage bacteria convert this into **histamine** which causes the so-called **scombrotoxic** poisoning (*scomber* is Latin for mackerel). Onset is extremely rapid, sometimes taking less than one hour. Symptoms are like those of allergic reactions (which are also caused by histamine). There may be a burning or dry sensation in the mouth and throat, a headache and nettlerash. There is usually also vomiting, diarrhoea and abdominal pain.

Tropical reef fish may contain a toxin called **ciguatera**. It is produced by **dinoflagellates**, a type of algae. These are eaten by fish and accumulate in the food chain so that the largest species; groupers, bass and barracuda, may contain considerable quantities of toxin. Affected fish smell and taste the same as harmless ones. Onset of poisoning is rapid, i.e. 1–6 hours. Symptoms are blurred vision, weakness, paralysis, numbness of the mouth and throat. There may also be vomiting and diarrhoea. Grouper, barracuda and other exotic fishes are available frozen in the UK and a small number of ciguatera cases occur here each year.

Shellfish

The flesh of shellfish is watery and has a rather high pH like that of fish. Shellfish tend to live in shallow waters close to the shore, where they may be contaminated by sewage. Like fish, shellfish are easily contaminated from hands and utensils. The common types of shellfish eaten in the UK can be classified as crustaceans, bivalves and gastropods.

Crustaceans include shrimps, prawns, lobsters and crabs. Those from British waters are sold live or ready-boiled. Provided the membrane joining the sections of shell remains intact during boiling, bacterial contamination cannot enter the animal. Crabs and lobsters bought ready-boiled should be inspected to ensure that cooking water has not entered them. Crustaceans require a good deal of handling during shelling and dressing. During these operations pathogenic bacteria may be transferred to the flesh. They multiply rapidly unless the seafood is adequately refrigerated. Boiled crustaceans are usually eaten without any further heat processing which might kill bacteria. Thus peeled prawns, dressed crabs and lobsters should be handled as hygienically as possible, and refrigerated at all times until they are eaten.

Raw, unpeeled prawns imported from the Far East may contain *Vibrio parahaemolyticus*. Cooked peeled prawns may also become cross-contaminated from raw products during storage or transit. *Vibrio* may also be transferred on the hands of process workers. However a study of the

Sri Lankan prawn industry (Sumner *et al.*, 1982) suggests that *Staphylococcus aureus* and coliforms are more likely to be transferred in this way. 'Crab Stix', 'Ocean Tails' and similar shellfish-like products are made by a process called **Surimi**. Waste or unsaleable fish such as Arctic Pollack, and sometimes shellfish, such as krill, are ground to a fine pulp. This is dissolved in a special alkaline medium and then extruded into dilute acid, where it sets into the desired shape. The mixture is not cooked but bacteria are removed by micro-filtration or pasteurization. Surimi products are usually of high microbiological quality when sold, but they can acquire bacteria by cross-contamination and will deteriorate rapidly if not refrigerated.

Bivalves are molluscs with two shells, e.g. oysters, cockles, mussels, scallops and clams. These animals filter their food from sea water, which they constantly pass through their bodies. Bivalves living in polluted water may thus become grossly contaminated with faecal bacteria and viruses. Long cooking tends to spoil the quality of these foods: cockles, mussels and clams are best boiled or steamed for about ten minutes. Scallops are sold in the raw, shelled (shucked) state and are usually sautéd briefly. Oysters are eaten raw. Thus contamination may well survive preparation for the table. The gathering and sale of shellfish should be carefully controlled.

The *Public Health (shellfish) Regulations, 1934* empower local authorities to forbid commercial gathering of bivalves from known polluted areas. Environmental Health Departments in coastal areas monitor bivalve shellfish quality. If indicator organisms such as coliforms appear, growers may be required to purify their shellfish before sale (Thomsett, 1986). Two techniques are used: relaying and depuration.

Relaying means removing the shellfish from a polluted area and transferring to a non-polluted area. This is rarely done just to purify the animals, but it is common practice to move farmed shellfish around. For example they can be transferred from a poor growing area to a good one. Alternatively they may be overwintered in clean holding basins.

Depuration involves holding the bivalves in a specially designed tank. Water circulating through the tank is sterilized either with chlorine or with ultraviolet light. The latter is now the most used method. Chlorination has to be very carefully controlled, as too little will not kill the bacteria, while too much will kill the shellfish.

Bivalves also filter and accumulate viruses from sewage. Norwalk-like virus has been reported in oysters and other bivalves. During the winter these animals metabolize slowly and normal depuration times are not sufficient to free them of viruses. Hepatitis A and polio viruses may also be transferred. Power and Collins (1986) comment: 'Heavily contaminated shellfish . . . [should] enter the food chain only through a certified heat-processing facility. Depuration cannot be relied upon to produce virus-pathogen-free shellfish.'

Cooked bivalve shellfish offer the same opportunities for bacterial growth as cooked fish or meat. They are easily contaminated during handling. Like crustaceans, they are not usually reheated before serving, so great care should be taken with processing and storage.

One of the algae on which bivalves feed during the summer months is a dinoflagellate (a reddish, single-celled plant with a silica skeleton) called *Gonyaulix*. This species produces a toxin called *saxitoxin* which becomes stored in the flesh of oysters and mussels. Saxitoxin is the cause of *paralytic shellfish poisoning (PSP)* in man. Onset is within one to three hours. The first symptom is usually lolling of the head due to loss of control in the neck muscles. General paralysis ensues and in severe cases death may occur by respiratory failure. PSP has a fatality rate of about 10%. Cases are uncommon and sporadic, as is the distribution of *Gonyaulix*. PSP is most likely to occur in the summer months, during exceptionally warm weather. Oysters do not retain the toxin for long and can be freed from it by depuration. Mussels hold high levels of saxitoxin for three weeks or longer and cannot be regarded as safe to eat during the summer months. Boiling does not destroy the toxin.

Gastropods (literally 'stomach feet') are molluscs with a single shell, such as winkles, whelks and snails. Winkles and whelks thrive in polluted water and may be contaminated by sewage, but they are usually boiled well before use. Whelks are shelled by hand after boiling. They may thus become contaminated with *Staphylococcus aureus* and coliforms in the same way as crustaceans. Certain species of marine snails, for example red whelks, produce toxins. These gastropods occasionally cause illness when they are picked and eaten in error with winkles.

Question

What action should caterers take if they wish to offer these foods?

> Boiled whelks should only be bought from a reputable supplier. It is best to buy winkles live. Any shells which appear different from the others should be rejected and the winkles should be cooked for at least 20 minutes.

Snails (*escargots*) frequently accumulate toxins from the plants on which they feed. Normally they are fed on oatmeal or bran for 10 days before sale, to clean them. Live, imported snails may be contaminated with *Salmonella* (Hobbs, 1976). No information is available about those farmed in the UK. Harmful bacteria are destroyed by adequate cooking, but snails may be contaminated during subsequent preparation.

Herbs and spices

Herbs and spices are mostly grown and gathered in hot climates, many from the Third World. Opportunities for contamination by bacteria and parasite eggs are many. Spices possess some antimicrobial activity, but this is narrow in spectrum. Chattopadhyay and Teli (1986) found large numbers of coliforms and *Bacillus* species in curry powder and spices from the Indian subcontinent. *Salmonella* and *E. coli* were absent. No similar report is available for herbs, but it is likely that these too are contaminated with soil and faecal bacteria. Fumigation of spices destroys pathogens and pests. The process is being phased out in the UK and many spices are still packaged and sold without treatment.

Beverages

Brews and infusions such as tea, coffee, cocoa and the increasingly popular *tisanes* (herb and fruit teas) have no health risk. Probably the raw materials become quite contaminated during picking, processing and drying. However any pathogens in coffee and cocoa beans are likely to be killed during roasting. Bacteria on teas and herbs are destroyed during infusion. Pathogens are only likely to survive if the teas are used in food without prior infusion.

Freshly squeezed fruit drinks offer bacteria a poor medium for growth. Their high acidity (pH 3.5 or less) means that in the short term only wild yeasts can grow. Affected juices are cloudier than usual and may bubble. Occasionally they may be discoloured. Yeast-contaminated drinks are not harmful as such but they indicate poor quality and should not be sold. Freshly squeezed juices should be kept as cold as possible i.e. 0–2°C. This not only inhibits the yeasts but also preserves the ascorbic acid content and the delicate flavour components.

Dispensed drinks include beer, lager and, increasingly, carbonated soft drinks. They are usually supplied pasteurized or sterilized to the retailer, and any contamination commonly comes from the dispensing system. Pipes leading from beer barrels to the bar taps become contaminated when barrels are changed. They must be cleaned regularly, but are often inaccessible to manual cleaning with brushes or pull-throughs. Instead, highly corrosive chemicals must be passed through the dispensing system to remove all traces of bacteria. Beer-line cleaning must be carried out very strictly and carefully. If the chemicals are allowed inadequate time to act the lines remain contaminated. If the lines are inadequately rinsed, the first few pints of beer may be seriously contaminated.

Soft-drink dispensers mix flavoured syrups with mains water and pressurize with carbon dioxide. The quality of the product is micro-biologically only as good as that of the water supply (see the section below on water). Tap lines also need periodic cleaning, like those supplying beer. Many dispensed products are low-calorie items. Unlike beer they contain few nutrients for bacteria, so line-cleaning may be somewhat less critical.

'Real ales' are unpasteurized and still contain live yeast. They are dispensed from the barrel or pumped through traditional, hand-operated bar pumps. Here too, the pipes need regular, careful cleaning and rinsing. Because they have not been pasteurized real ales are still in the process of fermentation. This tends to enhance keeping quality by protecting the beer from other microbial invaders. The brewing process involves boiling before fermentation, so it is unlikely that pathogenic bacteria could survive from the raw materials. However, spoilage organisms can and do get into the barrels. All such beer should be used rapidly and rejected if deterioration of any kind is noticed. Real ale should be stored at or below 15°C, the optimum temperature for serving.

Wines and juices in Tetrapaks and cartons have been pasteurized or ultra-heat-treated and packed under sterile conditions. They are gener-ally of very good microbiological quality. Many of the cheaper bottled wines are also pasteurized. The more expensive fine wines rely on fermentation to destroy spoilage organisms; any that survive are identi-fied by quality control during the ageing process. Bottles of fine wines are usually fitted with lead capsules. During ageing in the bottle, a little of the wine may leak past the cork into the capsule, where the acids in it may react with the lead. The resulting *lead salts* could cause serious illness if they found their way into the wine when the bottle was opened.

Question

How can the problem of lead poisoning from wine be systematically avoided?

Wine waiters should be trained to wipe the tops of bottles with a damp cloth between peeling off the capsule and drawing the cork.

Water and ice

Under the *Food Hygiene (General) Regulations, 1970*, food premises are required to have a sufficient, constant supply of clean, wholesome water. Most food operations use filtered, chlorinated water from the main supply, but a few are supplied from private wells or boreholes. Treated mains water is one of the purest 'food' products available, often with less than 10 bacterial cells per millilitre. Water from boreholes and wells should be tested before use. The acceptance criterion is that no coliforms are found per 100 ml in 95% of samples or in any two consecutive samples (Jacob, 1988).

Roof space storage tanks are widely used to ensure a good pressure of hot and cold water. Uncovered tanks in the roof space tend to become contaminated from dust and wind-blown particles. Insects, birds and rodents may use it as their water supply and contaminate it with pathogens, feathers, droppings and dead bodies. Even a covered tank is at some risk of contamination. Water from storage tanks may be used for cooking, but not for drinks or food preparation. Only water from the rising main can be regarded as completely safe for drinking. Soft-drink dispensers and vending machines should be connected directly to the mains. Water from the hot supply should always be regarded as potentially contaminated.

Ice machines should also be operated from the main water supply. Ice storage bins in machines should be regularly cleaned. Ice buckets in bars are a common source of contamination. Murphy and Mepham (1988) showed that stored ice in machines contained on average 12 times more bacteria than are present in water supplies. Ice buckets contained 56 times as many bacteria.

Study example 3.1

When presented with a list of food commodities and their hazards, many people ask 'What can we eat then?' What is safe?' No human activity is completely free of risk, particularly not a frequent activity such as eating. But individuals should be be allowed to eat what they like as long as they are prepared to take the consequences. Food risks underline the duties of the caterer: customers must be given what they want, but the risks must be minimized. It is important for caterers to understand the risks associated with different food commodities and seek to control them.

1. Describe three risks associated with sleeping (another frequent human activity).
2. Rare roast venison and raw oysters are examples of high risk foods. What might be the consequences of eating them?
3. What can caterers do to minimize the risks from these two products?

> 4. In general there are three ways in which the caterer can control risks by using his/her knowledge of commodities. What are they?

Processed and preserved foods

In general, food processing companies are able to exert much higher standards of microbial quality control than the caterer. Highly processed foods can therefore be regarded as safe in terms of food-borne illness. However, traditional products such as smoked and cured foods often need careful storage to maintain their safety. They may also cross-contaminate other, more sensitive products. It is therefore important for the food premises manager to understand:

- Food spoilage and food processing treatments.
- The likely surviving bacterial content in processed foods.
- Storage procedures for processed foods.

Food spoilage

Spoilage is anything which makes food unfit to eat, for example deterioration of appearance, texture, flavour and aroma. Spoilage includes physical contamination, e.g. by dead insects or rodent droppings. Food poisoning and spoilage are traditionally regarded as linked, for example in 'ptomaine poisoning'. Ptomaine (a name coined by Professor Selmi of Bologna, Italy, in 1880) was supposed to be an alkaloidal poison produced during food spoilage. We now know that there is no direct relationship; specific bacteria and/or toxins have to be present to cause food poisoning. Often these agents are present in food which is not apparently 'spoiled' at all. Food spoilage is caused in three main ways: growth of living things, oxidation and enzyme reactions.

Growth of living things usually involves bacteria, yeasts or moulds. These organisms convert some of the constituents of foods into undesirable substances: taints, discoloration, slime etc. A list of typical organisms and the spoilage they cause is shown in Table 3.1. Other living things which may contaminate food are insects, larvae and rodents.

Oxidation means the reaction of food constituents with oxygen from the air. For instance meats and meat products turn brown as the red pigment *myoglobin* is slowly oxidized to *metmyoglobin*. Fats become

Table 3.1 Typical spoilage organisms of foods

Species	Foods affected	Signs of spoilage
Bacteria:		
Clostridium	fresh and processed meats and fish	putrefaction, off-odours and flavours. Soft rot etc
Pseudomonas	fresh and processed meats and fish	spots (surface colonies), off-odours and flavours
Acetobacter	wine and beer	souring and cloudiness
Lactobacillus	vacuum packed and processed meats, bacon	slime, off-odours, gas production
	milk	souring
	wine	'rope' and 'graisse'
Streptococcus/ Micrococcus	fresh and processed meats and milk	tainting, off-flavours and odours
Bacillus	cooked products, milk, bread	off-odours and flavours, 'rope' in bread
Moulds.		
Botrytis,	fruit and vegetables	softening, 'furriness'
Penicillium/ Rhizopus	cheese, bread, cooked foods	off-flavours, black or green patches
Yeasts:	jams and preserves	'winey' flavour, runny texture,
	cheese	slime, greyish discoloration, 'wet' spots, off-odours
	wine and beer	off-flavours, souring, cloudiness

rancid by reacting with oxygen and producing tainting by-products. Very little fat need be present. For example wholemeal flour and coffee have short shelf lives because their small fat content is easily oxidized.

Enzyme reactions cause spoilage whenever living cells are ruptured. The natural, enzyme-regulated cellular processes get out of control and some of the constituents of foods may be converted into undesirable colours, taints or off-flavours. When vegetable cells are killed, undesirable enzyme reactions may result. For instance peeled apples and potatoes brown due to the enzyme *polyphenol oxidase*. Enzymes in broccoli and brussels sprouts cause gross tainting and loss of colour if the vegetables are not blanched before freezing. Wholemeal flour requires oxygen to become rancid, but the reaction is rapid because it is catalyzed by an enzyme released during milling. Enzyme reactions also occur in freshly-slaughtered meats (described earlier in this chapter), but these are mostly beneficial.

Food preservation techniques

There are a wide variety of food processing techniques in use. Some are solely concerned with preservation. Others, such as smoking, are more important for the way they enhance food quality than for actual preservation. Food processing techniques can be loosely classified into two groups, depending on whether they:

- Prevent or inhibit microbial growth.
- Destroy micro-organisms.

Most processes rely on one or other of these approaches. A few employ both.

Inhibiting microbial growth

The factors which bacteria need in order to grow were discussed in Chapter 1. It is possible to preserve food by restricting one or more of these, as follows.

- Keep the food at a lower temperature (i.e. chill or freeze).
- Lower the water activity (by drying, salting etc.).
- Change the atmosphere (pack under vacuum etc.).
- Lower the pH (by adding acids: vinegar, lactic or citric acid).
- Add preservatives (sulphur dioxide, nitrites etc.).

Lowering the storage temperature

Chilled foods

Many raw commodities are supplied chilled. Some processed foods also need the protection of refrigeration, for example ham, salami and smoked fish. Chilling and refrigeration do not destroy bacteria. Mesophilic species mostly decline in numbers, while psychrophilic bacteria are encouraged. The mesophiles thus tend over a period of days to give way to an increasing psychrophile population (see Figure 3.1).

Cross-contamination occurs easily in refrigerated foods and microbiological growth does not stop, it is is only slowed. For this reason, chilled items should be clearly labelled and regularly inspected. Stock rotation should be carefully observed. All refrigerated foods should be wrapped. Cross-contamination should be minimized by keeping raw and cooked foods apart.

Question
How should this be done?

Separate refrigerator cabinets (or separate shelves in a walk-in unit) should be available for different categories of foodstuffs. Raw foods should always be stored below cooked ones.

Chilled catered products

Cook–chill systems involve pre-cooking the food, rapidly chilling it and holding it refrigerated until use. It is then *regenerated*, i.e. heated to the original, just-cooked temperature, before serving. Many airline meal operations rely on chilled storage of food, portioned onto special trays. Advantages are that the meals do not spoil if planes are delayed and they are convenient to store and regenerate during flight. Cook–chill production may also lead to increased productivity, more efficient purchasing and the elimination of unsocial (and expensive) shiftwork hours. Large quantities of single lines may be produced during the course of a normal working day.

Sous vide is a style of cook–chill production where foods (usually of the meat and vegetable entrée type) are partly cooked and then sealed under vacuum into special laminated plastic bags. The bags are rapidly chilled to minimize bacterial growth and can be held refrigerated for up to 21 days. Products are regenerated by immersing the bags in boiling water. An alternative to *sous vide* is the **Capkold system**. A batch of several bags, or a large container of food, can be evacuated, sealed and cooled in bulk in special equipment, permitting large-scale production. The combination of chilling and vacuum packing gives excellent quality and storage life. However time/temperature treatment of the food is critical, and pH should also be monitored. *Clostridium botulinum* bacteria may grow in the vacuum packed product if the pH rises above 4.5.

Frozen Foods

Commercial meats are frozen without any special pre-treatment. Whole or part carcasses are usually blast-frozen, then cut up with a band saw, wrapped and stored. Vegetables are usually peeled, cut into pieces and **blanched** to destroy the enzymes. This means immersing them in boiling water for a few minutes and then rapidly cooling. As long as there is a good quality water supply, blanching will reduce the bacterial population.

During freezing the water content of food is converted into ice. Freezing should be rapid, as slow freezing causes the formation of large ice crystals. These damage the internal structure of the food, producing a mushy texture. On thawing, much fluid (and flavour) leaches out and is lost. Freezing removes not only the sensible heat (measurable as temperature) but also the **latent heat** of the water. While ice is being formed the temperature drops less quickly (see Figure 3.2). Various techniques have been developed to ensure rapid freezing and to keep crystals small, as follows.

Figure 3.2   Effect of latent heat on freezing

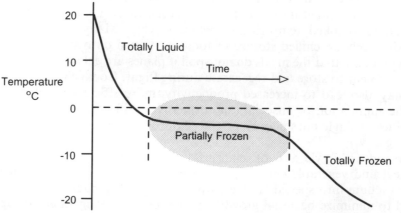

Blast freezing is used for meats, pies and vegetable products. The wrapped food is placed in a current of cold air at $-30°C$, moving at about 30 miles per hour. Heat is rapidly removed by forced convection. 'Separate-frozen' products like peas, mince and prawns are produced using a *fluidized bed*. Cold air is blasted upwards and food morsels are continuously loaded on to it. They float upon the cold air as they freeze and the frozen product is continuously removed.

Plate freezing, involves passing flat packs of fish fingers, burgers etc. over hollow metal plates, cooled by circulating refrigerant fluid. Heat passes from the food into the metal.

Immersion freezing is so called because the wrapped food is totally immersed in cooling fluid. The coolant is generally a concentrated solution of calcium chloride in water, which does not freeze at $-30°C$ or even below. Immersion freezing is used for packed fish, meat and vegetable products.

Cryogenic freezing is used for very delicate products, soft fruits such as strawberries, and fish. The food, which does not need to be wrapped, is first sprayed with liquid nitrogen. After this pre-cooling it is immersed in liquid nitrogen or liquid carbon dioxide (under pressure). These liquefied gases have temperatures below $-100°C$, so cooling is extremely rapid Products retain their texture well because the ice crystals are extremely small. They can also be kept much longer than frozen foods from other processes.

Microorganisms cannot grow in frozen food, because the water is unavailable. Most species survive freezing, however, and cross-contamination can occur. Frozen foods should always be wrapped. The correct operating temperature for a freezer cabinet is around $-20°C$ (at least $-18°C$). Ideally the temperature should not vary throughout the cabinet. If it does, ice will vaporize from the less cold areas and condense again in the colder parts. Unwrapped food easily loses ice in this way, becoming dry and discoloured, the effect known as 'freezer-burn'. Affected foods should be discarded because their wrapping is broken and they may have been contaminated. 'Warm' patches in freezers may also allow redistribution of ice within frozen food items. Crystals grow in some regions and contract in others. This spoils the texture and keeping qualities of the food.

Thawing

When food items thaw they must reabsorb the latent heat they lost during freezing. In theory it would be best to thaw in warm conditions to replace this heat quickly. In practice the latent heat of ice and the poor conductivity of food mean that thawing of large items may take many hours. During this time bacteria will grow on the surface even though the interior is still frozen. Foods should therefore always be thawed in the refrigerator. This takes longer than at room temperature so thawing time should be planned into the cooking process. Thawing charts are provided by some frozen food manufacturers. Most frozen foods lose some liquid during thawing. Frequently this is contaminated and must not be allowed to drip on to other foods. A refrigerator cabinet or cold-room area should be set aside exclusively for thawing.

Cook–freeze catering systems

Cook–freeze production means pre-cooking, freezing and storing food frozen before use. This has the same potential advantages as the cook–chill production discussed previously. However there are often problems with crystal growth because rapid, even freezing is difficult to achieve with plated or packed meals. Serious quality losses may result. In addition, freezing and regenerating the frozen product is expensive in energy terms.

Preservation by lowering water activity

Dried foods

Drying can be accomplished by sunshine in dry climates, by hot air, by contact with hot metal or under vacuum. Drying itself does not kill micro-organisms, spores or enzymes. Most foods are therefore blanched, cooked or chemically treated before drying.

Sun-dried foods are spread raw on mesh in the sun. Fruits such as apricots, which discolour seriously on drying, are treated with sulphur dioxide beforehand. This gas suppresses the browning reaction (Maillard's reaction) of drying fruit. It also helps to inhibit the growth of microorganisms. 'Unsulphured' dried fruits: most raisins, figs and prunes, contain large populations of microorganisms. These are mostly yeasts and moulds but some bacteria may also be present.

Spray-drying is used for milk, soups and some instant coffees. The pasteurized liquid is first pre-concentrated by boiling under vacuum. Then it is sprayed finely into the top of a tower, up which is passed a gentle current of hot air. The droplet size and air speed are adjusted so that the product arrives at the bottom as a fine powder. This can be made to agglomerate into granules by moistening and passing again down a drying tower.

Roller drying is used for milk, dried egg and other products. An internally heated steel roller dips into the pasteurized liquid. As it revolves a thin layer of product continuously dries and is scraped away as powder by an adjustable blade.

Accelerated freeze drying (AFD) involves quick-freezing of blanched or pasteurized food. This is then held in a gently warmed chamber under vacuum. The ice vaporizes without melting (as described above under freezing), leaving the dried food with its nutrients, its colours and most of its texture intact. AFD is used for high quality instant coffees and dried vegetables. It is more expensive than the other drying processes.

Question

Why is there such good retention of flavour, colour and nutrients?

During the AFD process the temperature of the food never rises above 0°C. Delicate chemical substances such as flavours, nutrients and colours are not destroyed by heat. Thus AFD produces a much higher quality product than is available from the other drying techniques.

If correctly packed, dried foods can be kept for long periods without deteriorating. However, if the packaging is ruptured, humid air can enter and cause damage. Most dried foods are hygroscopic, i.e. they can pick up moisture from the air. This happens readily in the moist UK climate and even more so in humid kitchens. The water activity in the dried food can increase sufficiently ($A_w > 0.65$) to support the growth of moulds and even some species of bacteria ($A_w > 0.90$). Dried foods should be kept in rodent-proof airtight containers. The store should be dry, well ventilated and ideally humidity-controlled.

Salted Foods

Very few foods rely entirely on salting for preservation. Products such as ham, bacon and bloaters are usually also smoked and some may contain preservatives such as nitrites and nitrates. Hams are pasteurized, and some fish hot-smoked to reduce their microbial population. Salt is not a very effective preserving agent, as many bacteria can grow in its presence. Its effectiveness for reducing water activity is also reduced by modern curing practice. Polyphosphates are often added and the meat massaged to make it take up more water, raising the A_w. Salted meat products become contaminated both at the factory and during subsequent handling. *E. coli*, *S. aureus* and *Clostridium* species are the most common contaminants (Dempster, Reid and Cody, 1973). Salted foods should be kept wrapped and refrigerated and should be regarded as a potential source of cross-contamination.

Sugar and alcohol preserves

Dried 'crystallized' products have usually been boiled in syrup so they have a low microorganism count when bought. Often they are very hygroscopic and therefore need to be stored in air-tight containers. Crystallized products are used infrequently and may become sticky and show mould growth after long storage. Alcohol preserves, e.g. maraschino cherries, are usually in no danger of spoiling but live bacteria undoubtedly fall into the jars and survive.

Preservation by changing oxygen availability

Microorganisms can grow under a wide range of oxygen concentrations, so it is impossible to prevent all growth by controlling the oxygen supply. However it is possible to selectively inhibit the species of bacteria which cause most problems. For instance vacuum-packed meat develops an unpleasant smell due to the growth of *Lactobacillus* species. Meat packed in a modified atmosphere containing oxygen does not develop the smell, although it must still be refrigerated and used quickly. Vacuum packing and modified atmosphere packaging (MAP) may also be used to prevent spoilage from other sources. Long-life, sterilized cream products are packaged in nitrogen or carbon dioxide to prevent rancidity. Coffee is vacuum-packed for the same reason. These products last well in their packs but oxidize rapidly after opening.

Preservation by lowering the pH

Pickled vegetables and eggs are made by boiling blanched produce in vinegar. Spoilage bacteria are thus absent until the container is opened. Growth is slow after opening because the pH is about 2.8: well below the normal growth range of most microorganisms. However, bacteria are not destroyed by vinegar and the vinegar itself may become a food source for certain species. When this happens the liquid becomes cloudy and off-flavours may be produced. Pickled herrings, such as rollmops, are not cooked. Those in sealed bottles or jars have usually been pasteurized and can be stored at room temperature. Opened jars must be refrigerated.

Preservation by adding chemicals

Antimicrobial compounds are of two types. **Bactericides** and **fungicides** destroy bacteria and moulds. **Bacteristats** and **fungistats** inhibit growth but do not actually destroy the microorganisms. Preservatives are mostly of the second type, so foods containing them can still carry live bacteria or spores and will usually spoil if given enough time.

Smoking covers the outside of foods with a layer of phenols which inhibit moulds and bacterial growth. Smoked foods are usually also salted (e.g. kippers and hams). They may contain lactic acid from fermentation (e.g. salami and cervelat sausages). Smoked products generally need to be refrigerated.

Sulphur dioxide is widely used to preserve sausages, processed meats, dried fruits, fruit juice and wine. It inhibits the growth of most bacteria, moulds and yeasts. It also inhibits the Maillard reaction, which otherwise causes browning of foods. **Sodium nitrate** and **sodium nitrite** are added to canned and preserved meat products. They inhibit the germination of *Clostridium botulinum* spores and also keep the meat a 'healthy' pink colour.

Propionates, sorbates and benzoates are used to preserve bread, flour confectionary, pickled herrings, salad cream, fruit yoghurt and other products. Their main function is to inhibit mould growth (i.e. they act as fungistats).

Destroying microorganisms in food

Food preservation techniques which aim to destroy microorganisms involve the input of energy in the form of radiation or heat. The main techniques are:

- Irradiation.
- Pasteurization.
- Canning/aseptic packaging.

Irradiation

Gamma rays are similar to X-rays, but carry greater energy. They are produced by the breakdown of certain radioactive substances. The irradiation process involves exposing food for a short time to rays from *cobalt-60*, a highly radioactive material. The rays destroy microorganisms and spores, particularly those on the surface of the food. Irradiation can be used to increase the useful life of frozen or chilled foods. It also inhibits the sprouting of potatoes and the natural enzymic spoilage of soft fruits such as strawberries.

Pasteurization, UHT and sterilization

These techniques have been described above in the context of dairy products. They are also used for fruit juices, wine and beer which require higher temperatures and longer times than milk. Some solid foods such as hams are pasteurized by heating in a special oven. The internal temperature is monitored with a probe, and must reach 65°C for at least 30 minutes. Pasteurization kills pathogenic bacteria but may allow some spoilage bacteria to survive. Ultra-high temperature processing kills spoilage bacteria but not spores. Sterilization destroys bacteria and spores.

Canned foods

The objective of canning is to kill bacteria and spores and then to isolate the food from further contamination. Foods are cleaned, blanched, cooked and dispensed into cans. Steam is used to drive out air and oxygen. Cans are made from steel sheet coated with tin to protect it, and lacquered on the inside. Despite these precautions oxygen left inside cans during filling may attack and corrode the steel. Acid foods may also dissolve some of the tin. After filling, cans are fitted with a lid and mechanically sealed.

Filled cans are heat-treated in different ways, depending on their contents. Those with a pH of less than 4.5 inhibit the growth of *Clostridium botulinum*. They can be pasteurized by immersion in boiling water or steam, as it is not necessary to ensure the destruction of all *Clostridium botulinum* spores. Cans containing less acidic products are pressure cooked at 120°C or above for several minutes.

Question

What may be done to ensure that surviving *C. botulinum* spores do not start to grow in high pH products, such as meat?

Salt and sodium nitrite are commonly added to inhibit growth. The two substances are **synergists**, that is, each enhances the activity of the other, so that a mixture of the two controls bacterial growth more effectively than the same quantity of either single substance.

Aseptic packaging

This process requires sterile containers. Cans may be used, or cardboard or plastic containers such as 'Tetrapaks' and 'Tetrabricks', which are sterilized with hydrogen peroxide. Food to be packaged is heated rapidly to 149°C, cooled quickly and filled under sterile conditions. The cooking stage does not kill *Clostridium botulinum* spores, so foods must be naturally acidic or be treated with citric acid to bring the pH below 4.5. Products will keep at room temperature for several months. Aseptic packaging is used for UHT milk, wine, fruit juices, and some solid foods in sauces.

Problems with canned goods

Thermophilic bacteria occasionally survive canning, if batches are underprocessed. Bacteria may also get into cans through pin-holes or end-seam flaws during cooling. Cooling water should be chlorinated and tested regularly to ensure that it is not a source of contamination. There are two main types of spoilage: blown cans and 'flat sours'.

'Blown' cans bulge, due to hydrogen or carbon dioxide gas produced by *Clostridium* species. The contents are generally foul-smelling and discoloured. If hydrogen sulphide is also produced there is a smell of rotten eggs and usually a black discoloration of ferrous sulphide.

'Flat sours' are produced by thermophilic *Bacillus* species. No gas is produced so the cans retain their shape, but the contents are sour and may have off-flavours.

In *dented cans*, the internal protective coating of lacquer may be broken, allowing acid foods to react with the metal. Toxic levels of tin may dissolve into the food, or it may become tainted and discoloured with metal salts.

Cans and aseptic packs should be handled carefully so as not to dent or distort them. They should be stored in cool conditions, as temperatures above 40°C encourage thermophiles to grow. Stocks should be rotated and, ideally, batch numbers should be noted in case spoiled cans are found. Cans and packs should be wiped carefully before opening and the contents should be transferred to another container as soon as possible. Once opened, these foods are highly susceptible to contamination and spoilage. They should be kept cool and used quickly.

Study example 3.2

The US National Academy of Sciences (NAS, 1969) suggests three basic criteria for rating the dangers inherent in foods:

1. The food is (+)/is not (0) likely to contain pathogens.
2. The food has not (+)/has (0) been heat-treated to kill pathogens.
3. The food will (+)/will not (0) support the growth of pathogens.

The three criteria are of particular use in **hazard analysis**, discussed in Chapter 9. They are also a convenient way of describing the microbiological safety of raw and processed foods. For example, raw chicken would be rated + + + because all three danger factors are present. Cornflour would be rated + + 0, because the first two factors are present, but not the third.
    Rate the following foods, using the three criteria:

1. Pasteurized milk.
2. Soup in the can.
3. Wholemeal flour.
4. Dried figs.
5. Frozen cooked prawns.

Summary – commodities and preserved foods

Do

- Buy from reputable wholesalers and manufacturers.
- Examine quality on purchase.

- Store preserved foods in an appropriate way.
- Reject items which show damaged packaging or spoilage.

Do not

- Store in dirty, warm or humid areas.
- Leave empty packaging or spilt foods about.

Cooking methods

All cooking processes involve the transfer of heat from a heat source (flame or element) to food. Heat transfer can occur by convection, radiation or conduction. *Convection* is the natural or forced movement of a fluid from the heat source to the food. Liquids hold much more heat, volume for volume than gases. Therefore liquid transfer media are generally much more efficient. *Forced convection* occurs when the fluid is pumped around (e.g. air in a fan oven) and improves heat transfer. Steam contains *latent heat of vaporization* as well as sensible heat and is therefore a more efficient cooking medium than air. *Radiation* occurs when heat energy is converted into a radiant form (infra-red or microwaves) and 'shines' onto food etc. Infra-red heats the surface only; microwaves penetrate several centimetres into the food. *Conduction* is the direct transfer of heat from one solid (e.g. a griddle surface) to another (e.g. the food). Any heat transferred to the surface of food items finds its way to the centre by conduction. Cooking techniques employ the whole range of heat transfer methods, as shown in Table 3.2.

Boiling, simmering and braising

These 'wet heat' methods generally give good heat transfer, as long as there is fairly vigorous boiling action the temperature of the water is around 100°C. Convection is good under these conditions and an even temperature is maintained. Microorganisms, many spores and most toxins are destroyed. However, oxygen is driven out of the boiling water, leaving the anaerobic conditions preferred by some bacteria. When large pots of stew or gravy cool, surviving spores of *Clostridium perfringens* may germinate. Problems of 'slow cookers' have been mentioned above, under pulse foods. In simmering too there may not

Table 3.2   Cooking techniques and heat transfer processes

Cooking method	Heat transfer method	Heat transfer medium
Boil, simmer, braise etc	Natural convection	Water
Steam, steam oven	Natural or forced convection	Steam
Deep fry, shallow fry	Natural convection, conduction	Oil or fat
Roast, bake	Forced (occasionally natural) convection plus some radiation	Air, long wave infra-red (radiant heat)
Grill, toast	Radiation	Short wave infra-red (radiant heat)
Microwave	Radiation	Microwaves (very short wave radio/radar)
Griddle	Conduction	Hot metal (good conductor)

be enough natural convection to ensure an even temperature. Convection currents in pans may by-pass certain 'cool spots' which lose heat to the room by radiation (see Figure 3.3). Microorganisms and toxins may survive

Question
What can be done to solve this problem in the kitchen?

Pans should be stirred regularly to keep the temperature evenly distributed within. Large pans should be boiled vigorously from time to time or moved about on the heat, to change the convection patterns.

107

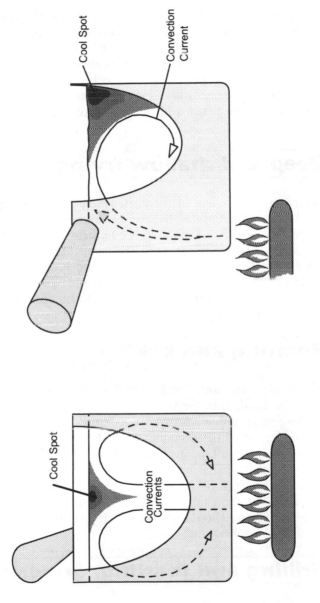

Figure 3.3 Cool spots in simmering pans

Steaming

Modern steamers are designed to give extremely good heat transfer. However they must be full of steam at all times during cooking. Otherwise some items will be surrounded by air, which is a less effective transfer medium. It is even more important that pressure cookers and autoclaves are filled with steam, as otherwise they do not reach the correct internal temperature. For this reason steamers and pressure cookers should be fitted with temperature gauges as well as pressure gauges.

Deep and shallow frying

Oil or fat is an excellent heat transfer medium because it can cook at a much higher temperature than water. Deep fryers commonly operate between 150–180°C and the food is completely surrounded by the frying medium. Even frozen products (if small) heat through rapidly enough to destroy almost all microorganisms. On the other hand, shallow frying only heats one surface at a time and heat is continuously lost by radiation from the top (see Figure 3.4). Inadequately thawed items may remain uncooked in the middle and pathogens can easily survive.

Roasting and baking

Commercial ovens are mostly fitted with fans. Hot air is circulated around the food, transferring heat by forced convection. In addition, some long-wave radiant heat is transferred from the oven walls to the food. Modern oven developments include infra-red elements to improve radiation and simultaneous steaming or microwaving. These greatly improve heat transfer and make destruction of bacteria etc. very efficient. Very large or imperfectly thawed items are at risk. Cooking temperatures at the centre of such foods should be monitored with a probe. Similar care should be taken with products which are deliberately undercooked i.e. beef and lamb.

Grilling and toasting, griddles

Infra-red radiation strikes the surface of food and is converted into heat. This then passes into the centre of the food by conduction. Grills usually heat one side of the food only. The most efficient units support the food on a surface of thick metal. This is heated by the element while the grill is empty and cooks the bottom of the food by conduction. Some grills heat

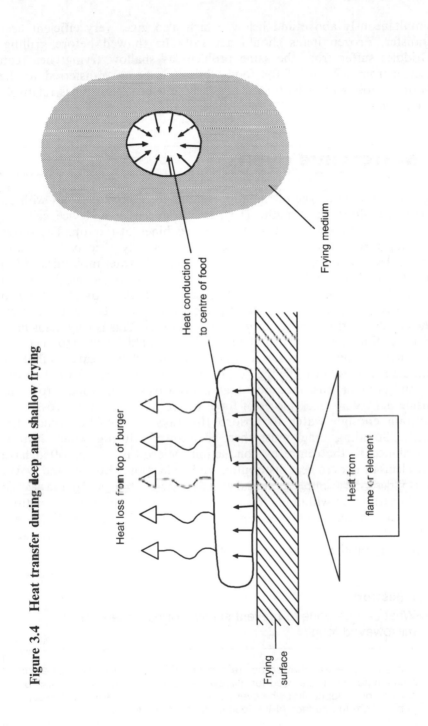

Figure 3.4 Heat transfer during deep and shallow frying

simultaneously above and below, which also gives very efficient heat transfer. Frozen items should generally be thawed before grilling. Griddles suffer from the same problem as shallow frying: heat can escape from the top of the food while it is being transferred to the bottom. Foods must be turned regularly and heat transfer is relatively inefficient.

Microwave ovens

Microwaves are a type of radiation similar to radio waves but with an extremely short wavelength. They are produced in a device called a *magnetron*, situated just outside the oven cabinet, at the top. The waves are adjusted to a particular frequency that is only absorbed by water molecules. As the microwaves pass through food, water molecules within it rotate and this molecular motion heats the food. A technical problem with all ovens is to get a completely even flux of waves over the food so that it is evenly heated. Any food placed in the cabinet further distorts the energy distribution by absorbing microwaves. This is why items have to be carefully and evenly spaced to cook thoroughly. As the food cooks, heat may escape from its surface as radiant energy and steam, so that the middle becomes hot while the outside may only be warm. This gives rise to the popular misconception that microwaves cook food 'from the inside out'. Very thick pieces of food, (more than 100 mm across) may contain enough water to absorb the rays before they reach the centre.'Standing time' must then be allowed, during which heat is distributed to the centre by conduction. Microwave ovens often have problems of uneven heat distribution and 'cold spots'. Bobeng and David (1975) describe a simple, practical way for caterers to measure the electric field distribution within microwave ovens. They use measured quantities of water contained in plastic cups, distributed inside the oven. These are all at the same initial temperature, but heat up at different rates, depending on the localized electric field.

Question
What can be done to prevent survival of pathogens in microwaved food?

Foods must be well thawed before cooking. Only the specified recipe and programme should be used for microwave cooking. Foods should also be covered or wrapped first wherever possible. This helps prevent the escape of heat from the surface of the food in the form of steam.

Study example 3.3

The microbiological quality of underdone roast beef depends on a number of factors. Most important is how long the beef has been stored hot after cooking. Boned/rolled joints and large pieces made up from re-formed chunks usually contain more bacteria than does meat on the bone. Storage times before use do not seem to affect the quality of meat on the bone, but may influence that of other roasting joints. Generally it can be said that bacteria are efficiently killed during roasting except near the centre of the meat.

1. Where are bacteria mostly located on whole, bone-in pieces of meat?
2. What effect will boning, rolling or re-forming have on the distribution of bacteria?
3. How is heat transferred to the centre of a roasting joint?
4. Why, in this example, are the bacteria at the centre unlikely to be killed?
5. Why is the storage time of the cooked beef the most important factor?

Summary – cooking methods

Do

- Use commercial equipment, which is designed for good heat transfer.
- Follow recipes carefully and allow adequate cooking times; alternatively use a temperature probe to check internal heating during a 'trial run'.
- Defrost food efficiently before cooking.
- Wrap or cover microwaved foods if possible.

Do not

- Use shallow frying as a substitute for deep-frying.
- Cook frozen foods, except for small items designed for use in this way.
- Take chances with faulty cooking appliances or automatic temperature probes.

Hot-holding techniques

Hot-holding relies on maintaining the temperature of food above 63°C, so that bacteria cannot multiply. A number of techniques are available, all of which have drawbacks as well as advantages.

Bain-marie

Food is held in a container immersed in boiling water or steam. Heat can be lost from the top when the lid is removed. Sometimes pots of food are not completely immersed. An even temperature then depends on circulation of the liquid by convection. This process may be poor in thick, viscous liquids and a cool spot develops at the top (see Figure 3.5). Temperatures should be checked regularly and water baths refilled when necessary. Thin liquids such as soup or gravy are more likely to maintain an even temperature throughout.

Hot table

Meats for carveries and hot buffets are often displayed on a hot table. They are heated from below, but large joints can easily lose heat from the top and microorganisms can multiply. Display and presentation are usually important, so few items are covered and this tends to increase the heat loss.

Infra-red lamps

Thin food items such as bacon are often held under a rack of heat-lamps interspersed with ordinary lamps. This arrangement holds food at a good temperature and allows for effective presentation. However foods must be used up quickly as they tend to dry and shrivel. Infra-red lamps can be used in conjunction with a hot table for large items, which are then heated from above and below. However items such as rare beef tend to go on cooking under the lamps.

Hot cabinets

These are used for pies, fish and chips, and sometimes plated meats. They should be held at 65°C, to allow for possible cooling due to draughts.

Figure 3.5 Heat loss from items held in *bain-maries*

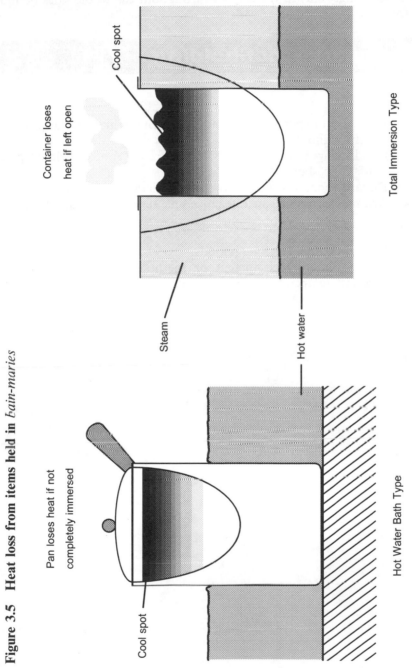

Container loses
heat if left open

Cool spot

Steam

Total Immersion Type

Pan loses heat if not
completely immersed

Cool spot

Hot water

Hot Water Bath Type

Temperatures should be checked regularly and stock rotated. Otherwise some items may stay in the cabinet throughout the whole sales period.

Summary – hot-holding

Do

- Choose equipment and techniques which are likely to keep food hot throughout.
- Check temperatures regularly to ensure the food is held evenly at 65°C or above.
- Discard foods which have been held inadequately hot.
- Arrange for regular maintenance and servicing of equipment.

Do not

- Hold foods hot for long periods.
- Use hot-holding equipment or methods that may not give adequate temperature maintenance.
- Overfill pots which are to stand in the *bain-marie*.

4   Food Hygiene and the Law

Objectives

To explain how food hygiene legislation fits into the British legal system. To describe the sources and content of food hygiene law and how the law is enforced. To discuss the interrelationships between food hygiene law and other areas of legislation, and with official publications such as codes of practice and British Standards.

Introduction

Legal aspects of food safety and hygiene are of great significance to the food premises manager. The law sets minimum acceptable standards of practice, it codifies managers' moral obligations to the public and it penalizes those who fail in these obligations. This chapter examines the nature and workings of food law and how these relate to the rest of the British legal system.

Types of law

Two types of legal action are recognized in the British Isles: civil law and criminal law. *Civil law* deals with disputes between individuals and corporate bodies such as limited liability companies. A court case involves a *plaintiff*, who brings the suit and a *defendant*, against whom it is brought. A judge decides who is the injured party; the other individual or body is then required to pay compensation.

Criminal law, on the other hand, deals with offences against the state, i.e. against the common good. Court cases are between the *Crown* (the State), who prosecutes, and the *defendant*, who is accused of the crime. Lesser offences are usually tried by magistrates, who decide the guilt of the defendant. More serious crimes are tried by judge and jury. If the defendant is found guilty the sentence of the court is a punishment. Compensation is not the aim of the sentence and is not usual, though it may sometimes be awarded. Food hygiene cases are generally criminal cases, though it is possible for recipients of contaminated food to sue the supplier. Grounds for such civil action might be breach of contract (because the food was not of the specified quality) or negligence (if the supplier had not taken due care in its preparation). A suit of this kind would usually stand more chance of success if the supplier had already been successfully prosecuted in a criminal case involving food safety or hygiene.

Sources of law

Common law, including much civil law, is based on **precedent** – i.e. legal decisions about previous, similar cases. Many of the more important cases are recorded and documented for future reference. Criminal law, and particularly food law, mostly depends upon **legislation** i.e. written laws (**statutes**) passed by Acts of Parliament. A statute begins life as a **Bill**, presented to Parliament by a private member or sponsored by the Government. The Bill is successively debated and voted in both Houses and may undergo considerable modification in the process. Finally it must receive Royal Assent before it becomes law. Acts of Parliament are required whenever statutes are created, amended or repealed. UK food legislation seeks to:

- Protect the public and public health.
- Limit the opportunities for food fraud.

Acts concerned with food date back into the last century. The most recent have had the following functions:

- Consolidating previous legislation.
- Updating legislation in the face of technological advance.
- Bringing British practice into line with European Community obligations.
- Bringing food handling practice into line with changing consumer expectations and opinions.

Some of these functions may be linked. For instance technological change and consumer expectations are also concerns of the European Community. In terms of food hygiene however, the EC has repeatedly been criticized (e.g. Green, 1989) for failing to issue directives.

Primary and secondary legislation

Laws authorized by Acts of Parliament are known as *primary legislation*. However, an Act of Parliament may be a cumbersome way to produce legislation. This is particularly the case when detailed stipulations are needed or when rapid technological advance means successive amendment. In such cases Acts usually empower Government ministers to make further provisions. Delegated *statutory implements* of this kind are called *secondary legislation*. They are usually titled Regulations or Orders, whereas items of primary legislation are always Acts.

Food law centres around the *Food Safety Act, 1990* (primary legislation). Food hygiene is specifically dealt with by secondary legislation empowered under section 16 of the Act. An example of this is the *Food Hygiene (General) Regulations, 1970*. Secondary legislation often predates the Act which apparently empowers it, and may be amended or revised quite independently of primary legislation.

Question

How can the Food Hygiene (General) Regulations, 1970 predate the primary legislation (Food Safety Act, 1990) which apparently empowers them?

> The Regulations were in fact made under an empowering clause in the *Food and Drugs Act, 1955*. The same empowering clause was included in the *Food Act, 1984* and the *Food Safety Act, 1990* so that the Regulations remain in force even though the original Act was repealed.

Interpretation of legislation

The job of a jury is to decide from the evidence whether an individual has contravened a particular statute. The judge's functions are to interpret the law and to pass sentence. If the legislation is ambiguous, three rules may be used in its interpretation.

The *Literal Rule* is the normal interpretation. It means that the court should apply the ordinary dictionary meaning of the printed wording of the statute. The *Golden Rule* is applied where there is doubt about the literal meaning of the printed word. It means that the court should take the natural, or commonly understood meaning of the law's words, provided these are not absurd. The *Mischief Rule* involves looking at the mischief which the legislation was intended to cure. This is done by considering the wording of the statute in the light of the Parliamentary debate from which it was passed.

The three rules may be used for interpreting either primary or secondary legislation. Precedent, i.e. decisions of the **Courts of Record** may also be used. In exceptional cases the wording of secondary legislation may also be declared invalid if it exceeds the power granted by the original Act of Parliament. Such wording may be interpreted as **ultra vires**, i.e. beyond the power of the authorizing minister.

European community legislation

Under Article 189 of the Treaty of Rome the Council and Commission of the European Community is permitted to influence the laws of member states by means of:

- Regulations.
- Directives.
- Decisions.
- Recommendations.

Regulations are legally binding. Their contravention infringes the European Economic Treaty and they are upheld in the European Court whether or not they have been supported by an Act of Parliament of a member state.

Directives are not binding like regulations. However, member states have an obligation to create legislation, e.g. by Act of Parliament, to put them into force.

Decisions of the European Court or Commission are a means of enforcing policy in a particular, limited area. Often they are the outcome of test cases brought from the courts of member states.

Recommendations are not binding, but would normally be expected to influence the policy of member states, without the need for a regulation or directive.

Existing EC legislation is much concerned with additives, processing techniques and the composition of foods. Directives permit sampling and compositional analysis. However there are none dealing with the hygiene or wholesomeness of food (Green, 1989). In 1985 the EC issued a White Paper declaring the intention to remove all barriers to trade between member states by 1992. A commission has been established which is responsible for harmonizing the health and safety standards of member states. It is expected that the Community will produce a food hygiene directive by 1992, when the provisions of member states have been fully examined (CEC, 1985)

Influence of the WHO

The World Health Organization (1977) has analyzed food hygiene regulations from a number of countries and produced its own model regulations. In many respects these are very similar to the Food Hygiene (General) Regulations, 1970. WHO recommendations have no binding force. They do, however, influence health and food experts. These in turn influence the British Government through such bodies as the *Food Advisory Committee* and the *Committee on Toxicology*, both of whom report regularly to Parliament.

The structure of food hygiene law In Britain

The primary legislation is the *Food Safety Act, 1990*. This has wider concerns than food hygiene, but in particular it lays down a framework within which food hygiene infringements can be detected and punished. In this respect its main functions are to:

- Define the terms within which the law works: 'food', 'sale', 'food authorities' etc.
- Set out the main offences: injury to health and food fraud.
- Set out control measures: inspection, prohibition and seizure.
- Empower Government ministers to make subsidiary (i.e. secondary) legislation.
- Set out permitted defences.
- Set out the powers of local authorities.
- Make provision for penalties and appeals.

Secondary food hygiene legislation is principally found in the *Food Hygiene (General) Regulations, 1970* and the *Food Hygiene (Markets, Stalls and Delivery Vehicles) Regulations, 1966*. There are also specific regulations aimed at the hygiene of food in transit through ports and at the hygiene of sensitive foods, for example meat and dairy products. The regulations generally:

- Define the foods and premises with which they are concerned.
- Specify particular hygiene requirements and standards for premises, plant/equipment, personnel and food handling processes.
- Specify exemptions.
- Specify powers of inspection and enforcement.
- Define offences and set out penalties.

Question

Why are penalties specified in both primary and secondary legislation?

Values of fines fall continuously due to inflation. They are therefore adjusted from time to time in:

- Primary food legislation such as the Food Safety Act 1990.
- Secondary food legislation such as the Food Hygiene (General) Regulations 1970, and amendments
- Other legislation such as the Magistrates Courts Acts, which specify the powers of the courts.

The Food Safety Act, 1990

The Act is divided into four parts.

Part I is concerned with definitions to specify and limit its scope.

Section 1	defines food, food premises and food businesses.
Section 2	establishes that the Act is concerned with food for sale for human consumption but enlarges the meaning of 'sale' to include food offered to guests as if it were on sale, and to prizes and promotional items.
Section 3	widens the scope of the Act to include materials, items and articles found on food premises but not obviously intended for sale; additives, ingredients and equipment, for example.
Section 4	specifies members of the Government who are concerned with the Act: the Minister of Agriculture, Fisheries and Food; the Secretary of State for Scotland; and Secretaries of State for Food and Health in England and Wales.

Section 5   designates *food authorities*. i.e. port health authorities, district or borough councils in England and Wales, and island or district councils in Scotland

Section 6   designates *enforcement authorities*. For most purposes these are the same as food authorities. However the Ministers and the Customs and Excise Commissions may also act as enforcement authorities.

Part II specifies the main provisions of the Food Safety Act. It sets out two main types of offence: selling or producing harmful food, and defrauding the customer. Part II also allows for inspection, prohibition, subsidiary legislation, defences, enforcement, penalties and appeals.

Offences

Section 7   Makes it an offence to render food harmful to health by

(i)   adding substances to it;
(ii)   removing substances from it;
(iii) using unsuitable articles or substances for handling it; or
(iv)   subjecting it to an unsuitable process or treatment.

All of these, but particularly the last two, have implications for food hygiene. Section 7(3) specifies that both acute and chronic injury to health are relevant to the Act.

Section 8   makes it an offence not merely to sell harmful food but also to store or supply it for sale.

Section 14   aims to prevent food fraud. It specifies that 'any person who sells to the purchaser's prejudice any food which is not of the *nature, substance* or *quality* demanded by the customer' is guilty of an offence. 'Not of the nature' is taken to mean a different food from that specified e.g. white fish sold as cod. 'Not of the substance' means non-food material i.e. foreign substances found in food: broken glass in a can of beans, for instance. 'Not of the quality' would mean tinned peaches in a 'fresh' fruit salad, for instance.

Section 14 has been criticized for not mentioning *composition*, so that poor-quality products may nevertheless comply with the law (Roberts, 1988).

Section 15   makes it an offence to falsely advertise, label or describe food so as to mislead the customer about its nature, substance or quality.

Control measures

Section 9   permits the official inspection of food which is offered for sale or in the possession of a seller. It allows prohibition of sale and empowers magistrates' and sheriffs' courts to issue destruction and confiscation orders. Compensation for wrongful prohibition or destruction is also permitted.

Question

What is the distinction between magistrates' and sheriffs' courts?

Magistrates' courts are found in England and Wales. Sheriffs' courts are the equivalent under Scottish law (discussed below). Both magistrates and sheriffs are designated *Justices of the Peace* in the Food Safety Act, 1990.

Section 10   empowers food authorities to issue an *Improvement Notice* requiring the proprietor of unsatisfactory or unhygienic premises to take specified action to improve them within fourteen days.

Section 11   empowers magistrates' and sheriffs' courts to issue a *Prohibition Order* preventing a food business from operating if the proprietor has been convicted under the Act and the court is satisfied that there is a *risk to public health* caused by:

(i)   a particular process or treatment;
(ii)   the construction of the premises; or
(iii) the state or condition of premises, plant or equipment.

One copy of the prohibition order must be served on the proprietor and another fixed conspicuously somewhere on the premises. A Prohibition Order is valid until the food authority or the court rescinds it.

Section 12   allows courts to issue an *Emergency Prohibition Order*. An Improvement Notice and one full day's notice of intent to serve the emergency order must be given to the proprietor. In addition the court must be satisfied that there is an 'imminent risk to health' from the process, premises or equipment. A emergency prohibition notice expires if no order is made within three days of its issue. A notice or order ceases to have effect if the proprietor can prove that the measures specified in the Improvement Notice have been carried out. Sundays and Bank Holidays are disregarded in the specified time periods. *Compensation* may be claimed if a food authority fails to apply for an order within three days of issuing a notice, or if the court is not satisfied that there is an *imminent risk to health*.

In practice an 'imminent risk' usually means evidence of gross infestation by rodents (Rock and Warren, 1986).

Section 13   allows Ministers to prohibit food production or processing operations with an *Emergency Control Order* if there is an imminent danger to health.

Direct ministerial intervention is used if the food chain is endangered in some way. An example was the contamination of cattle feed with lead during 1989–90.

Subsidiary legislation

Section 16   empowers ministers to make legislation to

  (i)   regulate the composition of foods;
  (ii)   ensure that food is safe for human consumption;
  (iii) require, prohibit or regulate processes used for treating foods;
  (iv)   ensure hygienic conditions and practices in commercial food operations
  (v)   regulate the labelling, marking, presenting and advertising of food;
  (vi)   cope with any new exigencies.

Section 17	authorizes Ministers to make regulations required by EC obligations.
Section 18	authorizes the making of regulations concerned with the manufacture and importation of novel foods. Recent examples of novel foods are fungal protein (myco-protein), and syrups derived from starch by enzymic hydrolysis.
Section 19	delegates to Ministers the power to require registration and licencing of food premises.
Section 31	empowers Ministers to make regulations about sampling and analysis of foods.

Permitted defences

| Section 20 | provides that if the offence is due to an act or default of somebody other than the defendant, then that person is guilty of an offence. |

A charge against the defendant is not necessarily withdrawn under this section, because there may have been complicity between the other guilty person and the defendant.

| Section 21 | permits a defendant to prove that *all reasonable precautions* were taken and *all due diligence* exercised to prevent the offence. Alternatively it is permissible to prove that the offence was due to an act or omission or to misinformation supplied by another person. The defendant must prove that all reasonable checks were made on the food and that (s)he could not know that an offence was being committed. The prosecutor must be notified in writing seven days before the hearing if the defence is to involve another person. |
| Section 22 | allows for similar defences when the offence involves advertising rather than sale of food. |

Powers of food authorities

| Section 23 | authorizes food authorities to provide food hygiene training for proprietors and employees in food |

businesses. Food authorities are also permitted to subsidize the cost of training.

The Food Safety Bill which was debated in Parliament in 1989–90 allowed for an additional payment of £30 million per year to food authorities to fund the training and extra expenditure required by the Act.

Section 24	permits food authorities to provide facilities for cleansing shellfish and for subsidizing this service, if necessary.
Section 26	permits food authorities to prohibit or regulate unsafe or unhygienic commercial food operations. Authorities may also require records to be kept and returns to be made so that they can control hygiene and safety.

Part III of the Food Safety Act deals with the administration of the Act: the food authorities, courts and procedures.

Section 27 & **Section 28**	allow food authorities to appoint and to pay *public analysts*. Authorities may also set up their own laboratories and facilities for the microbiological examination of food samples.

Sampling

Section 25	requires proprietors to provide samples of any food, substance or contact material which they sell or use to process food. A proprietor who fails to do this may be charged with obstruction.

(*Author's note*: Section 25 has been moved to this position from Part II of the Act so that all provisions concerned with sampling can be kept together.)

Section 29 & **Section 30**	permit authorized officers to take or purchase food samples and submit them to a public analyst or *food examiner*. This person shall analyze the sample as quickly as practicable and issue a *certificate of analysis*.

Question

What is a food examiner?

> Within the meaning of the Act, food examiners are microbiologists or food scientists who work in a laboratory administered by the food authority. Thus they are distinct from public analysts, who are private professionals, employed by the authority on a contract basis. Ministers are also empowered under Section 31 to make secondary legislation dealing with the way samples are to be taken, divided up and analyzed.

Entry and inspection

Section 32

permits an officer of the food authority to enter and inspect premises without notice at any reasonable hour; 24 hours' notice must be given before the inspection of domestic premises. If this would defeat the object of entry a warrant can be obtained from a magistrate. Officers must produce written authorization but may be accompanied by anyone they feel is necessary to the inspection. They may collect written or computerized evidence as well as samples. There is a clause preventing officers from disclosing trade secrets discovered in the course of their work.

Sections 33

sets out procedures and penalties for the offence of *obstruction*, defined as one or more of the following:

(i)   obstructing or denying access;
(ii) failing to give assistance or information requested; or
(iii) giving false information.

Prosecution and penalties

Section 34

states the expiry date for prosecution i.e. one year from the discovery of the offence by the prosecutor or three years from commission of the offence, whichever is the earlier.

Section 35	sets a penalty of two years' imprisonment and/or a maximum fine of £20,000 for hygiene, safety or fraud offences (i.e. offences under Sections 7, 8 or 14).
Section 36	permits directors, managers, secretaries etc. of limited companies to be prosecuted if consent, connivance or negligence can be proved in connection with an offence. Normally the officers of a company will be prosecuted as well as the company itself.

Appeals

Section 37 & **Section 38**	permit injured parties to appeal against wrongful: (i) issue of an Improvement Notice (ii) refusal of a Certificate of Compliance, indicating that work required in an Improvement Notice had been satisfactorily completed. (iii) cancellation of a licence Initial appeals must be made to a Magistrates' court or in Scotland to a Sheriffs' court. Appeals against decisions by a Magistrate or Sheriff can be made to the Crown Court, the Court of Appeal, or in Scotland to the Scottish High Court, or the Court of Session.

Part IV is a supplement to the Act. It details amendments to other Acts and clarifies various terms, to aid interpretation in the courts. In addition:

Section 39 **Section 40 &** **Section 41**	permit Ministers to guide and control the way food authorities exercise their powers. Codes of practice may be issued and action taken against authorities who fail to discharge their responsibilities.
Section 42	clarifies the position if a licence-holder dies
Section 43	protects food authority officers who are acting in good faith.
Section 44 **Section 45 &** **Section 46**	empower Ministers to regulate the charges made by food authorities.

Section 47   clarify the powers of Ministers in making second-
Section 48   ary legislation.
Section 49
Section 50

There are numerous documented cases illustrating the interpretation of food fraud under the Act. These are valid because the wording of the adulteration clauses (e.g. concerning 'nature', 'substance' and 'quality') has not changed through successive legislation since the 1930s. Specific fraud and adulteration cases have not been included in this book, which is primarily concerned with health and safety. At the time of writing there are no documented cases concerned with health and safety under the new terms of the 1990 Act. However, the following fictional study example draws on established practice to illustrate how the new Food Safety Act is likely to be interpreted.

Study example 4.1

A restaurant customer is served soup, in which a dead fly is floating. The customer complains and more soup (described on the menu as 'fresh spring vegetable') is brought. Within a few days the customer is seriously ill with botulin poisoning.

1. Which sections of the Act does the soup contravene?
2. Which prohibition applies to the dead fly: 'not of the nature', 'not of the substance', or 'not of the quality'?
3. What is the most likely way for botulin toxin to have got into the soup?
4. Which defence could most reasonably be brought by the proprietor of the restaurant?
5. How does the menu designation of the soup contravene the Food Safety Act, 1990?

The National Health Service (Amendment) Act, 1986

Passing of this Act removed *Crown immunity* from National Health Service catering establishments. The principle of Crown immunity dates back to mediaeval times. In effect it means that the monarch can do no wrong and cannot therefore be criminally or civilly liable for any action of the State. Before 1986 there was no requirement for NHS catering to abide by food hygiene legislation. NHS immunity has now been lifted, but other Crown institutions, such as the armed forces, are still exempt.

Question

Why did Crown immunity apply to the National Health Service?

> The National Health Service is owned and administered by HM Government. It is therefore legally under the direct control of the monarch, who cannot be prosecuted.

The Food Hygiene (General) Regulations, 1970 (as amended 1989)

The Regulations were originally issued under an empowering clause in the *Food and Drugs Act, 1955*. The same clause appeared in the *Food Act, 1984* and in Section 16 of the *Food Safety Act, 1990*. The Regulations have thus been kept in force through major changes in the primary legislation. The Regulations define terms and state their general requirements. Provision is also made for exemptions, enforcement and penalties.

Definitions

Regulations 1–5   set out the scope of the legislation. 'Food', 'food premises', 'enforcement authorities' etc. are defined as in the Food Safety Act 1990. Other terms: 'food room', 'catering business', 'open food' etc. are additional to the Act. Certain wrapped or packaged items are specifically excluded.

General requirements

Cleanliness of premises, plant and equipment

Regulation 6   prohibits the running of a food business in insanitary premises. These are defined as:

(i)   infested;
(ii)   having defective or leaking drains; or
(ii)   being in a condition, situation or state of construction which exposes food to the risk of contamination.

Regulation 7   specifies that items of equipment which come into contact with food must be kept clean and must be constructed and maintained in such a way that they:

(i)   are easy to keep clean;
(ii)   do not absorb matter from the food; and
(iii) do not contaminate the food.

Containers must be protected and kept free from contamination.

Regulation 8   specifies that domestic premises may not be used for preparing and packing food unless:

(i)   the food business is run from there; and/or
(ii)   the food is shrimps or prawns, given out for peeling.

Protecting food from contamination

Regulation 9   requires open food to be protected from contamination. The following points are specified:

(i)   cooked and raw foods should be kept apart from food for sale;

(ii)   food deemed unfit for human consumption should be kept apart from food intended for sale;

(iii) open food should be kept more than 18 in (450 mm). above the ground in open yards or forecourts, unless it is adequately protected; and

(iv)   animal feed may only be stored in a food room if it is in a container which prevents risk of contamination.

Obligations of food handlers

Regulation 10   requires food handlers to keep clean:

(i)   parts of their body likely to come in contact with food (hands, forearms, neck and hair); and

(ii)   parts of their clothing likely to come in contact with food.

Food handlers must keep open wounds covered and must not spit, smoke or take snuff in the presence of open food.

Regulation 11   specifies that food handlers should wear clean, washable outer clothing. A sufficient supply should be available so that they can change as necessary. This regulation does not apply to staff handling raw vegetables or to bar or beverage service staff.

Regulation 12   prohibits the carriage of live animals or poultry together with open food, food containers or equipment. Clean materials must be used for packing or wrapping open food. Newspaper is prohibited as a wrapping.

Regulation 13   requires food handlers to notify the district Medical Officer of Health if they have any of these prescribed illnesses:

(i)   typhoid or paratyphoid fever;

(ii)   any other *Salmonella* infection;

(iii) amoebic or bacillary dysentery; or

(iv)   staphylococcal infections of the skin, throat or nose.

Question

What is the difference between amoebic and bacillary dysentery?

Amoebic dysentery is caused by a species of protozoa (amoeba) usually contracted abroad in a tropical country. Bacillary dysentery is caused by *Shigella* bacteria. *Shigella sonnei* is the species which most commonly causes dysentery in the UK.

Specific requirements for food rooms

Regulation 14 specifies that drainage systems should not be vented into food rooms. All entrances to the system should be fitted with a water-sealed trap.

Regulation 15 requires that tanks supplying water to food rooms should not be directly connected with WCs or urinals.

It is permissible for flushing cisterns to be filled from the cold water supply tank. It would not be acceptable to use a flushing cistern as a supply tank.

Regulation 16 requires that lavatories are kept clean, and arranged so that odours cannot enter the food room. They should be well-lit and ventilated and contain a prominent notice to wash the hands after use. Lavatories must not be used as food rooms, nor may they open directly on to a food room.

Usual practice is to provide a corridor or lobby space with separate doors to the food room and lavatory. The intervening space should be separately ventilated.

Regulation 17 specifies that water supplies must be clean, wholesome, constant and of sufficient quantity.

Regulation 18 stipulates the provision of personal washing facilities, including:

(i) suitable and sufficient washbasins;
(ii) basins in food preparation areas, as well as lavatories;

	(iii) hot and cold water supply (cold alone is required where only wrapped food is handled);
	(iv) adequate soap and detergent;
	(v) nailbrushes; and
	(vi) clean towel or other hygienic drying facilities.
Regulation 19	requires first aid materials to be provided, i.e. a supply of bandages and waterproof dressings.
Regulation 20	specifies that accommodation must be provided for outdoor clothing and footwear. This must consist of lockers or cupboards if it is in a room where open food is handled.
Regulation 21	requires that sinks be provided for washing food and equipment. Sinks must be kept clean and well-maintained. They must have both hot and cold water unless their use is restricted to:
	(i) raw fish;
	(ii) raw fruit and vegetables; or
	(iii) glasses or ice-cream scoops (when a suitable bactericide must also be used).
Regulation 22	requires 'suitable and sufficient' lighting in all food rooms.

Lighting levels are not specified, but for example the Illumination Engineering Society has published guidelines, Hygiene Regulations of a few European countries specify levels e.g. a minimum of 215 lux.

Regulation 23	specifies 'suitable and sufficient', well-maintained ventilation. The regulation does not apply in rooms where humidity or temperature are specifically controlled.
Regulation 24	requires that rooms used for sleeping must not communicate directly with rooms where open food is handled.

A corridor with doors at each end would normally be required between bedrooms and food production areas.

Regulation 25	specifies that food rooms should be constructed in a way that:

    (i)   allows effective cleaning; and

    (ii) prevents the entry of birds, rats, mice, insects or other pests, as far as possible.

Regulation 26 requires that sufficient space be allowed for the removal and storage of waste or of unfit food. No refuse must be allowed to remain in a food room, unless this is temporary and unavoidable.

Hot- and cold-holding of foods

Regulation 27 specifies that high-risk foods must be heated to 63°C or above, or chilled and held in cold storage as soon as possible after production. Two classes of high-risk food are specified.

(a)   The following must be held at or below 5°C:

- Cut soft cheeses ripening at a pH above 4.5.
- Cooked products intended for eating without further cooking, containing meat, meat substitutes, fish, egg, dairy products or vegetables.
- Smoked or cured fish or meats, unless canned or otherwise aseptically packed.

(b)   The following must be held at 8°C or below:

- Whole soft cheeses ripening at a pH above 4.5.
- Cooked or partly-cooked products intended for cooking or reheating (to at least 70°C for at least 2 minutes) before eating, and containing meat, meat substitutes, fish, egg, dairy products or vegetables.
- Yoghurts and other desserts with a pH above 4.5.
- Prepared salads.
- Cooked pies, pasties etc.
- Uncooked or partly cooked products containing pastry or dough and meat, meat substitutes or fish.
- Sandwiches, filled rolls etc. if they are for sale within 24 hours of preparation.

Regulation 27 does not apply to bread or biscuits containing eggs and milk or to cooked pies intended for sale within 24 hours. Ice-cream, which is controlled by other regulations, is not included. Neither are dried, canned or aseptically packaged products, cheese with a pH below 4.5, uncooked bacon or ham. Food intended for sale within two hours is also exempt. Temperatures stated in the regulations may be exceeded or reduced by 2°C as long as this deviation is temporary and unavoidable.

Question

Which soft cheeses ripen above pH 4.5, and why is 4.5 a significant value?

Cheeses are produced by the souring of milk (see Chapter 3). Lactic acid is formed and the pH falls. Several types of soft cheese are matured by the action of yeasts or moulds. These digest the cheese, converting part of the protein into ammonia, which is alkaline. The ammonia progressively neutralizes the lactic acid originally present in the cheese, so that the pH rises. Examples of such cheeses are Camembert, Brie, Lymeswold and Limburger. Growth of pathogenic bacteria is inhibited in young, acidic cheese (pH below 4.5). However, once the pH rises above 4.5 pathogens can grow to significant numbers.

Exemptions and enforcement

Regulation 28   provides local authority employees (i.e. Environmental Health Officers) with:

    (i)   powers of entry;
   (ii)   duties of sampling, inspection and issuing Improvement Notices; and
  (iii)   obtaining of warrants.

This Regulation also permits food authorities to grant a certificate of exemption where food premises cannot reasonably be expected to meet the conditions required in terms of:

    (i)   water supply;
   (ii)   accommodation for outdoor clothing;
  (iii)   a sleeping place which communicates with a food room.

Penalties

Regulation 29   sets maximum penalties as follows:

- A maximum fine of £2000 on conviction by a magistrates court.
- A fine (as specified in the Food Safety Act, 1990) and for imprisonment for up to two years on conviction by the Crown Court.
- Prohibition orders, as specified in the 1990 Act.

Study example 4.2

Operational responsibilities of management can generally be classified into four areas of concern. These are:

- Premises
- Plant/equipment
- Personnel
- Process

The requirements of the Food Hygiene Regulations, 1970 can be classified into these four areas. This is a useful exercise in analytical thinking, as well as being a helpful way to study the legislation.

1. Identify the Regulations which are concerned with Premises (i.e. which require the manager to design, maintain or clean the food premises). How many such Regulations are there?
2. Identify and count the Regulations concerned with Plant or equipment, Personnel and the Process of food production/ service. Summarize your findings in a table.
3. Which areas do the Regulations emphasize?
4. Why do you think they have this emphasis?
5. Which of the four areas is in fact most directly concerned with food hygiene?

Scottish food hygiene legislation

The Scottish legal system is different from that in England and Wales. It is based upon a system known as **Roman Common Law**, which has a different structure from English Common Law. For this reason the

British Government has in the past produced special legislation specifically for Scotland. However there is currently a move to rationalize British law under the two systems. Until 1990 Scottish food law centred around the *Food and Drugs (Scotland) Act, 1956*. This Act was repealed and consolidated into the Food Safety Act 1990, which is the primary food legislation in force throughout the British Isles.

The *Food Hygiene (Scotland) Regulations, 1959* were drawn up under the provisions of the 1956 Act and have been amended several times. They compare with the English Regulations in the following ways:

Premises

No significant differences.

Plant/equipment

Scottish Regulation 10 specifies the way in which utensils (other than drinking vessels) should be washed.

(i) Rinsing water should be at or above 72.6°C or contain a bactericide; and
(ii) Drying is specified.

Hot water is not required for rinsing drinking vessels. Scottish Regulation 11 makes similar stipulations for cleaning other equipment.

Personnel

Scottish Regulation 6 specifies that hands and fingernails be kept clean and that personnel must wash after using the lavatory.

Process

Scottish Regulation 14 requires that food be brought to at least 82.2°C (185°F) during reheating. Scottish Regulation 15 specifies the treatment of gelatine. Scottish Regulation 16 deals with the handling and processing of bakers' confectionery filling.

In addition, the Scottish Regulations permit an unlimited fine plus one year's imprisonment per offence, upon indictment.

Question

What is the status of this specific, Scottish legislation?

> The Food and Drugs (Scotland) Act, 1956, remained in force until the passing of the Food Safety Act, 1990. Under the latter, the Secretary of State for Scotland has authority to make secondary food hygiene legislation. It is not clear whether the Scottish Regulations will remain or be repealed as being unnecessary under the new Act.

How food hygiene law is enforced

Food authorities are the Borough and District councils in England and Wales and in Scotland the Island and District councils. Officers responsible for detecting food offences belong to the Environmental Health Departments of councils in England and Wales. These bodies have five major law enforcement duties:

- Food fraud and food hygiene legislation.
- Legislation for the protection of people at work.
- Clean air legislation.
- General pollution control legislation (e.g. noise control).
- Housing legislation.

Environmental Health Officers therefore tend to specialize, dealing for instance only with food hygiene offences. The same specialist officers regularly visit all establishments within a particular area, getting to know all the proprietors.

Registration

Local authorities must register all premises producing, processing or selling food for public consumption. Mobile catering or retail units and vehicles for refrigerated food transport also have to be registered. Registration consists of filling in a form like that shown in Figure 4.1. Inspection is not a pre-requisite of registering, but newly registered businesses can normally expect a prompt visit and inspection by Food Authority officers before they begin trading.

Environmental Health Officers should be consulted by management before new premises are registered. The officers will give free advice on design, operation and maintenance of premises, plant and equipment.

Figure 4.1   Registration form for food premises

---

1   Address of premises...
    ....
    ....
    Telephone number...

---

2   Name of business ....
    ....

---

3   Name of owner(s)..

    Address of Head Office ....
    or Registered Office ....
    (if different from address of premises) ....

---

4   Name of manager ....
    (If different from owner)

---

5   Number of people engaged   1–10   11–50   over 50
    in food operators (tick as appropriate)   [ ]   [ ]   [ ]
    (count part-times as one-half)

---

6   If this is a new business
    Date you intend to open ....

---

7   Type of premises
    please tick all the boxes that apply

Restaurant/cafe/snack bar	[ ]	Farm	[ ]	Food Manufacturing producing:		
Hotel/guest house	[ ]	Farm with shop	[ ]	Dairy produce	[ ]
Public house/club	[ ]	Wholesale warehouse	[ ]	Canned food	[ ]
Institutional kitchen	[ ]	Private house used		Frozen food	[ ]
Staff restaurant/canteen	[ ]	for a food business	[ ]	Chilled food	[ ]
Takeaway food business	[ ]	Village/Church hall/		Aseptically packed food	[ ]
Supermarket/grocer	[ ]	community centre	[ ]	Food packed in a	
Bakery/baker's shop	[ ]	Confectioner/tobaconist	[ ]	modified atmosphere	[ ]
Dairy produce shop/		Greengrocer	[ ]	Vacuum packed food	[ ]
delicatessen	[ ]	Mobile food business	[ ]	None of the above	[ ]
Butcher	[ ]				
Fishmonger	[ ]	(how many vehicles?			

    Any other type of
    premises, please specify...
    ....

---

8   Signature..Date..................
    Name in block capitals ....
    Position in Company/business ....

Source: MAFF Press Release, 8 June, 1990.

Involving local authority officers from the outset reassures them of the manager's positive attitude towards food hygiene. Inspections are more likely to be trouble-free and anxiety is minimized.

Detection of offences

Officers may deliberately visit proprietors known for unsatisfactory practice. Such visits are carefully planned in advance. Officers are scheduled and a warrant may be sought from a magistrate, if necessary. However, Environmental Health Officers also make regular, routine visits to all proprietors in their area. If such a visit reveals gross infestation or deterioration the officer will usually telephone for assistance.

Equipment

Considerable equipment is required for a full inspection. It is usually carried in a plain, inconspicuous case so that the arrival of EHOs equipped for an inspection does not prejudice the establishment's reputation. Inspection equipment usually includes:

Protective clothing

White coat, trilby, rubber gloves and boots.

Sampling equipment

Sterile swabs, sample pots, glass jars (to preserve live samples of insects in visible condition), polythene bags, labels, spatulae and scoops.

Inspection equipment

Camera, torch, digital thermometer and cassette tape recorder.

Note-taking equipment

Pens, paper, clipboard and stationery.

Inspection procedure

Officers are recommended to carry out a quick initial inspection of all premises they visit (Rock and Warren, 1986). This enables them to identify:

- Whether proceedings ought to be taken.
- Whether they should call for extra assistance or equipment
- Any points which might otherwise have been hastily cleared up.
- Any obvious danger spots.

Two or more officers carry out the inspection, as this prevents later allegations of unfair treatment or false evidence. Large establishments may be inspected by several pairs of Environmental Health Officers, each being allotted a different floor or section. Officers must announce what they are going to do, e.g. inspect, take samples etc. Objections of the proprietor should be noted and may be counted as the separate offence of *obstruction*.

Environmental Health Officers often take photographs as part of their inspection. The Food Safety Act, 1990 makes no specific provision for this. However the *Health and Safety at Work Act, 1974*, which also comes under the jurisdiction of Environmental Health Departments, specifically authorizes the use of photography for gathering evidence. However, photographs are much more effective proof of unhygienic premises than verbal testimony, as witnesses may be discredited in court. Photographs are invalid if their authenticity can be questioned. Development and handling of the negatives must be conducted with scrupulous care so that the subject matter and date cannot be questioned later.

Sampling is specifically permitted under the Food Safety Act 1990 and is an important part of an Environmental Health Officer's duties. Items sampled will generally include:

- Spoiled food, e.g. 'blown' cans, mouldy items etc.
- Unsatisfactory wrapping materials, utensils and equipment.
- Evidence of infestation: live insects, larvae, droppings etc.

Samples for analysis are usually divided into three if possible. One part should be left with the proprietor and one kept for comparison. The third is sent for analysis.

Question

Is this same procedure used in the case of food that a Justice of the Peace has ordered to be destroyed?

A sample of condemned food cannot be given to a proprietor as this would contravene the Destruction Order. The proprietor might, in theory, sell the condemned food, or offer it for consumption.

Food Authority Officers are recommended to collect samples of live insects. These are particularly convincing if produced in clear glass jars in court. Live insects can easily be taken from infested foods or caught by setting traps baited with foods or pheromones. Insects can also be flushed from crevices and corners using a pyrethroid aerosol spray.

Note-taking is an important part of inspection. Locations of photographs and samples must be noted, otherwise their evidence value is jeopardized. Verbal evidence is also noted, when employees or the proprietor of the food establishment are interviewed. Environmental Health Officers are bound by the *Police and Criminal Evidence Act, 1984*, which requires that suspected offenders are cautioned before the interview. Cautions must make it clear to suspects that they are not obliged to make a statement, but that anything they say may be taken down and used in evidence. A signed record of the caution must be kept with the interview notes. Officers may also tape-record and subsequently transcribe interviews.

Legal action

Improvement Notices

Environmental Health Departments are obliged to issue an *Improvement Notice* covering all defects observed during an inspection. Improvement Notices must also specify what must be done to put the defects right and allow the proprietor fourteen days to do this work. Notices may be accompanied by a warning letter, but will not normally become the subject of a court case unless:

- The Environmental Health Department believes the proprietor has no chance of completing the specified work within fourteen days.

- The Department feels that there is an imminent risk to the public health.
- The law is being flagrantly and deliberately broken (e.g. the same offence continually committed)

Under these circumstances application may be made for a Destruction or Prohibition Order.

Prohibition and Destruction Orders

Food Authorities are entitled to apply to a magistrate (or sheriff in Scotland) for an officially order to close a business down (prohibition) or to destroy food seized as not being fit to eat (destruction). Fourteen days' notice are given for a Prohibition Order, which is usually issued as the result of a prosecution. Thus the normal procedure is to issue an Improvement Notice and to return after two weeks. If the work specified has been carried out to the officers' satisfaction the Authority will issue a Certificate of Compliance. This effectively cancels the original Notice. A proprietor who has not done the necessary work after this time is prosecuted, usually through a magistrates' court. If the court is convinced that a danger to health exists it will prosecute the proprietor and may also grant a *Prohibition Order*. The Order must be served personally on the proprietor and is also displayed prominently on the premises.

Officers can also apply to a magistrate or sheriff for an *Emergency Prohibition Order*. In this case the proprietor is only given twenty-four hours' notice after the Improvement Notice is served. The court must be convinced that there is a serious risk to health, for example major infestation or contamination with *Salmonella* or *Clostridium botulinum*. Emergency Orders are difficult to coordinate and Environmental Health Departments must have clearly established procedures. It may be necessary to receive authorization from a committee to proceed with the Order. An Improvement Notice must be prepared and served, and a court booked for the following day. If the prosecuting Department omits any aspect of the full procedure the defendant is entitled to appeal or to ignore the Notice.

Environmental Health Officers can seize unfit food, or order its withdrawal from sale. The food must be sent for analysis. If it is confirmed as unfit for human consumption the officers apply to a magistrate's or sheriff's court for a *Destruction Order*. The unfit food must then be destroyed as soon as possible and the cost of destruction is charged to the defendant.

Prosecution

Two types of trial are available for food hygiene offences in England and Wales. These are:

- *Summary trial* in a Magistrates' Court.
- *Trial on indictment* in the Crown Court.

Magistrates' Court

Cases brought to summary trial are decided either by three lay magistrates or by one stipendiary magistrate presiding over the court. *Lay Magistrates* are not lawyers, but individuals from various walks of life who have applied and been selected to represent their community. They are known as Justices of the peace (JP), a term which also applies to sheriffs. *Stipendiary Magistrates* are qualified lawyers, employed by the Court. They are usually found in urban areas where the supply of voluntary magistrates is insufficient for the number of Courts.

A *Magistrates' Court* deals with local cases which can be brought very quickly. Defendants may be represented by a solicitor or a barrister, but also often appear without legal representation. Legal aid is not available. Previous convictions are not considered and the court's powers are limited. The maximum fine is £2000. Actual penalties are related to the number of *counts* on which conviction is obtained i.e. the number of clauses or regulations in the legislation which have been transgressed. A Magistrates' Court deals with minor criminal cases, prohibition and Destruction Orders, search warrants and licences. It can also refer serious cases to the Crown Court for trial. Alternatively, a defendant has the right to choose trial by the Crown Court for certain offences, which might otherwise be tried by a magistrate. Defendants cannot choose summary trial for an indictable offence.

Crown Court

Trial on indictment refers to the document which charges the defendant with an offence, called an *indictment*. It is drawn up by the prosecution before any case is heard in the Crown court and it records the reason why the case has been referred to the Crown Court (e.g. decision of a Magistrates' Court or of the defendant). The police search their records for any past offences and these are also considered by the Court when sentence is passed. A *judge* presides over the Crown Court and interprets legal matters. The case is actually decided by a *jury* consisting of twelve men and women chosen from the electorate. The Crown Court is usually located in a city or county town and deals with the more serious cases. Often these will take weeks or months to come to trial. A barrister appointed by the State brings the prosecution. The defendant is also usually represented by a barrister, as solicitors have no right of audience. Legal aid is available to defendants of limited means.

Question
Can individuals represent themselves at the Crown Court?

> In theory it is a defendants' right to plead his own case. However, few people have adequate legal knowledge or expertise. In practice this right usually only amounts to calling the defendant as a witness in the case.

The maximum penalty the Crown Court can impose is stated in the legislation; the Court itself is not restricted. Severity of the sentence depends on the judge's view of the magnitude of the crime. The number of counts does not automatically influence the penalty, but the Court does consider previous convictions. The Crown Court can make Confiscation and Compensation Orders. A *Compensation Order* may be awarded to victims of personal injury resulting from a criminal offence, for example to an individual whose health was damaged by broken glass ingested with tinned food. A *Confiscation Order* may apply to an individual who has made profits in excess of £10,000 from an illegal enterprise, such as dealing in knacker meat.

Appeal

Defendants may appeal to a Magistrate's Court against the decisions of a Local Authority. This usually means a dispute about Improvement Notices, Certificates of Compliance or licences. There is a standard format of complaint, set out in the *Magistrates' Courts Act, 1980*. Defendants who are aggrieved at the decision of a Magistrate's Court may take the matter to the Crown Court, or to the *Court of Appeal (Criminal Division)*. The ultimate Courts of Appeal are the House of Lords and the European Court.

Scottish courts

The equivalent in Scotland of a Magistrate's Court is the *Sheriff's Court*. As in England and Wales, these Courts hear most food hygiene cases. The sheriff is a paid, qualified legal officer similar to a stipendiary magistrate. Both magistrates and sheriffs are referred to in a general way as Justices of the Peace in the *Food Safety Act, 1990*. A Sheriff's Court does not grant licences like a Magistrate's Court. In Scotland this function is fulfilled by Licencing Committees, which are standing committees of the local councils. The Sheriffs' Courts also have limited penalties, like Magistrates' Courts.

The *Scottish High Court* is the equivalent of the Crown Court. It consists of a judge (a Scottish Law Lord) and fifteen (not twelve) jurors. The High Court is not permanently in session in one place, but operates a circuit around the country. The *Scottish Court of Session* is presided over by three Scottish Law Lords and is equivalent to the English Court of Appeal.

Other legislation relevant to food hygiene

Three categories of legislation can be considered relevant to food hygiene in the UK. These are:

- Regulations aimed specifically at the hygienic production and treatment of particular foods. (Mostly empowered by the Food Safety Act, 1990 itself.)
- Food packaging controls
- Acts and Regulations which partly overlap the requirements of the Food Safety Act or the Food Hygiene (General) Regulations.

Regulations affecting specific foods

Milk and dairy products

The *Milk and Dairies (General) Regulations, 1959* (plus various amendments) require the registration of dairies, milk distributors and transporters.

The *Milk (Special Designations) Regulations, 1986* deals with the bottling and designations of different types of milk. For instance 'gold top' is a high fat designation; pasteurized, homogenized and other milks have other specified colour codes. Sale of untreated (raw) milk is strictly controlled.

The *Liquid Egg (Pasteurization) Regulations, 1963* specify the time/temperature treatment and testing of raw egg

Question

The specified time/temperature treatment is 64.4°C for 2.5 minutes. Is this more or less drastic than that for milk (72°C for 15 seconds)?

The approximate D_{60} value for salmonella is 4 minutes. The z value (see Table 2.4) is 4°C. Therefore approximate D values are:

D_{64} = 0.4 min (24 sec)
D_{72} = 0.24 sec

Thus 2.5 minutes (150 sec) at 64°C would reduce the bacteria count by its D value 150/24 times (6.25 reductions); 15 seconds at 72°C would reduce the bacterial count to one tenth its value 15/0.24 times (62.5 reductions). This is much more drastic. Presumably egg would denature at the higher temperature.

The *Ice-cream (Heat Treatment etc) Regulations, 1959* (plus amendments) set out the times and temperatures for (a) pasteurizing and (b) sterilizing. Ice-cream holding temperatures are also specified.

Meat production regulations

The *Slaughterhouses (Hygiene) Regulations, 1977* and the *Poultry Meat (Hygiene) Regulations* specify hygiene of premises, plant/equipment, personnel and process in slaughterhouses. Requirements are similar to those of the Food Hygiene (General) Regulations, 1970 but generally stricter. For example, premises must be specifically designed to minimize cross-contamination routes, and taps on basins must not be hand-operable.

The *Meat Inspection Regulations, 1963* and the *Food (Meat Inspection) (Scotland) Regulations, 1961* (plus various amendments) require the provision and training of *meat inspectors* by local authorities. This legislation also sets out inspection procedures and the criteria for rejecting unfit carcasses. The *Meat (Sterilization and Staining) (Scot-*

land) Regulations, 1983 set out the procedure for dealing with unfit carcasses. Unfit meat must be stained black and heat-sterilized. Condemned meat must be stored and transported securely so that it is not used for human consumption.

The *Diseases of Animals (Waste Food) Order, 1983* is secondary legislation made under the *Diseases of Animals Act, 1950*. It requires individuals who feed waste human food to animals to be licenced by the Ministry of Agriculture, Fisheries and Food. Waste food intended as animal feed must also be transported in a hygienic manner and heat sterilized before use.

Shellfish regulations

Shellfish are currently protected by the *Public Health (Shellfish) Regulations, 1934* (as amended). This empowers local authorities to prohibit the sale of shellfish taken from known polluted layings without cleansing.

Food authorities' powers over the cleansing of shellfish have been considerably enhanced by the passing of the Food Safety Act, 1990. This permits specific new secondary legislation for shellfish.

Food packaging controls

The *Materials and Articles in Contact with Food Regulations, 1987* (also empowered under the Food Safety Act, 1990) seek to prevent food contamination by controlling the materials of which food packaging and food handling equipment are made.

Legislation overlapping with food hygiene provision

The *Health and Safety at Work Act, 1987* sets out the responsibilities of employers and employees in terms of health and safety. Although the Act specifically deals with the health and safety of workers, parts of it can be construed as a applying to the general public. For example:

Section 4   requires anyone who controls premises or processes to ensure that they are not a risk to the health and safety of 'persons who use, enter or leave the premises'.

Section 7 requires that employees must take reasonable care of the health and safety of themselves and other persons who may be affected by their acts or omissions at work

In restaurants and hotels the Health and Safety at Work Act, 1974 is enforced by Environmental Health Officers of the local authority. This provides another area of common ground with the Food Hygiene (General) Regulations. Officers may use inspection powers such as photography, which is specifically permitted under the Health and Safety at Work Act, but not under the Food Safety Act. Health and safety in food production factories is the responsibility of factory inspectors of the Health and Safety Executive, rather than the local authority.

The 1974 Act requires employers of more than five persons to have a written health and safety policy. Employees must be notified of the main points of the policy and must be allowed to read it on request. Although there is no overt overlap of the Health and Safety at Work Act with the Food Hygiene Regulations, employers frequently include food hygiene within their health and safety policy (see Chapter 9). This strengthens the management of food hygiene and reinforces the importance of it to employees. Food hygiene may also become a matter of regular inspection by safety officers and discussion at safety committees. The Health and Safety at Work Act, 1974 empowers various secondary legislation, dealing notably with hazardous substances and first aid.

The *Control of Substances Hazardous to Health Regulations, 1988* make employers responsible for controlling the exposure of employees to harmful chemicals. All substances likely to be harmful and, wherever possible, harmful exposure times and levels must be identified. Work schedules should be arranged so that employees do not exceed hazardous levels. Cleaning materials, disinfectants, food preservatives and allergenic foods are all potentially harmful to health and therefore subject to the Regulations.

The *Health and Safety (First Aid) Regulations, 1981* set out the proper contents of first aid boxes and specify numbers of personnel who must be trained in first aid. This somewhat overlaps the requirement, under the Food Hygiene (General) Regulations of providing bandages and dressings.

The *Offices, Shops and Railway Premises Act, 1963* is mainly concerned with the welfare of employees and customers in the Service industries, including catering. The Act specifies:

- Cleanliness of rooms, furniture and fittings.
- Overcrowding, in terms of floor area and room volume.
- A minimum temperature of 16°C for most work.
- Adequate ventilation.
- Adequate lighting.
- Adequate provision of sanitary conveniences.

The Act provides for secondary legislation, for example the *Offices, Shops and Railway Premises Sanitary Accommodation Regulations, 1960, the Washing Facilities Regulations, 1964* and the *Sanitary Conveniences Regulations, 1964*, which contain the necessary specific details. These are also taken as standards for food hygiene provision by local authorities. Lavatory provision may also be required for employees and others under the *Chronically Sick and Disabled Persons Act, 1970*. Environmental Health Departments are responsible for enforcing this legislation.

Question

Why is it significant that Environmental Health Departments enforce this legislation?

Environmental Health Departments tend to apply common standards where legislation overlaps. For example, standards for ventilation and sanitary provision specified under the Offices, Shops and Railway Premises Act, 1963 will generally also be applied when judging compliance with the Food Hygiene (General) Regulations 1970.

The *Local Government (Miscellaneous Provisions) Act, 1976* extends the provision of facilities for employees to include:

- Washing facilities.
- Availability of drinking water.
- Accommodation for clothing.
- Seating arrangements.
- Staff restaurant facilities .
- Safety and hygiene of floors, passages and stairs.
- Protection from dangerous machinery.

Secondary legislation empowered under the 1976 Act includes the *Prescribed Dangerous Machines Order, 1964*. This prohibits the cleaning of certain machines by operatives under 18 years old, and therefore has a potential effect upon workforce scheduling and indirectly upon food hygiene.

The *Public Health (Control of Disease) Act, 1984* requires the notification of scheduled diseases to the the Local Authority's Medical Officer of Health. The list of diseases is extensive, including severe

tropical diseases and the main childhood illnesses (measles, mumps etc)
Significantly the list includes:

- Dysentery (amoebic or bacillary).
- Poliomyelitis.
- Tuberculosis.
- Typhoid and paratyphoid fever.
- Viral hepatitis.

The **Medical Officer of Health** is usually the chief community
physician or pathologist at the district health authority. Generally this
individual has an office at the Environmental Health Department of the
Local Authority. It is to this office that notification should be made.

Codes of practice

The Government seeks to influence food hygiene indirectly, as well as
through legislation. The Ministry of Agriculture, Fisheries and Food,
and the Department of Health have produced a number of codes of
practice relating to various aspects of the food industry. These are as
follows:

- Hygiene in the retail meat trade (1959).
- Hygiene in the retail fish trade (1960).
- Poultry dressing and packing (1961).
- Hygiene in the bakery trade and industry (1966).
- Hygiene in the operation of coin-operated food vending
  machines (1967)
- Hygiene in the meat trades (1969).
- Guidance on pre-cooked frozen food (1970).
- Hygiene in microwave cooking (1972).
- Guidelines on pre-cooked chilled foods (1980) (revised 1989).
- The canning of low acid foods (1981).

These guidelines serve to inform managers of their legal responsibilities and to disseminate good practice. They also form a basis from which
Environmental Health Officers can judge plant and process hygiene in
particular branches of the food industry. In addition to official
government publications there are codes of practice drawn up by manufacturers' associations and other bodies. An example is the Food
Manufacturers' Federation/Food Machinery Association (1970) code
for the design of food machinery. The British Pest Control Association
also publishes a code of practice, with which Association members are
expected to comply.

British Standards

The British Standards Institute has produced a number of recommended standards for products which have an impact on food hygiene and food safety. These include:

- Disinfectants and disinfection, BS2462, BS5283.
- Sanitary appliances for hotels and restaurants, BS6465.
- Low lead paints BS4310.
- Refrigeration units BS2501, BS2509.
- Frozen storage units BS3053.
- Waste compactors BS5832.

In addition there are auxiliary standards published by other bodies, for example the Illumination Engineering Society has produced standards of lighting for public buildings. These may be used to decide whether practice at a particular establishment conforms with the law. British Standards and official codes of practice are available for reference at most college libraries and at the larger public libraries.

Other publications

The Hotel, Catering and Institutional Management Association (HCI-MA) also publishes guidelines on legal and technical issues. These sheets, produced by the Technical Advisory Group (TAG) are circulated free to members and are available from the Association (HCIMA, 191, Trinity Road, London SW17 1HN)

Study example 4.3

Provision of sanitary and washing facilities for staff is affected by primary and secondary legislation as well as by British Standards.

1. Indicate the primary legislation which relates to employees' sanitary and washing facilities
2. Indicate the secondary legislation which relates to employees' sanitary and washing facilities
3. How do British Standards affect interpretation of the law?

Summary – food hygiene law

Food hygiene law is criminal law, based on enforcing statutes, i.e. written laws passed by Parliament. The relevant primary legislation is the Food Safety Act, 1990, which deals with food hygiene, food safety and food fraud. The Act also empowers Ministers to make secondary legislation for food premises registration and food hygiene. Food hygiene law specifies the hygiene, construction and maintenance of premises, plant and equipment, the hygiene and behaviour of personnel, and the way certain food processes should be conducted.

Food hygiene law is enforced by Environmental Health Officers. These local authority employees have the following duties:

- Registration of premises.
- Inspection, sampling and seizure.
- Issue of Improvement Notices and Certificates of Compliance.
- Obtaining and enforcing Prohibition and Destruction Orders.
- Prosecution of offenders.

Environmental Health Officers should be consulted when any new food business is set up.

Prosecution can be summary, by a Magistrate's Court, or on indictment, in the Crown Court. The latter deals with more serious offences and can hand down heavier penalties. Appeals may be made against decisions of local authorities or Courts.

Food hygiene law mentions conditions such as toilet facilities, ventilation and lighting, but does not specify standards. These are drawn from other Acts and secondary legislation, official or industrial codes of practice, and British Standards.

5 Food Hygiene and the Management of Premises

Objectives

To identify the legal obligations of the food process manager with regard to premises. To discuss the principles and practice underlying planning, design, maintenance and cleaning of premises, in order to ensure food hygiene and customer safety.

Introduction

The design and upkeep of premises are a major concern of the Food Hygiene Regulations. Areas specifically mentioned by the Regulations are:

Infestation by pests	(Regulation 6)
Drains and drainage	(Regulations 6 and 14)
Water supplies	(Regulations 15 and 17)
Lavatories and hand basins	(Regulations 16 and 18)
Lockers	(Regulation 20)
Facilities for washing food and equipment	(Regulation 21)
Lighting and ventilation	(Regulations 22 and 23)
Isolation of food rooms from other rooms	(Regulations 16 and 24)
Cleanliness and repair	(Regulation 25)
Refuse storage and disposal	(Regulation 26)

Besides achieving compliance with the law, effective management of food premises can increase operational efficiency, improve staff morale, raise the value of premises and reduce energy costs. It is therefore in the manager's interests to pay careful attention to buildings, site and services. The two main management functions are *planning/design* and *upkeep*, which are dealt with separately in this chapter.

Planning and design

Planning and design can improve food hygiene by:

- Reducing cross-contamination.
- Reducing the likelihood of infestation.
- Increasing the efficiency of equipment for hot- and cold-holding of foods.

Cross-contamination opportunities are reduced if raw and cooked foods never have to occupy the same work surfaces or storage areas. Areas and equipment used in raw food preparation should be kept separate from areas where cooked food is handled.

Infestation begins when vermin are attracted by food and waste food. Pests can be kept out by screens or barriers. If they do manage to enter food premises, they can be discouraged by denying them shelter, moisture, warmth and food. This approach is called *ecological control*, as opposed to pest control by poisons or traps.

Question
What does the word 'ecological' signify?

> Ecology is the study of environments and habitats. Therefore ecological pest control aims to make food premises an unsuitable environment for pests.

Efficiency of equipment often depends upon services such as mains water, ventilation, drainage and the ambient temperature. Careful positioning of ventilation hoods and drains can improve the efficiency of cooking and cleaning appliances. Rooms for refrigerators should not heat up, e.g. by solar heat gain from windows. Areas containing *bain-maries* should not have such a through-draught that hot foods cool by forced convection.

The hospitality industry, like other service industries, is expanding and will continue to grow. There is considerable investment in new buildings and in the interior restructuring of older ones. Often a team of experts:

architects, specialist catering consultants and engineers, is involved in the design of new units. Wherever possible the manager and staff of the unit should participate in the process. Design of food service and production systems is a complex process involving a matrix of factors. Planning often involves a compromise between available space and the ideal design. It is important that food hygiene is given full consideration at this stage, so that it is adequately represented in the planning mix.

Planning means allocation of space and the positioning of work stations and amenities relative to one another. Interconnections, barriers and the layout of the work stations and amenities themselves also have to be planned. In this chapter *design* is taken as the detailed design of the site, structure and services, including such things as finishes, positioning of pipework and materials.

Planning considerations

Four basic principles should be considered in the hygienic planning of a food handling operation. These are concerned with:

- Workflow.
- Interaction between work-centres.
- Separation of functional areas.
- Economy of movement.

Workflow

The guiding principle is to have *linear* workflow as far as possible. In other words, raw materials should ideally pass in a direct line from the receiving area to the store, to preparation, cooking, the servery and the customer. There should be no points where the flow doubles back, or flow lines of different foods cross. In such a linear system cross-contamination cannot occur, because raw foods are separated from cooked ones in space and time. In practice a number of problems may arise. Available space is seldom suited to a linear distribution of work-centres. Some work-centres may have to serve others, breaking up the flow. An example of this is a kitchen with one chilled storage room. Staff will have to make trips to it to collect raw ingredients or to store intermediates such as prepared, stuffed poultry or dough for pastry. Finished products such as salads or chilled starters may have to be held in the same area. This storage problem may be solved by installing separate cabinets along the workflow instead of having a single walk-in refrigerator at one point along it. It is less easy to solve the problem for some other work-centres. For instance the waste collection area usually serves the preparation and washing-up areas. The washing-up area usually takes pots from the cooking area and dishes from the restaurant. It may also receive equipment from preparation areas. Such multi-interactions may or may not be of serious concern. Their impact on workflow and hygiene should, however, be carefully considered during planning to minimize contamination problems.

Interaction between work-centres

The best way to analyze interactions between centres is probably to use *relationship charts*. A typical chart is shown in Figure 5.1. Numbers at the intersections between work-centres indicate which should ideally be located close together. Such a chart may be produced by an individual or a working party deciding the layout. Alternatively staff may be consulted, using a questionnaire which allows them to rate the importance of locating the various centres together. Questionnaire scores can be averaged and the results entered in a relationship diagram similar to that shown in the figure. This is called a *consensus relationship chart*. However, the value of staff input may be affected by their level of hygiene training. Relationship charts can be used to identify and reduce likely movement of personnel between work-centres. This may also reduce contamination opportunities. Charts can also be used to make decisions about the locations and distances between centres. However, the linear workflow principle should generally take precedence over likely interactions in deciding layout.

Separation of functional areas

Food handling operations can be analyzed into 'clean' and 'dirty' areas.

Dirty areas are defined as anywhere where personnel, equipment or food might become contaminated. Typical dirty areas are lavatories, washrooms, raw meat and vegetable stores and preparation areas, waste storage or collection points, dish-washing and the restaurant.

Question
Why is the restaurant included in the list of 'dirty' areas?

Restaurants should be regarded as 'dirty' areas because they contain all the contaminants normally associated with humans: tobacco smoke, saliva and dirt from street clothes, for example. All these will find their way on to plates and return, with waste food, to the kitchen.

Figure 5.1   Work area relationship chart

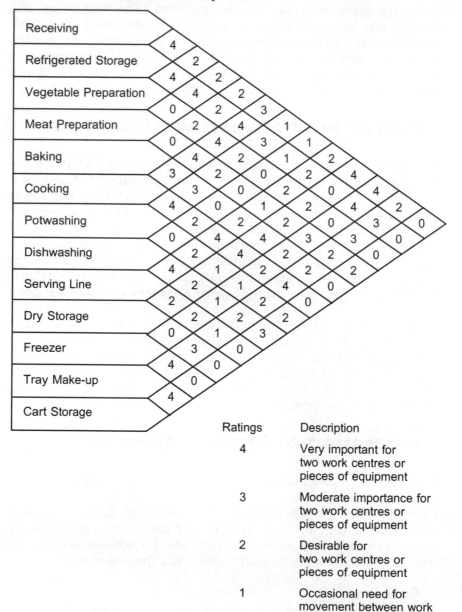

Ratings	Description
4	Very important for two work centres or pieces of equipment
3	Moderate importance for two work centres or pieces of equipment
2	Desirable for two work centres or pieces of equipment
1	Occasional need for movement between work centres or pieces of equipment
0	No need for consideration as to closeness

Source: Avery, 1973.

**Figure 5.2   Average frequency of isolation of Escherichia coli,
Streptococcus faecalis and total coliforms from
different kitchen areas**

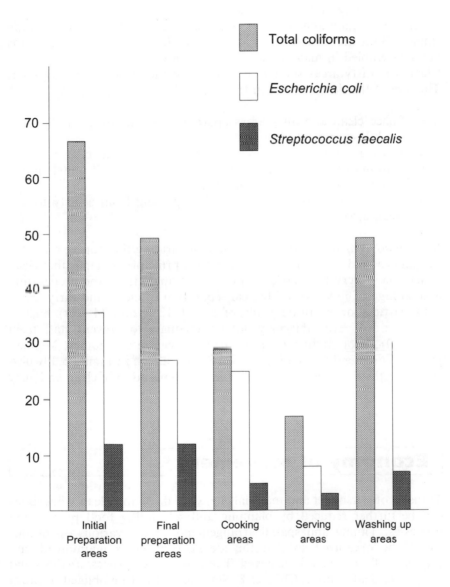

Source: Mendes, Lynch and Stanley, 1978, p. 228.

Clean areas of the food operation are locations where cooked and ready-to-eat foods are handled and stored. By definition any contamination of clean areas is harmful. Examples are hot-holding, plating-up, cooking and salad assembly areas. Mendes, Lynch and Stanley (1978) made a study of kitchens in the London area and obtained bacteriological data for typical clean and dirty areas. These are shown as a bar chart in Figure 5.2. These authors distinguished between *initial* food preparation (peeling, washing, unwrapping, can-opening) and *final* food preparation (boning, trimming and filleting), although the contamination levels are similar. Both are clearly 'dirty' areas. Mendes' group observed salads being assembled in many final preparation areas.

Clean and dirty areas should be marked on the layout plan in colour. The aim of the designer is then to:

- Space clean and dirty areas apart, if possible using the linear workflow principle.
- Physically separate clean and dirty areas by means of barriers.
- Rationalize and minimize the movement of personnel and materials from dirty to clean areas.
- Encourage personnel to wash when passing from a dirty to a clean area.

Spacing areas apart means, for example, separating the storage areas for raw and cooked meats. The linear workflow principle demands that clean areas (the servery for example) are located apart from the preparation and storage of raw foods. Physical separation of clean and dirty areas, with barriers or partition walls of about 1230 mm (4 feet) high is recommended. Even this may not be adequate to prevent staff from passing foods or equipment from one work-centre to another. Mendes' group recommend the outline kitchen design shown in Figure 5.3, which combines the linear workflow principle with separation of clean and dirty areas.

Economy of movement

Transfer of personnel and materials between dirty and clean work areas can be further reduced by planning and scheduling food preparation processes. Timing and spatial arrangements of the various operations should be organized so that the ideal workflow is maintained and economy of movement is achieved. These aspects of process analysis and design are dealt with in Chapter 8. Staff should not be obliged to move back and forth unnecessarily between work-centres, and particularly not

Figure 5.3   Suggested kitchen flow layout

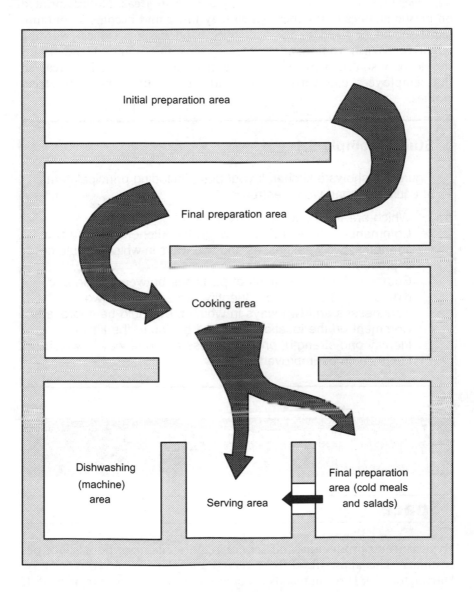

Source: Mendes, Lynch and Stanley, 1978, p. 228.

between clean and dirty areas. Hygienic layout, workflow and process design should be explained to staff at induction and training sessions.

Personnel can be encouraged to wash by installing hand basins wherever they must pass between dirty and clean areas. Notices printed on plastic plaques (not paper, which may tatter and become a contaminant) should be fixed to the wall over hand basins. Typical wording might be: 'Wash your hands before passing this point'. Hand basins should be installed between locker rooms and food handling areas so that employees can wash their hands after changing their street clothes.

Study example 5.1

Figure 5.4 shows a kitchen layout plan, including principal items of equipment and work-centres.

1. Which are the clean and dirty areas?
2. Comment on the workflow through the kitchen. Identify two strengths, two weaknesses and two ways in which it could be improved.
3. Comment on the locations of partitions between clean and dirty areas of the kitchen. Identify two strengths, two weaknesses and two ways in which they could be improved.
4. Comment on the locations of hand basins in the kitchen. Identify one strength, one weakness and one way in which these could be improved.

Planning of work-centres and amenities

Space

Hygienic food production and service require adequate floor space per customer. This allows food to be served and plates removed efficiently. Harrington (1981) recommends the space allowances shown in Table 5.1. It is impossible to give precise guidelines for kitchen areas based on staff numbers. Food production operations and the movements they necessitate vary widely. Other important considerations are subdivision of space, provision of facilities and the layout of the work-centres themselves.

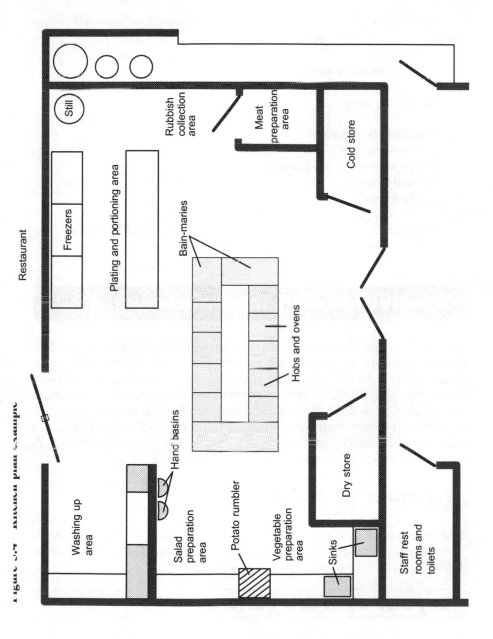

Figure 5.7 Kitchen plan example

Table 5.1   Space allowances for food production and service operations

Functional area	Allowance: m^2/person
Public areas:	
Cocktail parties/receptions	0.46
Banqueting rounds	1.11
Banqueting sprigs	0.93
Restaurants and bars:	
Luxury restaurant	1.7
Coffee shop/medium restaurant	1.3
Bar and lounge	1.7
Staff canteen	1.6
Kitchens	25–30% of restaurant

Subdivision and separation

General flow and layout considerations have already been discussed. It is also important to separate certain areas from the atmosphere of the main kitchen. For example, heat and moisture should be kept away from stores. The planning team may consider that other sensitive work-centres should also be isolated. In addition there are legal considerations. For example, amenities such as toilets, locker rooms and sleeping quarters must not open directly onto any area where food is stored or handled. A corridor and two doors must separate the two.

Number of facilities

Requirements of staff and public water closets, urinals and work wash basins are laid down by various pieces of legislation. These are shown in Table 5.2.

Layout of work-centres

Economy of movement between work-centres has already been discussed as an important factor in the overall plan. Economy of movement *within* each work-centre is another important consideration. Inadequately designed work-centres contribute to fatigue, inefficiency and human

Table 5.2   Staff and public sanitary accommodation

No. male/female staff	WCs.	Urinals	Washbasins
Hotels, restaurants, shops			
up to – 15	1	–	1
– 30	2	Not	2
– 50	3	speci-	3
– 75	4	fied	4
–100	5	–	5
Factories			
up to – 25	1	Not	1
– 50	2	speci-	2
– 75	3	fied	3
Male public			
up to –100	1	4	3
–200	2	8	5
–300	3	12	7
etc			

(A separate cleaner's sink should also be provided.)

error, all of which may result in poor food hygiene. A number of analytical techniques are available to assist the ergonomic design of work-centres. These include *string diagrams*, *value* and *efficiency ratings* and *photographic techniques* (stroboscopic pictures and cyclegraphs). All are discussed in detail by Kotschevar (1968). Work-centre layout may require the repositioning of items of equipment and this may mean that services have to be moved. It is therefore important to plan work-centres in advance. Because operatives differ in physique, it is frequently necessary to use movable equipment to achieve full workplace efficiency. Movable items also permit easier cleaning and contribute to food hygiene.

Ease of cleaning partly depends on the type of construction materials and on the style of features such as architrave and skirting. These are discussed separately below. The positioning of fixed equipment such as shelves, surfaces and machinery also has an effect. Where possible, movable equipment such as shelved trolleys and cookers on castors should be used. Fixed items should be spaced at least 300 mm (12 in.) from one another and from walls so that all sides are accessible to mops or cleaning lances.

Equipment should be positioned so that it functions effectively. For example, refrigerators and freezers are inefficient and costly to operate in a high ambient temperature. They should not be exposed to heat from kitchens or placed in rooms with south- or west-facing windows, where there may be high solar heat gain. Fixed appliances such as ovens or potato rumblers usually require power, gas, ventilation hoods, drains or water. It is important to plan locations carefully. Otherwise equipment will operate inefficiently or need costly repositioning of services.

Detailed design considerations

Site, foundations and drainage

The site may have a considerable impact upon hygienic operation. Site and buildings should be carefully planned and ideally should permit the whole food production service operation to be located on one level. This makes transfer of materials easier between departments. Trolleys laden with foods should not have to negotiate steps between stores, kitchen, servery and restaurants. Lifts are a possible solution to such problems, but they may waste time, jostle foods on trolleys and occasionally fail. However, a split-level site may be desirable on marketing grounds: a high-level restaurant with a panoramic view, for example. If use of a lift is inevitable, very careful thought should be given to its siting, operation and cleaning at the design stage. Sometimes a split-level site can be exploited by locating the rubbish collection point with chutes, directly below the kitchen. A split-level site may also grant access to sewers and other services beneath the floor of the food production area.

In theory sites should be located away from potential sources of pests. In practice this may not be a realistic consideration. Clearly it would be ill-advised to build close to a tip for household rubbish where there may be rats or other vermin. On the other hand, sites by rivers or canals are also often frequented by brown rats. Such sites are becoming increasingly popular for hotels and restaurants. Catering units near beauty spots occasionally suffer invasions by ducks, pigeons or foxes. Visitors feed the creatures, which tend to remain in the area and forage from waste bins.

Foundations and site concrete-work are an important factor in deterring rats and mice. Brown rats generally scrape burrows in the soil under floors. This can be prevented and the rats discouraged by concreting all such areas. External walls should be rendered with smooth cement to a height of 500 mm (20 in.), preferably with an overhanging ridge to catch drops of water and also prevent rats climbing the walls. There should be a continuous cast concrete apron or border, 675–750 mm (27–30 in.) wide, abutting all outside walls. The concrete denies small animals cover and discourages them from seeking an entrance. Rubbish collection areas in particular should be concreted and constructed so that they can easily be swept and washed down. Foundations, oversite concreting and the bases of walls (see Figure 5.5) should contain a damp proof membrane. 'Rising damp' can be an important source of moisture to rats, cockroaches and other pests. Damp also supports fungal growth such as 'wet' and 'dry' rot. Apart from attacking the structure of the building this growth provides food and shelter for various insects, including some pests. Cellars should be *tanked*, i.e. surrounded inside or out with an impermeable, moisture-proof barrier. Most of this work is required by law for a new building, under the Building Regulations. Local authorities may also demand improvements of this kind when an older building is converted for catering use. Managers should be aware of the way in which construction may affect food hygiene and consider these points when viewing new plans or inspecting work.

Figure 5.5   Pest-proof structure of floor and foundations

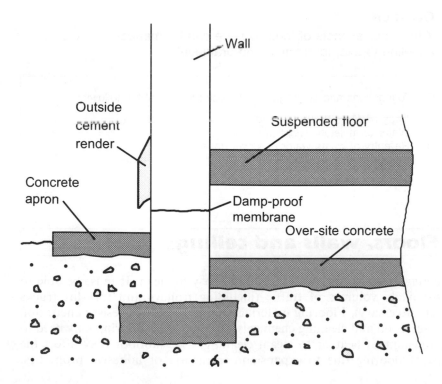

Drainage is particularly important at food preparation sites, which usually produce large quantities of waste water. There should be two separate drainage systems. One system carries storm water to a soak-away, to the street drains, or to a waterway. The other carries waste water to a main sewer, to a septic tank, or to a private treatment unit. Drains should run beneath the ground with a fall of one part in one hundred (1/100). Capacity of drainage systems must be adequate to likely demand. Pipes should, however, be small enough in diameter so that occasional surges of waste water keep them clean by dislodging solid items. There should be access and inspection points (manholes) wherever drains join, turn corners, or are forced to fall more steeply than 1/100. In addition *rodding eyes* should be constructed in accessible positions wherever pipes are likely to become obstructed. These features are shown in Figure 5.6. Sewer and waste pipes can give access to pests. Ideally waste and overflow pipes should not project through walls close to the ground. If such pipes are essential they should be sealed into the surrounding wall with cement or mastic and open ends should be covered with wire cages. Pipes carrying waste water or sewage should leave the building either through a water-filled *gulley trap*, or through a vertical *breather pipe*. Vertical pipes should be fitted with collars of wire or plastic to prevent rats climbing them.

Question

Which four aspects of food hygiene can be managed by proper attention to site, foundation and drainage?

Site, foundations and drainage may be used to control the following:

(i)   Entry of pests to the building;
(ii)   Water or moisture supplies for pests;
(iii)   Re-entry of waste water or sewer gases; and
(iv)   Efficient transfer of foods and materials between departments.

Floors, walls and ceilings

Flooring must be safe, waterproof and easy to clean. It must be able to resist likely volumes of traffic (including trolleys and fork-lift trucks where necessary). Flooring materials should be able to resist penetration by grease, oil and cleaning chemicals. In some areas flooring may need to be resistant to heat or to steam cleaning. The subfloor may affect the type of flooring due to expansion/contraction or adhesive properties.

169

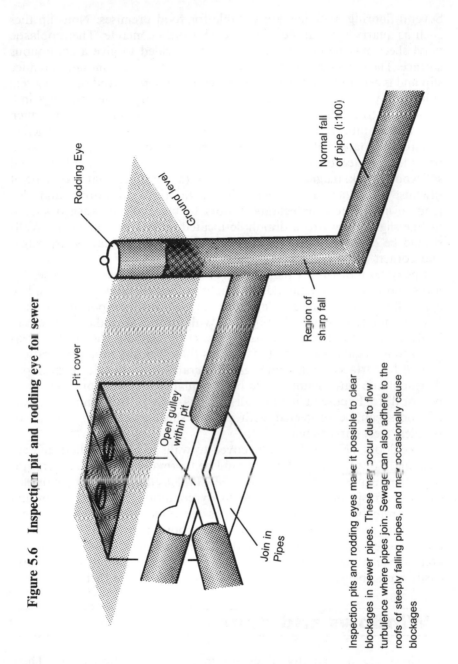

Figure 5.6 Inspection pit and rodding eye for sewer

Rodding Eye

Ground level

Normal fall
of pipe (1:100)

Pit cover

Region of
sharp fall

Open gulley
within pit

Join in
Pipes

Inspection pits and rodding eyes make it possible to clear blockages in sewer pipes. These may occur due to flow turbulence where pipes join. Sewage can also adhere to the roofs of steeply falling pipes, and may occasionally cause blockages

Several flooring materials are suitable for food premises. Non-slip tiles such as quarry tiles can be laid in cement onto concrete. Thermoplastic vinyl sheet may be laid in strips and edge-welded to give a continuous surface. The vinyl may contain granules of garnet or corundum to reduce slip and is generally laid onto a self-levelling mineral screed on a concrete subfloor. Alternatively, mineral flooring containing stone chippings in a cement matrix can be used. Examples are *granolithic* flooring, which contains granite, and *terrazzo*, containing marble chippings. Concrete can also be coated with *epoxy resin*, *rubber paint* or light-grade *asphalt* to provide a serviceable floor. Unsuitable flooring materials are hard- and softwoods, cork, magnesite and granwood (a composite material made of sawdust with fillers and cement). These floorings are porous and also tend to inactivate disinfectants. Floors to be regularly washed should incline slightly towards a drainhole located away from the walls. Walls should be *coved* to the floor without skirting, to eliminate sharp edges and corners (see Figure 5.7).

Epoxy resin or rubber paint are probably the best general finishes for *walls* and *ceilings* and should be a light colour to show up dirt and to assist illumination. Surfaces must be smooth and non-porous for easy cleaning and to deter crawling insects. Wall finishes should be resistant to likely conditions of heat, moisture, grease or cleaning chemicals. Areas likely to be regularly disinfected, such as those for raw food preparation, should be surfaced with white, glazed ceramic tiles or with continuous thermoplastic vinyl. Paint should be of a quality that will not crack, chip, peel or flake. Exposed parts of walls such as corners, piers and the reveals of doors can be protected with plastic sheet and polypropylene or stainless steel corner-guards.

Like floors, *ceilings* should be coved to walls to avoid corners and aid cleaning. Conventional ceilings should be thermally insulated, incorporating a moisture barrier to minimize condensation. Ceiling materials should be resistant to fire and to likely conditions of heat, steam and grease from below. Suspended ceilings are often used to conceal pipes and other services, but the dead space above them will attract pests unless visited and inspected regularly. There should be good access to the area above a suspended ceiling. Therefore large ceilings should have easily accessible entrance hatches and walkways above them.

Windows and doors

Windows are not strictly necessary in food production areas. There should always be artificial lighting and mechanical ventilation, so windows at best only have psychological importance. Unwanted and unnecessary windows can often be bricked up to good advantage. Food production and storage areas should not have south- or west-facing

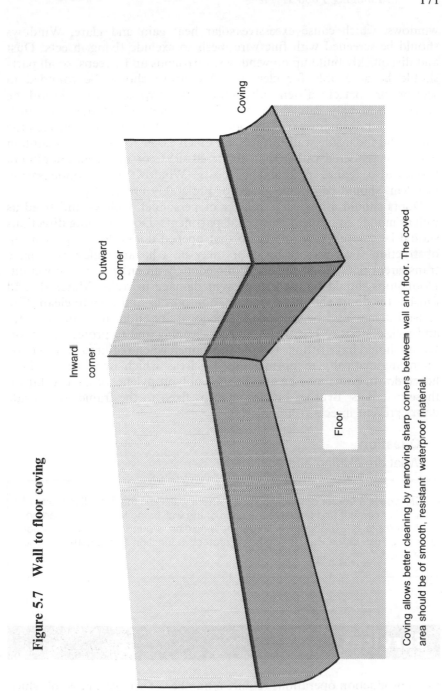

Figure 5.7 Wall to floor coving

Coving allows better cleaning by removing sharp corners between wall and floor. The coved area should be of smooth, resistant waterproof material.

Inward corner

Outward corner

Coving

Floor

windows, which cause excessive solar heat gain and glare. Windows should be screened with fine wire mesh to exclude flying insects. Dust and dirt quickly build up on windows, surrounds and screens, so all parts should be accessible for cleaning. Architrave should be rounded in section or, better, absent altogether. Window sills too should be absent, or steeply canted so that they do not collect dust and dirt. *Reveals* round windows (i.e. the sides and top of the window between the frame and the inside wall surface) are much easier to clean and maintain if tiled or rendered rather than timbered. PVC or anodized aluminium frames also reduce maintenance costs. Windows with condensation problems should be double-glazed or preferably bricked up.

Doors should allow easy transfer of personnel, trolleys and fixed as well as mobile equipment between departments. Door opening directions should be carefully considered so that opened doors do not present an obstruction. Two-way swing doors may be a hazard unless they have transparent panels and the areas immediately on either side are well-lit. Door-stops should be used to prevent damage to walls. Materials and finishes for doors should be smooth, non-porous and easy to clean. Fire resistance may also be specified by the local fire authority. Finger-plates and kick-plates can be fitted for easier cleaning and to protect the door. Doors should have fittings to hold them open when required and to close them automatically in normal use. In areas which must be regularly hosed down, doors may be of rubber or polypropylene, or have a skirt of these materials. Brushes or plastic strips fixed to the frames of outside doors prevent insects from entering.

Question
What are skirting and architrave?

Skirting is a border or moulding used where walls join the floor. It is made of wood or cement and prevents the base of the wall being knocked or marked. **Architrave** is a decorative border or moulding around a window or door frame, flush to the wall. It also has a protective function and is usually made of wood.

Services

Food production operations require a number of services, most of which are stipulated by law. These should be adequately provided at the planning stage. Supplying services to an existing building may be costly or even impractical. Services usually required are:

- Clean water.
- Drainage.
- Waste disposal.
- Electricity and gas.
- Lighting.
- Mechanical ventilation.

Water, drainage and waste disposal

Most areas of the UK are supplied with treated mains water of high microbiological quality. Premises without mains water may require wells or boreholes, which should be dug by a specialist contractor. Water samples from private supplies should be submitted to the local public analyst to ensure that they are of drinkable quality and that no seepage from sewers or septic tanks is occurring. Older premises may still have lead supply pipes, which should be replaced with polypropylene at the earliest opportunity. This not only removes the possibility of lead poisoning, but also usually improves the flow of the supply. Most food premises have a cold water storage tank in the roof space, which maintains a constant supply and pressure. Such tanks should be tightly covered to prevent contamination by dust and insects. There should be no back-siphonage of water from the tank into the mains. Water from the mains is often much colder than the air inside buildings. It may be necessary to lag cold water supply pipes to prevent condensation where they are exposed to warm, humid air. Pipes for water (and for other services) should be held clear of walls, ceilings and one another by brackets. A distance of 150–200 mm (6–8 in.) is usually enough to permit cleaning and maintenance, such as repainting.

Hot water is usually supplied at a temperature of 60–65°C. This may be unsatisfactory in food premises. Pedal- or elbow-operated taps are more hygienic for hand washing but are harder to control, so the water they deliver should be at 50°C or below, to avoid scalding. Rinse-water for manual dish-washing should preferably be at 85°C or more to ensure sterilization. A special supply may be required, e.g. from the still.

The number and positions of drain outlets must be carefully planned from the start. Dish-washers, potato rumblers and other appliances often need to have their own gulleys or to be connected directly to the drainage system. Without adequate planning, much time and money may be wasted in digging up floors to move services. Open, trough-style drains should not be used as they provide moisture and hiding places for cockroaches and other pests. *Waste disposal units* in kitchens and washing-up areas can be used to dispose of spoiled food, which would otherwise attract pests in the rubbish collection area. Waste disposal units must be plumbed directly to the drains, otherwise ground-up waste may accumulate around gulleys, or on floors.

Grease and *silt traps* prevent drains from becoming blocked with fat or with silt from rumblers etc. Traps should be located in an accessible position and be easy to clean. There should also be a hand basin nearby so that operatives can wash after emptying the trap.

Manholes and *inspection pits* should not be located in food areas. If this becomes unavoidable, double-sealed, screw-down covers should be used.

Question

How are odours and pests from the sewer system prevented from entering buildings through drains?

> Beneath each open drain there is a *U bend*, filled with water. Each time the drain is used this water is renewed so it does not become stagnant. Odours and insects cannot pass the water barrier, but rats may be able to swim through it. Drain holes are covered with a grille or gauze to deter them.

Waste disposal systems, such as the 'Garchey System', consist of waste disposal units fitted to sinks, which are separately plumbed to a collection chamber in the basement of the building. This is effectively a huge silt trap, into which the solid waste settles, while the liquid drains off it into the sewers. The collection chamber is emptied by a special tanker, which compacts the silt as it is removed from the chamber.

Dry waste should be compacted if possible, and stored in a collection area before disposal. A chute is an effective way of transferring rubbish to the collection area. Chutes should be easy to inspect and to clean and should deny access to insects and rodents. For example, flexible rubber flaps or trapdoors can be installed at the top and bottom. If a chute is impractical and the site is on one level, wheeled bins may be used to transfer rubbish to the collection area. The route should be slightly canted, and provided with drain holes so that it can be hosed down. Rubber skirted doors which sweep the ground help to exclude pests and will withstand regular washing.

A recent innovation in plant hygiene is *centralized cleaning*. This involves a centralized high-pressure pumping unit with a series of pipes connecting it to tapping points in all parts of the building. In this way a cleaning medium can be pumped to whatever it is needed. 'Single-line' systems dispense water at temperatures up to 80°C. Cleaning chemicals and disinfectants are added from metering dispensers located at the tapping points. This permits different types of cleaning at different locations. In 'multi-line' systems one universal mixture of cleaning chemicals is stored centrally and dispensed to all tapping points. A wide range of cleaning tools can be plugged into the tapping points, including cleaning lances, sprays, brushes and devices with rotating nozzles for cleaning the insides of tanks. Centralized cleaning requires good drainage and involves considerable installation of pipework. Therefore it should be allowed for at the planning stage. Very efficient cleaning is claimed and there are labour savings because there is no need to move heavy plant about or to measure out cleaning chemicals.

Electricity, gas, lighting and ventilation

Electrical wiring and controls should be accessible to inspection. They should also be moisture-proof and pest-proof. For example, electrical cable should be led through steel, rather than plastic conduit or trunking, so that cannot be gnawed by rats. Trunking, like pipework, should be held clear of walls and ceilings by brackets. Wiring should be installed by a competent electrician. *Gas* too, should be installed only by competent fitters. There should be a master valve near the exit of each room where gas is used, to shut off the supply in an emergency.

Adequate *lighting* of kitchens and other work areas is required by law under the Offices, Shops and Railway Premises Act, 1963. Lighting of washrooms is stipulated under the Food Hygiene (General) Regulations, 1970. Without proper lighting it is not possible to check cleaning standards. Lighting in lavatory cubicles is important in controlling transfer of bacteria by the faecal-oral route. Minimum recommended lighting levels are 500 lux for close work and inspection, 200–300 lux for general work and 75–100 lux for other areas, such as restaurants (Illuminating Engineering Society, 1977). It is better to err on the brighter side rather than to risk inadequate lighting, and to check levels with a meter just above wash basins or work surfaces. *Tungsten filament lamps*, (i.e. incandescent light bulbs) give out about 80% of their wattage as heat. The hot glass bulbs are also prone to shatter if splashed with water. Tungsten lamps are therefore unsuitable in kitchens, where they may add to overheating and contamination problems. The most economical illumination is provided by *fluorescent tubes*, which give three to four times as much light for their wattage and last three times as long as bulbs. Tubes should be covered with *diffusers* to protect them and to reduce glare and eyestrain. Light-coloured walls reflect light and help to raise illumination levels.

Mechanical ventilation should be used in kitchens to remove moisture, odours and waste heat. This helps prevent excess moisture from condensing on walls, and attracting insect pests. Ventilation hoods must be positioned directly over hobs, fryers and steamers, so it is important to decide the equipment layout before planning the ventilation. Ventilation lowers the air pressure slightly within the kitchen. Air is drawn in from other parts of the building, and sometimes from outside the building to replace the air expelled through the hoods. Air inlets from outside should be fitted with filters to remove insects, dirt and dust. Air should flow from the restaurant to the kitchen rather than vice versa, to minimize the spread of odours. It is even more important that the ventilation fans prevent kitchen odours from flowing to reception and accommodation areas. Extractor fans intended to ventilate stores should draw the air into, rather than from the kitchen. Otherwise the warm, humid kitchen air may spoil dry stores.

Question

How else may high humidity in the kitchen and stores jeopardize food hygiene?

Conditions of high humidity may cause personnel to sweat, to wipe themselves or to remove protective clothing. Humidity also encourages some species of insect pests, such as cockroaches.

Ventilation efficiency is assessed in terms of the number of air changes per hour. Between ten and twenty are recommended for kitchens. The law requires that lavatories are separately ventilated, and the recommended rate is six air changes per hour. Moisture may condense in ventilation trunking, which should therefore be rust-proof, e.g. of aluminium. Trunking also rapidly collects deposits of dust, fluff, insects and condensed grease from friers. This is a fire risk, as well as harbouring contamination and pests. Ducts can be fitted with filters to reduce this soiling, but a more satisfactory solution is to install a system that is easy to clean, and to clean it regularly. For example, ducting should be as short as possible and have large access ports. Fans, always difficult to clean, should be located at the outermost point of the system, preferably on the roof outside the kitchen. Accumulation of dirt is then slower and motor noise less of a problem.

Summary – planning and design

Do

- Plan for linear workflow as far as possible.
- Analyze and control interactions between work-centres.
- Separate 'clean' and 'dirty' areas.
- Aim for economy of movement.

- Plan work-centres and amenities.
- Design systematically, considering site, construction details, and services.

Do not

- Neglect food hygiene aspects in the total design.
- Overlook traffic between work-centres and stores, waste disposal areas, staff rest rooms or lavatories, in the total design.

Upkeep operations: maintenance, cleaning and pest control

Maintenance, cleaning and pest control are important hygiene aspects of premises management. Unless they are effectively organized the food premises will quickly deteriorate and contravene the law. Cleanliness, structural safety and freedom from vermin are specified in the *Food Hygiene (General) Regulations, 1970, The Health and Safety at Work Act, 1974* and the *Offices Shops and Railway Premises Act, 1963,* among others. Maintenance, cleaning and pest control are also important to the efficient operation of the food production system. Current trends towards customer hygiene-awareness mean that efficient operation is likely to have a marketing advantage as well.

Maintenance, cleaning and pest control are upkeep functions for which management has an ongoing responsibility. Chapter 1 dealt with the operational details of cleaning and pest control. This chapter shows how a single management approach can be used for all these functions.

Strategies

There are four approaches to managing ongoing aspects such as maintenance/cleaning/pest control. These are usually given as:

- Corrective.
- Preventive.
- Planned.
- Running.

The corrective approach

The corrective approach to upkeep functions involves putting something right as it goes wrong. If a light bulb fails, it is replaced (corrective maintenance). If something is dirty, it is cleaned (corrective cleaning). If pests are detectably present they are destroyed (corrective pest control). Corrective approaches rely on:

(i)   early, efficient reporting of faults; and
(ii)   quick, responsive action.

Even with these ideals, premises will be faulty, dirty or pest-ridden in the interval between noticing the problem and putting it right.

The preventive approach

The preventive approach involves estimating the time the next main-tenance, cleaning or pest control treatment will be needed. Treatment is then given slightly before the due date. An example of preventive maintenance is the block replacement of lamps. Light bulbs have an average life of 1000 hours and more than 90% give at least 800 hours' service. Therefore if all are changed together as soon as they have given 800 hours, a failure rate of 10% or less can be guaranteed. The 10% of bulbs which fail before the 800 hours may be replaced as they fail (i.e. on a corrective basis).

A preventive cleaning approach would be to clean down the kitchen at the close of every day. Preventive pest control involves the regular laying of traps or baits in case pests are present. Preventive strategies rely on:

- Accurate assessment of treatment life-span.
- Efficient scheduling of action, so that jobs get done.
- Efficient monitoring that the strategy is working.

In theory, preventive strategies should mean that problems never arise. However, as in the case of the light bulbs above there is always a chance of interim failure. In addition, preventive strategies usually need con-siderable administration and they may be costly.

Question
Is a preventive strategy is always more effective than a corrective one?

Preventive approaches are not necessarily better than corrective ones. They may be costly, and because they are rigidly systemized they may not allow adequately for emergency measures.

The planned approach

Both corrective and preventive maintenance can be planned. Planning means scheduling inspections, routine work, monitoring and documentation. Preventive maintenance is by nature planned, because it involves regular, scheduled operations. All planned systems should allow for regular monitoring and documentation of work done, as well as for inspections and the operations themselves. Thus it is also possible to have planned corrective maintenance which entails:

- Regular, scheduled inspections.
- A system for notifying operatives that the work needs doing.
- A system for monitoring and documenting what has been done.

For example, routine weekly inspections of the kitchen may reveal a fault in the wall tiling. The fault is noted in the fault book and corrected during one of the planned, monthly maintenance operations. Cleaning, particularly of areas that need infrequent attention, can be managed in the same way. Planned, corrective pest control often means the regular use of detector traps. Maintenance, cleaning and pest control standards are not constant. As time passes, expectations in terms of safety, hygiene and freedom from pests increase and technology advances to meet these expectations. At the same time the actual quantity of the premises deteriorates. Planned strategies should consider likely expectations and aim at future needs, not just at the standard of the original premises (see Figure 5.8)

Figure 5.8   Changes in maintenance standards with time

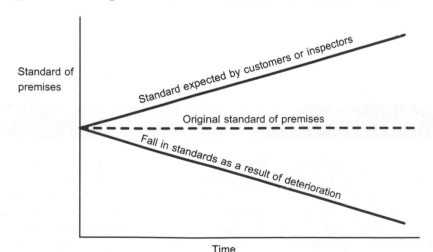

Running operations

Running upkeep operations are those which can be carried out while the food process is in operation. 'Clean-as-you-go' procedures are an example, where food handlers swab surfaces with sanitizer as soon as they have finished each job. Pest control procedures often have to be 'running' because the baits remain in the premises all the time. Many maintenance jobs (for example, replacing light bulbs) contain some risk of food contamination and therefore should not be done on a running basis. However, the concept of running maintenance is open to some interpretation. Most food production premises have a slack time during the afternoon or at night, when small 'running' upkeep jobs can be undertaken. For operations which cause dust, fumes or other hazards, production must be stopped.

Preventive versus corrective strategies

Corrective approaches always involve some temporary failure, so in theory they are inferior to preventive strategies. In practice, preventive strategies may be too unwieldy or expensive to use. Bushell (1979) gives five criteria for assessing preventive vs corrective strategies. Planned, preventive maintenance, cleaning or pest control is worthwhile if:

- It is cost effective.
- It is needed to meet statutory/legal requirements.
- It meets operating needs.
- It will reduce the incidence of running maintenance.
- There is a predominant need for work, rather than inspection.

Cost effectiveness

A quick cost calculation of materials and labour may decide whether a preventive or corrective strategy should be used. For instance, multiple replacement of light bulbs clearly involves less labour per bulb than fetching and installing a new replacement for every single failure. Savings on labour are generally greater than the loss on bulb-life incurred by block-replacing lamps before they have failed.

Statutory requirements

Any failure of maintenance, cleaning and pest control contravenes the law. It is therefore important that the food premises manager should be seen to take responsibility for these procedures. The only way to do this with complete confidence is through a preventive approach. Corrective strategies always involve some degree of failure, which may be unacceptable.

Clients' operating needs

Maintenance strategies have to fit in with the running of a business. Operations involving hazards or food contaminants often require special precautions and even closure of the plant. This will usually affect the choice of maintenance strategy.

Reducing the incidence of running maintenance

Preventive approaches can often help the manager control the need for running maintenance and hence eliminate some of the associated hazards. For instance, corrective replacement of electric lamps or tubes is normally carried out while food operations are running. There is therefore a danger that dust from fittings or glass from lamps will find their way into food. Running repairs can be minimized by replacing the lamps on a preventive basis. This might make it worthwhile closing down the operation, so that food contamination would be avoided.

Regularly cleaning down the premises at the close of work reduces the onus on clean-as-you-go discipline. Regular inspection and maintenance of window-screens, pipe-guards and other devices which check the entry of pests should reduce the need for on-going pest control.

Work versus inspection

Frequent operations such as cleaning windows, mopping floors, or changing lamps should generally be planned on a preventive basis.

Table 5.3 Typical building maintenance cycles

Site of Work	Frequency (years)	Typical operation(s)
Roof	20	Patch/renew tiling
Exterior of walls	30	Repoint mortar seams
Doors	30	Renew/repair half the doors at a time
Ironmongery	20	Replace rusted items etc.
Interior of walls, and ceilings	30	Replaster/make good
Flooring Finish	10	Re-lay screed, vinyl or terrazzo
Seal	1–2	Renew (if used)
Wall/ceiling paintwork	5*	Strip or scarify and reapply
Doors windows etc. paintwork internal/ external	5*	Strip and reapply
Water/sanitation	40	Clean/replace pipes, sewers gulleys etc.
Sanitary fittings	15*	Renew lavatories, urinals, basins etc.
Boiler	20	Replace
Heating pipes and radiators	40	Replace/partially/ completely
Electrical Wiring	30	Rewire completely
Light fittings	15	Replace

*In public areas, changes in taste and the requirements of branding or other marketing policies may shorten these cycle times appreciably.

Once the required frequency is known there is little point in regular inspection. Managing the problem consists of drawing up a schedule of work and setting up a system for monitoring and documentation. On the other hand, a planned, corrective strategy may be more suitable for infrequent operations such as repainting, roof repairs, or dusting stored surplus equipment. This means scheduled inspections and a report system, with operations attended to as necessary. Thus cycles of inspections, maintenance, cleaning and pest control are an important consideration in deciding strategy.

Maintenance, cleaning and pest control cycles

'Cycles' are the time intervals between inspections or between one preventive operation and the next. Table 5.3 shows the cycles for some typical building maintenance operations.

It is also necessary to check other aspects such as guttering, foundations and external airbricks. Maintenance may be needed to prevent moisture and pests entering the building. Walls, floors, skirting, door reveals and so on should be regularly checked to ensure they are withstanding daily wear and tear, are adequately clean, and do not harbour pests. An example of a possible maintenance inspection checklist is shown in Table 5.4.

Table 5.4   Example of a maintenance inspection list

Inspection area	Typical frequency	Typical points to note
Building exterior	6 monthly: Spring, Autumn and after storms	No soil, grass or weeds on surrounding concrete. No breach of d.p.c. No blocked air vents. No breached pest screens. No leaking gutters. No tiles slipped, lost or broken.
Building interior	Monthly	Wall paint and tile work intact. Door/window reveals intact and clean. Door fit to jamb still good. Window screens intact. No internal signs of entering moisture. No condensation. No signs of infestation etc.

Question

Explain the two items 'No soil, grass or weeds on surrounding concrete' and 'No breach of d.p.c.' in Table 5.4.

Soil, grass and weeds near the walls may allow damp to enter, may block air bricks and may provide cover for pests trying to enter the premises. D.p.c. stands for damp-proof course. If this is breached moisture may enter the building as 'rising damp'.

Cleaning, pest control and maintenance inspections should be incorporated into the same cycle. Most cleaning should be so regular that formal, scheduled inspection is unnecessary. A clean-as-you-go system should be followed, together with routine daily cleaning of all production areas and at least weekly cleaning of stoves and other 'dry' areas. If this is done, inspection can focus on wear and tear, maintenance and possible entry of pests. As far as cleaning is concerned it is only a final check that systems are working correctly.

Frequency and standards

Frequency of inspection and correction depend upon the standard of maintenance, cleanliness or infestation-status required. It is therefore important to set standards. The frequency of operations is then

Figure 5.9(a)   Maintaining building to constant standard

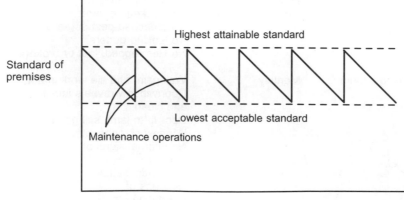

determined by the highest possible standard and the lowest acceptable standard. This is shown in Figure 5.9(a).

In practice, technological developments are constantly improving the maximum standards attainable. At the same time expectations of quality are increasing (see Figure 5.8, p. 179), so the graph of maintenance procedure against time is more like that shown in Figure 5.9 (b). Two aspects differentiate 5.8(b) from figure 5.9(a):

Figure 5.9(b)   Maintaining building to increasing standard

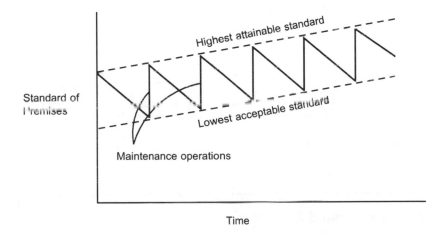

1.   The time span between maintenance/cleaning/pest control operations becomes shorter as quality expectations rise more steeply.
2.   The quality of each maintenance operation: i.e. the difference between the lower and upper line, increases as quality expectations rise more steeply.

The use of pheromones in pest control means that lower and lower levels of infestation can be detected. Eventually it may be possible to get down to non-viable population numbers and the infestation will die out (Robinson, 1987). The traditional approach, of treating infestation only when it reaches the complaint level, leaves a residual, viable population (see Figure 5.10).

Figure 5.10   Riddance and maintenance for cockroach control

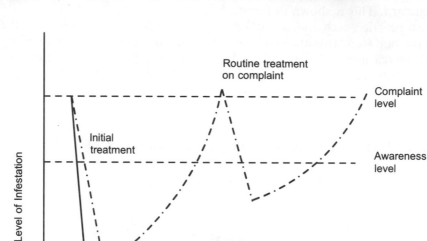

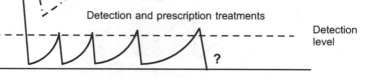

Study example 5.2

Look carefully at Figure 5.10 and then answer the following questions:

1. Explain what is meant by the 'complaint level' and the 'awareness level'.
2. What are pheromones? How can they detect pests when numbers are very small?
3. How can very small pest populations become 'non-viable'?
4. Pheromones may prevent insects breeding for another reason. What is this?
5. The graph implies that it is impossible to eradicate pests without a sensitive detection technique. Why is this likely to be the case?

In-house versus outside contract work

Many aspects of maintenance, pest control and even some cleaning work may best be contracted to outside specialists. This does not absolve the manager from all responsibility in these matters, but it will reduce the number and complexity of managerial tasks. In addition, substantial savings may be made on personnel and infrequently-used equipment. Criteria for choosing between a contractor and an in-house capability are shown in Table 5.5. Specialists should have the skilled personnel, technical backup, equipment and insurance necessary for the task. Contractors vary in reputation and performance and should be selected in a methodical way.

Table 5.5   Criteria for choosing between in-house and contract work

In-house operations	Outside contractor operations
Frequent	Infrequent
Time-consuming	Need short visits
Labour intensive	Capital intensive
Unskilled/semiskilled	Skilled
Low technical content	High technical content
Low risk	High risk

Selection of specialist contractors

Selecting contractors should be carried out on objective lines, like any other management evaluation process. A list of criteria should be drawn up. As much information as possible should be obtained about the available contractors. Each contractor should then be assessed against the list of criteria. The main areas to consider are:

- Cost.
- Service offered.
- Co-operation with outsiders (EHOs etc).
- Co-operation with client.

Cost

Quotes for the work should be obtained from all the contractors. Formal tendering is probably more trouble than it is worth. It is not unknown for pest control and maintenance firms to deliberately overestimate the extent of work needed. Therefore the manager or supervisor should accompany the contractor's inspector on an initial survey of the premises. Firms may also cut corners with specifications in order to make the lowest bid. The cost of the job should be carefully considered in the light of the service offered.

Service offered

Services offered are usually described in the sales brochure, but it is often worth asking the representative a few questions. Pest control firms should make it clear whether they offer:

- Diagnosis/detection.
- Baiting, trapping.
- Spraying, dusting.
- Prevention of pest entry.
- Monitoring – the level of detection is important.

Maintenance contractors should specify:

- Inspection.
- Strategy: planned/corrective/preventive.
- Monitoring and documentation.

It is also worthwhile asking other caterers or retailers who have used the firm. In particular, do building contractors leave a mess? Are they sensitive to the needs of food handlers? Do pest control agencies deliberately leave survivors, so that their services will be needed again? It is worth checking whether firms operate in a methodical way, scheduling the work and documenting progress. Pest control firms, for instance, should keep plans or lists showing where traps and bait have been laid. They should also document any rodent runs or nests they discover. For safety's sake, employees should be kept away from these areas.

Question

What is the danger from rat runs and nests?

Rats' saliva and urine may contain Weil's disease bacteria (*Leptospirae*). In addition, employees may be bitten by sick or injured rats near these areas.

Contract firms may offer useful advice or training. Sometimes this is worth the extra cost of the service. In addition, contractors may rent insect electrocutors or sell and maintain such equipment at a special rate. Flying-insect killers are not usually considered part of a pest control contract, but environmental health officers include them in hygiene inspections.

Co-operation with Environmental Health Departments

An important objective of maintenance, pest control and cleaning is compliance with the law. Both food hygiene and health/safety legislation may be involved. Food premises managers often receive advice on laws and by-laws from the local Environmental Health Department. Contractors engaged to do the work should therefore have a good track record of co-operation with local Environmental Health Officers. This can be established by enquiring from the local Department. Do contractors:

- Take advice when it is given?
- Use approved materials, methods and equipment?
- Discuss any problems or difficulties that arise?

Building contractors may also have to deal with other parties, such as architects or kitchen design consultants. This should be made clear when the contract is drawn up. The frequency and terms of reference of meetings to monitor the project should also be specified.

Co-operation with the client

Food premises managers should make sure that they will be able to liaise properly with the contractor. It is the manager, not the contractor, who is responsible for the upkeep of the premises. Therefore there should be no feeling on either part that the manager is 'leaving it to the contractor'. In particular contractors should be prepared to:

- Allow the manager or his staff to accompany personnel on inspection rounds.
- Advise the manager of all action taken.

- Advise the manager of any hazards or risks associated with the work.
- Keep to a strict routine and communicate this to the manager and staff.

It is usually possible to find out whether a contractor is prepared to do this, by asking other clients. It may be useful to specify the points listed above in the contract.

Management systems for cleaning and maintenance

Pest control and specialized aspects of maintenance are often contracted to an outside firm. Most cleaning and minor maintenance is under the direct control of the food premises manager. Management of ongoing operations of this kind consists of:

1. Designing a system for doing the work; and
2. Ensuring that the work runs smoothly and the job gets done.

Designing a cleaning/maintenance system

Any system for ongoing work should have the following features:

- A schedule of jobs.
- Job cards.
- Task record sheets.
- A procedure.

Schedules

Schedules are essential for all planned operations. The term 'cleaning schedule' varies in interpretation, and as a result standards vary between different organizations. A job schedule should list:

- The job to be done.
- Equipment, materials or chemicals required.
- An estimate of man-hours.
- Relevant safety points.

Jobs and frequencies

Premises should be carefully inspected and notes made of areas which need attention and the likely time scale. For instance, kitchen floors should be cleaned once a day, while stores areas may only need to be swept weekly. A systematic way to assess this is to have the floor in question cleaned and then note the interval until it becomes unacceptably dirty. Standards of cleanliness, such as 'no spilled food visible' should be set. With this information the necessary jobs and their frequencies can be defined.

Equipment, materials and chemicals

There is a tendency to duplicate materials for cleaning and maintenance jobs. This stems from regarding jobs in isolation and should be avoided. The list of jobs and frequencies should be drawn up as fully as possible and carefully scrutinized. Usually the number of different job types varies little. The number of cleaning products used should be no greater than the number of job types. An inventory of cleaning materials in current use should be drawn up and apparent duplication of items investigated. Suppliers should be approached for price lists, product specifications and details of any services they offer. Training or advisory services are usually worthwhile. 'Off-the-peg' cleaning schedules are not usually so valuable because they have to be adapted to a particular work situation. Dispensing/mixing systems or equipment will help prevent the makeshift use of food containers for chemicals. Some manufacturers colour code cleaning powders and liquids for 'food-use' or 'non-food use', further reducing the chance of a mistake. Limiting the range of cleaning material stock also reduces the numbers of operating instructions and simplifies training.

Estimating man-hours

Cleaning and maintenance jobs are labour-intensive, i.e. wages make up most of the cost. Estimating the labour requirement and likely wage cost is therefore important. A number of specialized work study techniques exist for doing this: stop-watch time studies, predetermined motion times, standard data and work sampling. Of these, the stop-watch time study is probably most simple and suitable for cleaning jobs in food premises. Work study techniques take a mechanistic view of the worker which may not always be acceptable in a service industry culture. An alternative is to work out man-hour requirements from task sheet records. It may also be possible to shorten job durations by motivating staff (see Chapter 7)

Safety points

Some cleaning and maintenance jobs involve health, safety or contamination hazards. For instance, changing lamps involves handling glass; window cleaners may risk falling; cleaning chemicals may contaminate food or drink. It may be possible to remove or reduce these dangers at the scheduling stage. In any case the schedule should note any hazards, for the benefit of the supervisor.

Question
Give an example of a cleaning process which may contaminate drinks.

Chemicals used for cleaning beer lines frequently contain corrosive chemicals such as caustic soda. They will therefore cause serious contamination unless rinsed out thoroughly before the line is used again.

Job cards

The function of a job card is to specify the job in detail. Operatives can use the cards to aid their memory as they are doing the job. Job cards cannot *replace* training, they are only aids to the operative's memory. However, cards are useful if a new operative suddenly arrives, or if supervisors are short-staffed and have to take over jobs they have not done for a while. Job cards make it easier to set, monitor and improve standards, labour costs and efficiency. A job card should list:

- The title of the job.
- The equipment, materials or chemicals needed.
- The detailed method to be followed.
- The standard to be achieved.
- Safety notes and details of hazards.

A specimen job card for floor cleaning might read like this:

Specimen Job Card

Job title: Cleaning kitchen floor

Equipment: Brush, dustpan, sponge mop, bucket

Materials: Non-food (blue) cleaning powder

Detailed method:

1.   Remove all mobile units, equipment from the area to be cleaned.
2.   Sweep up all loose dirt, rubbish, pieces of food etc. Collect in dustpan and throw away in waste bin.
3.   Set up a 'danger cleaning in progress' sign outside each door to the kitchen.
4.   Sprinkle all areas with cleaning powder (blue).
5.   Mop with hot water. Make sure to remove all stains and marks. Pick up any surface water with the sponge mop to leave the floor dry as you go.
6.   Make sure that areas behind and between fixed equipment are clean.
7.   Move any items on castors and clean under them.
8.   Quickly check the whole floor to make sure it is clean, dry and free from loose dirt, rubbish and food.
9.   Replace the movable items of equipment where you found them.

Safety notes: The blue powder is alkaline and will cause dermatitis after a few hours' contact. It is quite safe if it is washed off quickly, or plastic gloves are worn.

Study example 5.3

1.   There is no 'standards' heading in the specimen job card above. What standards (if any) are given for the job?
2.   Which safety points does the job card make?
3.   Give three examples where the job card could be made more precise or more specific.
4.   What are the advantages of having a blue powder for cleaning this floor?
5.   What are the probable disadvantages of the blue powder?

Task record sheets

Once a schedule has been drawn up it is necessary to allocate the work to individual staff and to check that the designated jobs have been done. A *task record sheet* is used to document this process. It should contain:

- A list of tasks.
- Methods, or reference to job cards.
- Names of staff to whom tasks have been allocated.
- Timing.
- A note that work has been checked

List of tasks

The schedule should indicate when the cleaning/maintenance tasks are due to be carried out. Each day the supervisor should refer to the schedule and identify which jobs are to be done. These are listed on the task sheet. Usually there is a core of regular tasks, which can be preprinted on task record forms to save time. Space should be allowed for other jobs which may crop up.

Methods

Sometimes it is adequate to note down the task method in a brief form. This relies on all staff knowing what to do and being highly trained and motivated. A better system is to use job cards, and to refer to them in the task sheet.

Names of staff

The task sheet's function is to ensure the work gets done, by assigning clear tasks to the staff. Names of individuals should be used, because individuals are then more likely to accept the responsibility. If roles are used instead: 'kitchen porter', 'chef' etc. individuals may leave the work to one another. What is 'nobody's job' never gets done.

Timing

Time estimates for jobs appear on the schedule. The task sheet translates these durations into hours of the day, and includes time for tea breaks, for moving from task to task and so on. Sheets should be used to plan the day and to record that tasks have actually been achieved, so that the supervisor can keep track of jobs and personnel.

Checking and documentation

Task sheets should allow space for comments about the quality of the work. Any problems can also be noted. There should also be space for the initials of the supervisor, or possibly the operative, that the job has been checked.

Summary – cleaning, maintenance and pest control

Do

- Formulate a logical strategy for the work, e.g. corrective/ preventive, in-house/contract.
- Plan work and inspections.
- Evaluate potential contractors.
- Use systems – schedules, job cards and records, to ensure the work is done.

Do not

- Simply go for the cheapest contract.
- Leave jobs to contractors without monitoring them.

6 Food Hygiene and the Management of Plant and Equipment

Objectives

To identify the legal obligations of the food process manager regarding plant and equipment. To discuss the theory and practice of selecting, cleaning and operating all types of equipment in order to ensure food hygiene and customer safety.

Introduction

Plant and equipment affect the hygiene of catering operations in various ways. Food processing equipment may touch food directly, so that there is a potential for contamination or cross-contamination. Such equipment may also harbour pockets of bacteria, foreign bodies or pests. Current trends towards larger, more complex, 'self-cleaning' equipment tend to increase these problems.

The selection, maintenance and operation of equipment also affect time/temperature control. This does not only apply to cooking, holding and storage equipment. Food processing may take so long that bacteria even multiply within processing machines themselves.

Cleaning operations themselves employ equipment. Cloths, mops and cleaning machines are required for the hygiene of premises and processing equipment. Soap dispensers and hand driers are needed for the personal hygiene of staff.

Legal aspects

The *Food Hygiene (General) Regulations, 1970*, make a number of stipulations about the hygiene of plant and equipment. *Regulation 7* requires that utensils and equipment which come into contact with food must be properly constructed of safe, hygienic materials. They must be easy to clean and must not contaminate food on contact. *Regulation 18* specifies equipment and services for the personal hygiene of food handlers. Nail brushes, soap dispensers and facilities for drying hands must be provided, as well as wash basins and hot/cold water supplies. *Regulation 19* sets out the first aid materials which should be available. *Regulation 27* specifies the temperatures at which certain foods should be held or stored. Holding equipment should be capable of keeping food within $\pm 2°C$ of the specified temperature. This implies that such equipment must be well monitored and maintained.

The **Materials and Articles in Contact with Food Regulations, 1987**, make two further stipulations about equipment and packaging used for handling food. *Regulation 4* requires such items to be manufactured in accordance with good practice. Under normal or foreseeable conditions of use they should not transfer harmful constituents to food during contact.

The Ministry of Agriculture, Fisheries and Food encourages manufacturers of food equipment and packaging to publish codes of good practice, which are accepted as standards under the Regulations. *Regulation 7* requires food containers to be protected and kept free from contamination.

The **Food Hygiene (Markets, Stalls and Delivery Vehicles) Regulations, 1966** specifically require the hygiene of coin-operated automatic vending machines, and delivery vehicles used for food or drink.

Contamination levels of plant/equipment

Mendes, Lynch and Stanley (1978) report a survey of kitchens where items of equipment were sampled to assess contamination levels. Their results are presented in Table 6.1.

Question

Can the contamination levels shown in Table 6.1 be grouped according to use?

The table shows that equipment which came into contact with waste (sinks and draining boards) had the highest contamination levels. Next came items such as chopping blocks and potato peelers, which came into contact with raw foods. Handles and parts of equipment which were regularly touched had a low, but significant contamination level.

Table 6.1   Frequency of contamination of various kitchen equipment

	% w coliforms	% w *E.coli*
Cooking/holding equipment		
Oven/hotplate control knobs	16	11
Oven canopy	4	2
Hot cupboard handles	30	17
Refrigerator handles	47	29
Preparation/handling equipment		
Chopping blocks	61	49
Potato peeler	54	26
Meat slicer	41	29
Worktop surfaces	34	24
Food mixer	21	13
Can opener	18	10
Washing/cleaning equipment		
Hand basins: drainhole	74	34
hot tap	34	14
cold tap	35	17
Sinks: drainhole	72	49
hot tap	31	24
cold tap	40	30
Draining boards	66	51
Washing machine	24	18

Source: Mendes, Lynch and Stanley (1978).

The hygienic management of premises and equipment involves scheduled cleaning and maintenance. Critical selection and evaluation of items for purchase is also important. These aspects are discussed in this chapter.

Keeping plant and equipment clean

Two approaches may be used for cleaning in food operations: clean-as-you-go, and deep cleaning. Both should be used for plant and equipment if adequate food hygiene is to be maintained.

Clean-as-you-go systems incorporate an element of cleaning into each task. Under such systems the task of meat preparation, for example, would also include washing up the knife and chopping board and wiping over the work surface with sanitizer. Cleaning procedures can be written into job cards or recipe cards and should also be stressed at training sessions. Clean-as-you-go systems make departments responsible for the equipment they use and can promote team-work and friendly rivalry through inter-departmental competition. However, clean-as-you-go systems cannot get equipment completely clean and should not be expected to do so.

Deep-cleaning operations are tasks in their own right. Separate job cards should be produced for them, as discussed in Chapter 5, rather than incorporating such jobs into food production tasks. Instead, deep-cleaning should be carried out during slack periods, or better still when production is closed down completely. Scrupulous monitoring and documentation of cleaning should be observed so that standards are maintained and any deterioration reported. Standards for both routine and deep cleaning can be established by microbiological analysis, i.e. by swabbing and plating. Easy-to-use assay systems such as the 'Tillomed' range are available. These will usually give results within a few days, without laboratory facilities or highly trained technicians. Standards can also be set on the basis of apparent cleanliness. Alternatively the detail of the procedure itself may suffice. For example, 'wipe down slicer blade with a damp cloth' is clearly an inferior standard to 'dismantle slicer and soak components for one hour in sterilant solution.' The ideal standard of cleaning will seldom be practical on a regular, short-term basis. Routine and deep cleaning operations should be scheduled so that any residual accumulation of dirt or bacteria is regularly removed (see Figure 6.1).

Cleaning methods

Equipment may be cleaned manually, automatically, or in a machine. *Manual cleaning* is generally more expensive and more susceptible to human error and quality fluctuations. However, it is more flexible and versatile and, with well-trained staff, more thorough. With large or awkward items, manual cleaning is often the only way. *Automatic cleaning* (or clean-in-place) is a feature of some large food processing plant items. Cleaning is achieved by passing a solution of chemical cleaner through pipes and vessels. Clean-in-place systems can give good, consistent results, but sometimes contain design faults, discussed later in

Figure 6.1   Routine and deep cleaning cycles

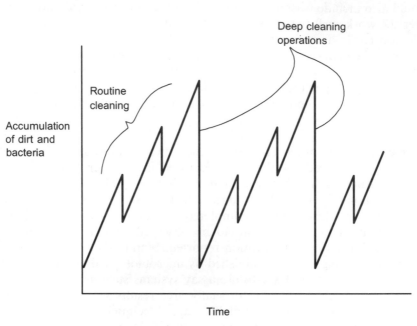

this chapter. Dishwashing machines usually clean to a more consistent standard than manual washing. However, food-handling equipment must be compatible. For instance components from food machines should fit into dishwashers, and not be damaged in washing.

Cleaning methods for equipment should follow the sequence outlined in Chapter 1, i.e. the *five stages* of cleaning. Clean, dry equipment and utensils should be stored where they cannot become wet, contaminated or dusty.

Study example 6.1

Meat slicers have a high potential for cross-contamination. They may need to be used with raw or cooked meats, and the mechanical intricacies often provide nooks and crannies in which food particles can collect and bacteria grow. A typical cleaning procedure for a meat-slicer is as follows:

(a) Unplug the machine and move it away from the socket.
(b) Dismantle the guard, blade and other moving parts as far as possible. Refer to the operating manual.

(c) Remove any adhering food particles.

(d) Wash, rinse, disinfect and dry all the detachable parts by hand, or in a dishwasher.

(e) Wash/wipe the body of the machine with detergent solution, using a scourer on any stubborn grease or dirt. Scrub into recessed areas with a brush. Rinse.

(f) Rinse the body of the machine and wipe over with a food-compatible disinfectant (e.g. amphotenside).

(g) Dry the body of the machine thoroughly with disposable paper towels.

(h) Reassemble the machine, plug it in and check that it runs smoothly.

1. What are the five stages of cleaning? (See Chapter 1.)
2. How do operations (a) – (h) refer to the five stages of cleaning?
3. The example given here is a deep-clean. Suggest instructions for a clean-as-you-go procedure.
4. What instructions should be given for storing or protecting the machine after cleaning?

Codes of practice may provide useful guidelines for cleaning certain items of equipment. For example, the Ministry of Agriculture, Fisheries and Food has issued codes for the hygiene of vending machines and for microwave ovens. Equipment manufacturers may also have codes and guidelines which they will supply on request. Large plant is often best cleaned using a spray lance, with hot water or steam. This may be supplied from a centralized cleaning system or from a mobile pressure cleaner (discussed later in this chapter).

Maintenance

Maintenance of plant and equipment involves similar strategies and systems to premises maintenance, discussed in Chapter 5. Usually maintenance cycles are short (a year or less) and specialist labour is often required.

Question
Which maintenance strategy (see Chapter 5) is most likely to be required in these circumstances?

Planned preventive maintenance is commonly used where cycles are short and where a visit from specialist personnel is likely to be needed. For most food production operations this means contracting the work out to specialist firms. Contractors should plan and monitor maintenance systematically. They should announce schedules to the food premises manager in good time, in case operations need to be shut down. They should maintain detailed records of maintenance work, faults and likely problems. Copies of these should be available to the catering manager. These aspects should be carefully considered before choosing contractors or renewing maintenance contracts.

Equipment on which time/temperature treatment of food depends: e.g. cookers, cooker thermometers and hot- and cold-holding equipment, should be regularly monitored. Faults should be quickly diagnosed and documented so that corrective action can be taken (see also 'Monitoring and Control', on pages 213–14).

Selection of equipment

Three categories of plant/equipment have an influence on food hygiene. These are:

- Items which come into direct contact with food.
- Items on which correct time/temperature relationships depend.
- Items used for cleaning premises, personnel or other plant/ equipment.

The three types differ in selection criteria, although there is often overlap between the first two categories. (For example Holding equipment often comes in contact with the food.) However, the selection process should always follow a logical sequence. There are usually four distinct stages:

1. Identify requirements.
2. Draw up a purchase specification.
3. Compare this with manufacturer's specifications.
4. Evaluate.

Identifying requirements involves analyzing present and future needs. Volume output tends to increase as businesses grow. Hygiene and safety needs also tend to become more stringent with time and are not necessarily compatible with greater volume. Thus there is a double pressure on the performance of all categories of equipment, which must have sufficient capacity to cope with the increasing workloads and standards projected during their lifespan. Newly-purchased equipment should have the best hygiene standards available, because these may rapidly become the minimum standards of the future.

A purchase specification is a list of the equipment characteristics required and is based on the identified needs of the operation. Lists compiled in this way are, however, based on ideal characteristics. Probably no actual equipment will possess all of them. Therefore the purchase specification should indicate which characteristics are essential and which are merely desirable. For example, a floor scrubber must be capable of scrubbing floors at a specified rate (essential). A desirable feature may be the machine's optional use as a polisher, or for disinfecting.

Manufacturer's specifications list the characteristics of the particular makes of equipment. They should be carefully compared with the essential and desirable characteristics listed in the purchase specification. It is best to draw up a table showing positive and negative features of each make or model of equipment. This makes it easier to compare makes with one another and with the original purchase specification.

Evaluation should take into account the features of each make or model of equipment. In order to make a logical selection, the model selected should fulfil the maximum number of purchase criteria for the budgeted price. Ideally the chosen model should be viewed and tested before purchase, to ensure that it meets the job requirements in all respects.

Equipment used for handling or holding food

Codes of practice

The Food Manufacturers' Federation (FMF) and the Food Machinery Association (FMA) (1970) have produced a code of good practice for the design of food machinery. This is one of the areas of good practice referred to in the Materials and Articles in Contact with Food Regulations, 1987. Main points of the code are that:

- The design should be properly cleanable.
- The exterior should not be able to harbour dirt, waste food, or pests.
- All surfaces in contact with food should be inert, both to foods and to cleaning chemicals.

- Surfaces in contact with food should be smooth, non-porous and not liable to buckle, bend, crack, chip or pit.
- There should be no dead spaces, crevices or corners in the region containing the food.
- Food should be protected from contamination in the form of screws, nuts, or grease from the mechanism.

Even equipment designed within this code of practice can vary widely in hygiene efficiency.

Question

Why does the code of practice not simply require the highest hygiene efficiency standard?

The FMF/FMA code of practice has to cover a range of different manufacturers, price ranges and market niches. It is therefore only aimed at the lowest common denominator: the minimum acceptable hygiene and safety standards. The code forms a useful starting point for selecting plant and equipment. Main points of the code are considered in more detail below. Most of the points are relevant to small equipment such as tools and utensils, as well as to machinery.

Cleanability

'Properly cleanable' should mean both easy and quick to clean. Machines are easier to clean if they have the minimum of working parts. They should also be simple to strip down. Removable parts should have integral screw devices, rather than removable nuts or bolts. Mechanical components should have clips or bayonet fittings where possible, rather than screw threads, which need more labour time to remove. Large plant or equipment which must be cleaned in situ should have safe, convenient access points. Internal visibility is also important in equipment hygiene. All parts likely to become soiled should be available to easy inspection, i.e. without mirrors or special lenses. Insides of machines should be uniformly white or metallic and should never be allowed to become stained or discoloured. External parts should be in a colour such as blue, which contrasts strongly with residues of processed food. Seals and gaskets around inspection hatches or refrigerator doors should be capable of removal without tools and without dismantling the appliance. This makes for easier inspection and quicker, more efficient cleaning.

The weight and dimensions of a machine and of its components affect ease of cleaning. North (1987) recommends that removable parts be no more than 20 kg in weight. Dimensions should generally be no more than 1000 x 700 x 100 mm (400 x 28 x 4 in.). These limits represent the practical maximum that can be lifted, manoeuvred and mechanically cleaned. Components with one linear dimension of up to 1400 mm (56 in.) can be considered if they are within the weight restriction and the other two dimensions are less than 1,000 x 400 mm. Cleanability of vessels, openings and channels depends on their depth, width and height. Ideal dimensions are shown in Table 6.2.

Table 6.2   Recommended cleanable dimensions for channels and recesses in food equipment

Depth	Width and height
Up to 100 mm	At least 100 mm
Up to 500 mm	At least 200 mm
Up to 1000 mm	At least 500 mm
Over 1000 mm	At least 750 mm

Source: North (1987).

It is often worthwhile timing the cleaning of machines before buying them. Clean-as-you-go procedures should take no longer than 15 minutes. The same is true of the intermediate cleaning of production-line machines: routine cleaning should be achievable within the space of a tea-break. Deep-cleaning should not require more than one hour, so that at a pinch it can be accomplished during the lunch break. Stripping and cleaning machines should require the minimum of labour skill and training. Hayes (1979) makes the comment that 'equipment that is difficult to clean will be cleaned as infrequently and as indifferently as the operative can get away with'.

Question
Does this comment reflect a very poor opinion of worker attitude and responsibility?

This statement may seem to hold workers' motivation in low esteem. However, it is up to management to provide the necessary systems and means to do the job. If management demand quick efficient work, but make it difficult or inconvenient to do the job, their attitude is at fault, not that of the workers.

Machines designed to run continuously are generally more difficult to clean than batch units. Their construction is usually more complex and it is more difficult to find a time for stripping and cleaning. It is particularly important to assess cleaning times for such machinery. Some items have built-in 'clean-in-place' systems. These pump hot water or chemical solutions through all the parts which come in contact with food. Clean-in-place systems rely on the turbulence of the cleaning medium to remove food particles. Cleaning is poor if the internal design allows air pockets or 'dead spaces' to develop along the flow route (see Figure 6.2). An alternative is to use centralized cleaning with specialized spray heads for tanks and containers. All such vessels should have good drainage with the drain cock at the lowest point and the outlet pipe flush to the inside wall. Flat bed equipment such as *bain-maries* should be mounted with a slight fall towards the drain cock.

Ease of cleaning should also be considered when choosing tools and utensils. Dark and food-like colours should be avoided, e.g. for knife-handles and chopping boards. Items should preferably not have decorative grooves or holes for hanging them up. Aluminium items corrode and darken in dishwashers. On-glaze decorated crockery should not be used in a dishwasher.

Exterior

All equipment should have a smooth exterior, free of crevices. There should be no dips or dents in which moisture may collect and no unlagged cold water or coolant pipes to cause condensation. There should be integral hoppers and funnels, allowing food materials to be fed into the machine easily with the minimum of spillage. External surfaces should be accessible and preferably glossy, to aid the removal of spoilt food. There should be no recesses which could harbour pests. Unavoidable recessed areas should be screened with fine wire mesh. Panels containing thermal insulation material should be sealed and water-tight. Otherwise the insulation will become water-logged and harbour microorganisms.

Electrical components should ideally be contained within a purpose-built housing. Failing this they should be enclosed in a polythene bag to protect them during cleaning. Some machines have removable electrical units, but there should also be some means of sealing the socket while the unit is detached for cleaning. Safety equipment such as fuses and circuit-breaks should be capable of immediate access, without specialist tools. Exteriors of large machines should be free of protruding corners and external fixings. These jeopardize food hygiene as well as efficiency and safety.

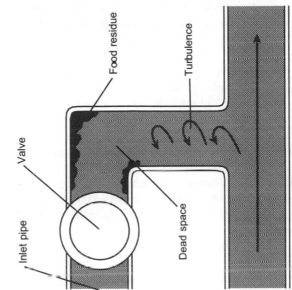

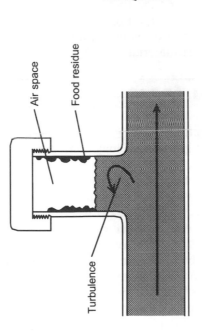

Figure 6.2 Problems in clean-in-place systems

Inert materials

Surfaces with which food is in contact must not absorb food or water. Otherwise pathogenic bacteria may be absorbed as well, grow within the material and leak back into the food. Some materials contain constituents which may migrate into the food. For example polyvinyl chloride (PVC) and polyvinylidene dichloride may contain **plasticizers**, chronically toxic chemicals which dissolve out of the plastic into fats and oils. Some kinds of wood contain water-soluble poisons.

Many metals are corroded by acids, salty foods, alkaline cleaning materials or chlorine disinfectants. These include iron, aluminium, galvanized steel, chromium plate and some types of stainless steel. Several metals also catalyze chemical changes in food and in cleaning chemicals. For example hot chromium, vanadium and manganese in steels and stainless steels may catalyze the oxidation of **dichloromethane** (used in some food and cleaning processes) to the highly poisonous gas **phosgene**.

Knife blades should be of food grade stainless steel, not carbon steel. Aluminium and galvanized equipment and vessels should be avoided. Copper pots and pans should not be used with acid foods. Their use should be kept to a minimum, though they may be appropriate in visual situations such as *flambé* work. Draining boards should be of stainless steel or inert plastic, rather than of wood. Knife handles and chopping boards should also be of inert materials (see below).

Non-porous surfaces

Pores, chips, cracks and pitting harbour bacteria and resist effective cleaning. Materials which chip or crack may contaminate the food with particles of foreign matter. Chipped, cracked or pitted areas are more prone to attack by cleaning chemicals and foods, which deteriorates the surface even further. Inner walls of food equipment must not bend or buckle, otherwise dead spaces may develop where pockets of bacterial growth can occur. Flexing weakens inner walls, forming hairline cracks and increasing the likelihood of corrosion, pitting or chipping.

Chopping boards should be of plastic, rather than wood. The plastic must be food-grade, non-porous and must not yellow with use (This indicates absorption of constituents from the food.) Chopping boards should not score deeply in use, otherwise crevices are generated, in which bacteria can grow. Handles of equipment such as knives and saucepans should also be of plastic, rather than wood. If polypropylene or nylon boards become deeply scored they can be given a new lease of life by planing off the old surface. Some commercial boards have layers of adhesive plastic which can be peeled off successively as they become scored.

Dead spaces

Crevices, corners and blind pipes within food equipment create dead spaces. These tend to hold back pockets of partly processed food. Bacteria may grow unchecked and survive from batch to batch, because these areas are difficult to clean. Dead spaces are by nature inaccessible to good visibility and to cleaning equipment. Spaces at the top may fill with air and resist flushing with cleaning media. Internal corners are more prone to corrosion or erosion than flat, rounded surfaces. North (1987) recommends that all internal bends and corners in food machines should be curved to a radius of at least 50 mm (2 in.). Joints in the internal walls of vessels should be set at least 25 mm away from any natural 'corner' that would otherwise be made (see Figure 6.3).

Figure 6.3   Welded joints in food equipment

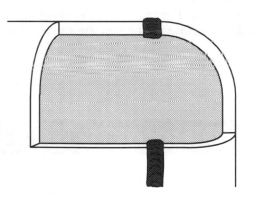
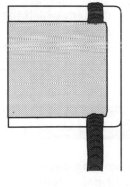

Good design, with weld set away
from rounded corner

Poor design, with weld
at sharp corner

Contamination by mechanical components

Nuts and bolts should be externally mounted and should be prevented from working loose by vibration etc. Components such as motors should be housed separately, so that they can never come into contact with the food. Glands and bushes should be of food grade nylon rather than grease-packed metal. Special precautions should be taken if poisonous chemical lubricants are used anywhere in the machine. Knives and other kitchen tools should be assembled with firm, robust rivets rather than nuts and bolts. If screw fixings are essential they should have anti-slip washers and their heads should be recessed into the tool. Plastic components should be supple, not brittle. Handles or other plastic parts which begin to crack, flake or chip should be replaced or rejected.

Study example 6.2

Apply the criteria discussed above to the purchase of a slicer like the one discussed in Study example 6.1 on pages 200–1.
Identify the following:

1. Eight features which make for easy cleanability.
2. Four general safety features.
3. Ideal materials for: the blade, the table and the bearing through which the main shaft passes (from the motor to the blade).
4. An ideal finish for the exterior.

Time/temperature aspects

Cold-holding equipment, i.e. refrigerators, freezers, chilled display and vending units should have *integral thermometers*. Temperature displays should be on the outside of the cabinet and should clearly indicate any rise above the proper storage temperature. With hot-holding equipment it is generally more important to monitor the temperature of food items than that of the unit. This is best done using an electronic pocket thermometer, which can be sterilized regularly and will not contaminate food with glass or mercury. Hot cabinets should have integral monitoring thermometers.

Cooking equipment should be capable of efficient heat transfer. Integral probe thermometers are useful for monitoring the internal temperatures of large joints during roasting. This may be critical if pathogenic bacteria are present in food. D and z values should be used to estimate the likely destruction of bacteria (see Chapter 1).

Preparation and processing equipment may generate warm pockets in the food, encouraging bacterial growth. Table 6.3 shows the effect of a rise in temperature on this growth. A rise of 10°C may make a dramatic difference, depending on the starting temperature. Cell division is roughly three times as rapid at 35°C as it is at 25°C. At 25°C it is roughly twice as fast as at 15°C.

Table 6.3   Multiplication of bacteria at different temperatures

| | | Relative Contamination Level at Temperature | | | |
Hours	35°C	30°C	25°C	20°C	15°C
0	1	1	1	1	1
1	8	4	2	2	1
2	64	16	4	3	2
3	512	64	8	4	3
4	4096	256	16	6	4
5	32768	1024	32	10	6
6	262144	4096	64	16	8
Doubling interval	20 min	30 min	60 min	90 min	120 min

Question

If the rate of cell division is three times as fast at 35°C as at 25°C, why does the number of cells rise to 8 in one hour at 35°C when it is only 2 at 25°C?

At 35°C doubling takes 20 min; at 25°C it takes 60 min. In 60 minutes at 35°C the number of bacteria doubles three times, so that:

$$2 \times 2 \times 2 = 8$$

Thus tripling the rate of cell division actually increases the number of cells by eight times, not three.

Long time intervals (several hours) are needed to multiply numbers by a factor of 1000, even at optimum temperatures. In normal operation, food does not spend long enough in batch-operated equipment such as mincers or mixers for microbial numbers to grow substantially. Cross-contamination is a much greater danger with this type of equipment. However, growth may occur if production is poorly scheduled and food has to wait for a while in the machine before the next step in the process.

Growth may reach dangerous levels in machines designed for continuous operation. Such machines apply considerable power, which tends to warm the food. A longer flow path within the machine may mean that food remains at the optimum growth temperature for a considerable time. There is also a chance that dead spaces and air pockets will develop, increasing the likelihood of contamination. It is best to chill food before continuous processing and also before large batch treatments. Operations such as mixing fish cakes, which are normally carried out warm (at 40°C) should be reviewed. It is often possible to carry them out at lower temperatures, if the ingredients are modified (Hayes, 1977).

Cooling of solid and semi-solid foods between processing operations should be carried out in a **blast chiller**. This appliance cools food rapidly by forced convection, using a blast of cold air. Centres of large items thus remain within the temperature danger zone for the shortest possible time. Items for blast chilling should always be wrapped or covered and must be transferred to a holding refrigerator as soon as possible. Similar considerations apply to blast freezers, which should be used wherever a substantial amount of food must be frozen.

Some continuous processing plant may be fitted with an integral cooler unit, so that food never rises above 10°C during processing. Liquid ingredients such as batters can be passed through a separate cooler unit. Danger of microbial growth may also be reduced by changing the ingredients slightly. For instance the pH may be lowered by adding acids, or the A_w raised by adding more salt or sugar. However, the ideal food processing equipment should operate outside the range of rapid bacterial growth, i.e. below 10°C or above 63°C.

Location of equipment

Access to large items should be safe and convenient to clean. Ladders, gantries and even specially constructed mezzanine floors may be necessary for the safe cleaning of tall plant. Heights and diameters of equipment should be carefully considered before purchase. Medium-sized appliances such as cookers or refrigerators should be on castors. Fixed items should stand at least 300 mm (12 in.) from the wall and from each other. This distance should be greater still for equipment more than

1000 mm wide or deep. Services such as drains and centralized cleaning points should be located conveniently close.

Display equipment should be placed so as to minimize contamination. Low-fronted chilled cabinets should not be sited where children or adults can use the glass front as a temporary seat. Eye level displays should be protected with a sneeze-guard. Chilled storage units should not be sited in hot or sunlit rooms. Hot-holding equipment should not be located in draughty areas.

Monitoring and control

Equipment which comes in contact with raw foods should not be used with cooked items. The best way to prevent cross-contamination is to colour code equipment with a dot of paint. For example, green may be used to indicate raw vegetables and red raw meat. Equipment for handling cooked food can be coded yellow, or white. Paints used on food equipment should be non toxic (e.g. guaranteed lead-free). Items to be marked should be properly prepared, i.e. by sanding and washing with sugar soap, and two or more coats should be applied. This makes cracking, flaking and wear less likely. Paint marks should be applied through a stencil. A circle cut from cardboard is adequate, but the outline should be smooth so that chipping, flaking and erosion will show up. Large plant and equipment often requires safety notices. For example, notices prohibiting cleaning by under-eighteens should be placed near prescribed dangerous machines. Three-phase equipment should bear a sign reading 'high voltage: 415V'.

It may also be helpful to fix operating or cleaning instructions close to machines to which they apply. Painted signs should conform to the criteria for painted code marks described above. Signs printed on paper or cardboard should not be used. Inked, engraved signs on blue plastic plaques are the ideal.

Question
Why are blue plastic plaques ideal?

Rigid plastic is recommended because paper or card may tear, while paint may chip or wear. Plastic plaques are also much less likely to be detached from walls or to shatter. In the event that this does occur, blue colouring makes the pieces easier to see if they get into food.

The temperature of holding equipment such as refrigerators, freezers and hot or cold display units should be monitored regularly. Readings should be recorded daily and documented to give an early indication of faults. The best way to do this is by cards in waterproof plastic mountings, fixed firmly to the sides of cabinets. The temperature inside the unit is read daily from a thermometer built into the equipment itself, or from a portable, digital probe. Temperatures are noted on the control card, which should have thirty-one spaces for entries and signatures (see Figure 6.4). At the end of each month the card is replaced. The old card should be kept on file until the following year end.

Figure 6.4   Temperature control card for a refrigerator

PQR Hospitality Ltd

Meat Refrigerator: Correct Temperature 5°C

Month ....

Date	Temp.	Initials	Date	Temp.	Initials
1			16		
2			17		
3			18		
4			19		
5			20		
6			21		
7			22		
8			23		
9			24		
10			25		
11			26		
12			27		
13			28		
15			30		
			31		

Summary – equipment used for processing or holding food

Cleaning

Do
- Use the five stages: pre-clean, clean, rinse, disinfect and dry.
- Intersperse clean-as-you-go with deep cleaning operations.
- Try to set standards for cleanliness.
- Consult codes of practice before drawing up schedules or job cards.

Maintenance

Do
- Decide maintenance strategy according to the guidelines given in Chapter 5.
- Select contractors who will work systematically and report their activities and any problems.
- Monitor and document the operation of:
  - hot and cold-holding equipment; and
  - cookers and integral probe-thermometers.

Do not
- Leave maintenance to the contractor, without taking any further interest in it.

Selection

Do
- Use the FMF/FMA code of practice as a checklist.
- Eliminate porous or chemically reactive materials from food use, as far as possible.
- Colour code equipment for use with different types of food.
- Ensure that foods are chilled or held above 63°C when undergoing continuous processing.

Do not
- Locate equipment so that it is difficult or inconvenient to clean.
- Use paper, card or toxic paint in signs and notices.

Other equipment involved in food hygiene

As well as food handling utensils and machines, three classes of equipment play a major part in food hygiene. These are concerned with the hygiene of:

- Premises, e.g. general cleaning, waste disposal equipment.
- Other plant/equipment, e.g. cleaning, dishwashing and textile washing machines.
- Personnel, e.g. articles for hand washing, drying and personal hygiene.

Careful selection and provision of these categories of equipment will greatly improve efficiency, food hygiene and staff morale. Criteria for selection are discussed below.

Equipment for the hygiene of premises

Manual cleaning equipment

Clean-as-you-go systems often involve manual cleaning because there is neither time nor scope to use mechanical methods. It is important that the correct tools are available for manual cleaning and that they can be kept hygienic and stored conveniently for quick use between food handling operations. The equipment required for manual kitchen cleaning includes cloths, brushes, mops and buckets.

Wiping cloths should be of heavy cotton cloth. They will need to be boiled periodically to sterilize them. Boiling does not rot the fabric like chlorine bleach and is much more effective against bacteria than the other available disinfectants. Cotton cloths are less satisfactory for wiping down items like chopping-blocks, which come into regular contact with food. It is impossible to boil or disinfect such cloths regularly enough to prevent bacteria from growing on absorbed particles of food. A survey by Tebbutt (1984) found wiping cloths to be a frequent source of contamination (see Table 6.4).

Table 6.4   Frequency of contamination of personnel and equipment items

Organism (% contaminated by)	Finger rinse 247[*]	Nail brushes 193[*]	Wiping cloths 224[*]	Cutting boards 169[*]	Bar soap 4[*]	Communal towels 5[*]
Escherichia Coli	25	22	48	18	75	100
Stapliylococcus aureus	19	2	0	0	25	20
Streptococcus faecalis	0	7	4	5	25	20

[*] Number of samples surveyed'.

Source: Tebbutt (1984)

Question

Why would chlorine bleach be specifically recommended for disinfecting floor cloths?

Chlorine bleach is ideal for disinfecting cloths because it is powerful and leaves little residue or odour. Other types of disinfectant may also be inactivated by gross food residues or by the cloth itself (see Chapter 1).

Semi-disposable cellulose wiping cloths are the most satisfactory for food-contact surfaces. The thin fabric can be washed, rinsed and disinfected quickly. In addition, the cloths can (and should) be thrown away at the end of the day so that growth opportunities are limited. Even better are the cloths which are ready-impregnated with sanitizer.

Correct use of cloths is important. Wet wiping cloths should not be used for mopping up spillages, where a paper towel should be employed. Food absorbed in a wet cloth becomes an unnecessary breeding ground for bacteria, but a paper towel is simply thrown away after use. Chefs' cloths are intended for dry use and should not be employed for mopping-up operations. A large concentration of spilt food will inactivate the sanitizer in an impregnated cloth, so it is better to use paper towels first.

Abrasive nylon cloths for scouring dirty pots may also become a source of contamination. Like cotton, they are rotted by long soaking in chlorine bleach and so should be disinfected by boiling in water with a little detergent, preferably daily.

Brushes should have polypropylene or nylon heads and bristles. Brush heads of wood and natural bristle are not satisfactory for any type of kitchen use, as they absorb moisture, harbour contamination and inactivate many disinfectants. Brush heads should be boiled, bleached and dried between use. The same applies to plastic brushes used for cleaning pots.

Mops of several different types are available. The traditional style with a fixed head should not be used in kitchens. It is difficult to sterilize and dry and the metal attachment which holds the strings of the mop head may react with bleach. Better are the Kentucky or Foss type mops with string heads which can be sterilized by boiling. Such mops usually require a specialized bucket and press.

Buckets should be of polypropylene or other plastic. These are lighter, cheaper and less liable to corrosion than galvanized steel. Buckets should be the correct size for the mop with which they will be used. They should be mounted on a trolley, with a mop press for easy use. Light mopping jobs and clean-as-you-go can use *single-solution mopping*. This requires a two-bucket assembly: one containing detergent solution and the other water. Dilute bleach can be used instead of water for particularly dirty areas. Deep cleaning and very soiled areas require *double-solution mopping*. A three-bucket assembly is used: one with detergent, one with disinfectant and one with rinse water. Equipment used in lavatories and washrooms must be kept separate from that used in food rooms.

Question
How can this best be prevented?

Mops, buckets and trolleys for the kitchen should be colour coded to distinguish them from those for lavatory use. Mop heads can be sewn with coloured thread, provided this will not be bleached during sterilization. Handles and metal parts may be coded with coloured paint.

Mechanical cleaning equipment

High-pressure cleaners

Centralized cleaning systems, which pump cleaning medium to tapping points were described in Chapter 5. An alternative is the mobile high-pressure cleaner, which heats water or generates steam at the site where it is needed. The machine contains a reservoir of water, a pump, a heater and a device to meter cleaning agent into the water as it pumps out. A lance or specialized spray head can be used to direct the cleaning medium. Pressure cleaners for use in food preparation areas should be powered by electricity, not petrol or propane-driven. They are rather heavy appliances and this may limit accessibility and use. A much cheaper alternative may sometimes be to use a **tap proportioner** device. This can be fitted to a tap and will meter cleaning chemical solution into the flow of water at a constant rate. A stream of cleaning medium can thus be provided, at tap pressure. However, pressures and temperatures are much less than those supplied by a pressure cleaner.

Floor scrubbers/polishers

These versatile machines will scarify, scour, scrub and spray-clean as well as buff and polish. Models may have one, two or three brushing/buffing rotors. Three-rotor models are the most satisfactory because they neither pull to one side nor leave a 'dead space' on the floor surface between the rotors. Larger, heavier machines are more efficient because they can apply more pressure and power to the rotors. Floor scrubbers are very much more efficient than manual sweeping or mopping.

Study example 6.3

The rate at which a floor polisher will clean can be calculated approximately from the following formula.

$$\text{work rate (sq. metre/hour)} = \frac{0.05 \times D^2 \times \sqrt{r} \times \sqrt[3]{W}}{1000}$$

where:

D = rotor-wheel diameter (mm)
r = revolution rate (rev/min)
W = machine weight (kg)

This formula is for a single-rotor machine. An estimate for a triple-rotor appliance can be made by using the manufacturers r and W values, but calculating the diameter (D) value as twice the diameter of any of the three rotors (see Figure 6.5)

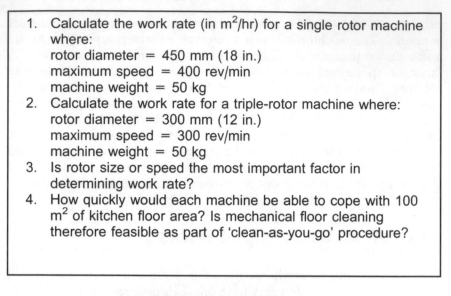

1. Calculate the work rate (in m²/hr) for a single rotor machine where:
   rotor diameter = 450 mm (18 in.)
   maximum speed = 400 rev/min
   machine weight = 50 kg
2. Calculate the work rate for a triple-rotor machine where:
   rotor diameter = 300 mm (12 in.)
   maximum speed = 300 rev/min
   machine weight = 50 kg
3. Is rotor size or speed the most important factor in determining work rate?
4. How quickly would each machine be able to cope with 100 m² of kitchen floor area? Is mechanical floor cleaning therefore feasible as part of 'clean-as-you-go' procedure?

Figure 6.5   Relationship between rotor diameters of triple- and single-rotor floor cleaners

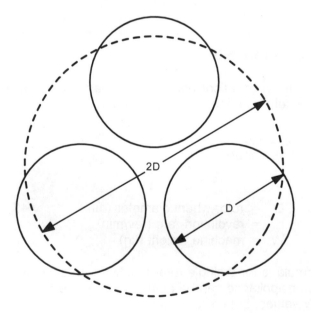

A wide range of detachable, sterilizable brushes and muffs is available for different jobs. Machines should also have detachable solution tanks for distributing disinfectant or detergent onto the floor. Scrubbers for use in food areas should be powered by low-voltage electricity or compressed air. Petrol and propane models are not suitable. Scrubbers should have a 'dead man's handle' device to switch them off automatically when released.

Suction cleaners

Three types of suction (vacuum) cleaner are available: ***horizontal cylinders***, ***upright models*** and ***canisters***. The latter (see Figure 6.6) can be used on both wet and dry surfaces. They are therefore the most suitable type for use in kitchens and food areas. Suction cleaning is better than manual sweeping from the food hygiene point of view. Dust,

Figure 6.6   Cyclone-type canister suction cleaner

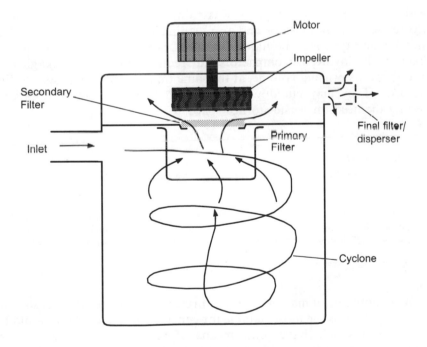

Source: Adapted from Allen (1983) p. 121.

cobwebs and other potential physical contamination can be completely removed. Almost all models are electrically powered. Appliances which use a low voltage supply are safer for kitchen conditions.

Waste disposal equipment

Waste disposal units should be fitted to sinks in food preparation and washing up areas. They substantially reduce the amount of waste food that must be stored, so there is less attraction for pests in the waste collection area. Waste disposal units should be powerful enough to cope with bones, which will attract pests if stored.

Glass-breaking machines should be purchased if there are large numbers of bottles, jars or light bulbs to be disposed of. Glass-breakers reduce the risk of injuries and of physical contamination, as well as helping to minimize the storage space needed for waste. They also aid recycling by keeping glass separate from other waste.

Rubbish compactors compress waste into a steel chamber, using a hydraulic ram. Both side- and top-loading models are available. The side-loading type may be more suitable if heavy items or materials are likely to be involved. Compactors can reduce cardboard packaging to about half its original volume, at the same time minimizing pests and fire hazards. They may cut down odours and their use can substantially reduce the need for waste-storage space.

Question
Will all waste be reduced as much as cardboard?

Rubbish compactors work to a set maximum pressure. Thus the amount of compaction depends on the type of rubbish. Corrugated card and boxes can be very efficiently compressed. More rigid materials will resist compaction.

Bins should be of manageable size, preferably wheeled. Plastic, such as polypropylene, is the most suitable for general use. Bin trolleys should be robust and should have some means of braking. All waste disposal equipment should be capable of regular, thorough cleaning and disinfection.

Equipment for cleaning utensils etc.

Manual dishwashing

Adequate manual dishwashing requires two sinks; draining boards (of stainless steel or plastic, not wood); cloths of cotton and nylon (for scouring); nylon or polypropylene brushes; and gloves. Criteria for selecting these items are discussed elsewhere. The procedure is as follows:

1. Scrape plates free of waste food and soak pots in hot water.
2. Scrub all items with a cloth or brush in the first sink, which should contain an approximately 1:100 solution of detergent in hand hot water (50–55°C).
3. Rinse items free of visible food particles in the first sink.
4. Transfer to the second sink containing water at 80–85°C plus bactericide. Items must remain in this sink for at least one minute.
5. Transfer to the draining board and allow to air dry. Items for immediate use can be wiped with paper towels.

Mechanical dishwashing

Dishwashing machines range from worktop cabinets for small batches to large, continuous, automated systems. Machines should be convenient to load, unload and charge with chemicals. Internal dimensions and load capacity should be checked against likely loads of both crockery and dismantled equipment parts. Dishwashers should be capable of at least three functions:

(i) Wash with detergent at 65°C (some energy-saving models operate at 55°C);
(ii) Rinse with a spray jet at 65°C–75°C; and
(iii) Sterilize with hot water at 85°C.

More sophisticated models may also dry the washed utensils in a stream of hot air, and burnish cutlery. Dishwashers generally need to be stacked in a particular way, e.g. with the utensils handle-down, the pots inverted, and crockery oriented in a particular way. Instructions and notices about proper use should be available and staff should be trained to operate the machine. Dishwashers also need minor, routine servicing to clear filters, or to replenish chemicals such as salt for water softeners. These operations should be regularly scheduled. Clean utensils should be stored in an enclosed, clean, dry area, preferably away from busy walkways and at least 450 mm (18 in.) from the ground to avoid contamination by dust.

Laundering

Food handlers' protective clothing should be laundered separately. Often it may need a biological prewash, below 40°C to remove protein-bound dirt. Protective clothing, chefs' cloths etc. should be sterilized by washing at the hottest cycle available i.e. 95°C. Most detergent powders contain **perborate** which is converted to hydrogen peroxide at this temperature and has excellent bactericidal properties. Use of starch on protective clothing should be minimal as it offers a potential hiding place and food source for bacteria. Washing machines for protective clothing should be capable of pre-wash and boil cycles. They should be located well away from food rooms in an area which can be cleaned and disinfected if necessary. Storage space should be provided for dirty items awaiting washing, as well as for laundered clothing.

Equipment for personal hygiene

Mendes and Lynch (1976) describe a survey of washrooms and toilets. A summary of their results (Table 6.5) shows that items such as taps, which are regularly handled, are very likely to be contaminated. As Table 6.4 (p. 217) indicates, towels, nail-brushes and even bars of soap may carry harmful bacteria.

Taps

Non-manual taps should always be used. The best type are operated by pedals or an infra-red sensor. Elbow-operated taps like those in hospitals are less suitable for food premises as manual operation is still possible. Staff have to be specially trained not to touch them.

Showers

Relatively few staff washrooms have showers. Yet these can play a useful part in promoting hygiene. Kitchen heat and humidity encourage staff to mop their brows and scratch their heads and bodies, thus transferring bacteria to their hands. Showering promotes comfort and ultimately contributes to hygiene.

Table 6.5   Results of a bacteriological survey of washrooms and toilets

	% frequency of contamination by faecal bacteria	
Sample point	Male	Female
Cubicle door lock	5	4
Cubicle door handles	5	6
Flush handle	6	5
Entrance door:		
outside handle	12	8
inside handle	23	20
Tap handles	25	29
Water in WC pedestal	38	24
Floor in cubicle	39	46
Under flushing rim	53	38
Wash basin overflow	55	59
WC seat	68	58
Urinals	89	–

Source: Mendes and Lynch (1976).

Soap dispensers

Liquid soap from a dispenser should be used rather than bar soap, which is a source of contamination (see Table 6.4 on page 217). The formulation should contain a bactericide such as ***chlorhexidine*** and should be unscented. Areas below soap dispensers should be wiped down regularly, so that spilled soap does not collect there.

Nail brushes

Like the brushes discussed above, nail brushes should be of polypropylene or nylon, not wood and bristle. They should be boiled occasionally to clean them, and stored in disinfectant solution when not in use. Unless this is done, nail brushes will carry high levels of contamination (see Table 6.4).

Hand driers

Communal towels (also shown in Table 6.4) are unsuitable for use by food handlers. Acceptable alternatives are hot-air driers, paper towel dispensers and continuous roller towel in a cabinet.

Hot-air driers should have a button which is easy to operate with the arm, rather than the hand. Alternatively, driers with infra-red sensor switches are available. It is recommended that there be one drier for every two hand basins, so that queues do not develop. Very frequent use of driers may cause chapped hands. Driers recycle the air within lavatories. There has been some unsubstantiated speculation that they may accumulate contamination from air-borne dust. Hot air driers should ideally be located away from cubicles and the area around them well ventilated. Paper towels from dispensers are claimed to remove more bacteria from hands than do hot air driers. They are also quicker to use, but operating costs are higher. Torn paper from towels may be carried into food rooms on clothing or in pockets, and become a contaminant.

Continuous roller cabinet towels remove bacteria efficiently, are quick to use and are not likely to release physical contaminants. However, mechanisms sometimes jam, converting a hygienic roller towel into an unhygienic communal one. Maintenance of the cabinets must therefore be efficient.

Question
Which means of hand drying is the most suitable?

All three means of hand drying have advantages and they also have limitations. The best choice will depend on the particular situation, i.e. the level of hygiene required, the rate of use and the amount of time available for drying. Personal preferences of workers and management may also need to be considered. The procedure for evaluating and selecting new purchases, discussed earlier in this chapter should also be applied to hand drying equipment.

Sanitary towels

There should be a vending machine selling tampons and towels in each ladies' lavatory area. Each cubicle should have a notice requesting that sanitary items are not discarded down WC pedestals, where they may block soil pipes and sewers. Sanitary disposal bags and a bin should be provided in cubicles. Bins should have plastic liners and close-fitting, odour-tight lids and they should be emptied daily. The contents should not be stored with other waste as they are a great contamination hazard. They can be incinerated on-site, but this equipment involves considerable capital outlay and may produce noxious odours and smoke. Alternatively, specialist contractors will refurbish and empty bins on a regular basis.

Summary – hygiene equipment

General hygiene

Do
- Select equipment which will do the job quickly in the likely conditions.
- Ensure that equipment can be easily washed and sterilized between use.

Do not
- Purchase combustion-driven (petrol or propane appliances) for use near food.

Washing equipment for clothing etc.

Do
- Select dishwashers with dimensions large enough for detached parts of food machines and other equipment.
- Ensure that dish and textile washers can sterilize as well as wash.
- Train and instruct staff in the correct use of hygiene equipment.

Personal hygiene

Do
- Anticipate staff hygiene needs (such as showering and sanitary towels) and make allowances for them.

Do not
- Install any equipment which must be switched off manually after washing the hands.

7 Food Hygiene and the Management of Personnel

Objectives

To identify the legal obligations of the food premises manager with respect to personnel. To set down hygiene standards for personnel. To discuss how these standards can be achieved through the selection, training, motivation, monitoring and support of staff.

Introduction

Food handlers have a major impact on food hygiene. They are potential vectors of contamination and their behaviour and efficiency at work determine the standards of premises, equipment and process hygiene. A whole section of the Food Hygiene (General) Regulations, 1970 is directed at the hygiene and behaviour of personnel.

Regulation 10 specifies personal hygiene 'as clean as is reasonably practical' of hands, forearms, neck, hair and any clothing liable to come into contact with food. Open cuts, wounds etc. must be covered with a waterproof dressing. Food handlers must not spit, smoke or take snuff near open food.

Regulations 11 and 12 require handlers of open food to wear clean over-clothing and head coverings and set out minimum hygiene requirements for the carriage and wrapping of food.

Regulation 13 requires food handlers to notify the local Medical Officer of Health if they contract typhoid, paratyphoid or salmonella infections, amoebic or bacillary dysentery or staphylococcal skin, nose or throat infections. *Regulation 14* requires notices in WC cubicles instructing employees to wash their hands after using the lavatory.

Regulation 29 classifies the responsibilities of personnel:

- *Food handlers* must comply with the provisions of the Regulations.

- *Proprietors* must take all reasonable steps to ensure the compliance of persons under their control.
- *Managers* (who are not owners of the premises) have the same responsibilities as proprietors.

In order to manage the personnel aspects of food hygiene, the manager needs to know:

- Detailed standards of personal hygiene required to ensure effective food hygiene.
- How to monitor the hygiene and health of personnel.
- How to train for hygiene.
- How to motivate for hygiene.

These aspects are discussed below.

Standards of personal health and hygiene

Hands

Hands come into frequent contact with food and have many opportunities to transfer contamination. They become contaminated from:

- Using the lavatory (faecal bacteria/coliforms).
- Scratching or wiping parts of the body, particularly infected parts of the skin (*Staphylococcus aureus*).
- Handling raw foods, particularly raw meat. (*Salmonella* species, *Clostridium* species, *Listeria monocytogenes*).

Most people's hands carry bacteria, particularly under the finger nails and under rings or ornaments. To a lesser extent they may be present in the lines, creases and pores of the palm. These areas are constantly warm and moist and particles of food collect there during work, so bacteria can multiply. The numbers of bacteria present on the hands can be minimized by good hygiene. The following points should be considered.

Visible cleanliness is important. There should be no stubborn residual stains of engine oil or nicotine. Clean hands cannot hide contamination and they indicate a positive attitude to hygiene. They are also noticed by customers.

Finger nails should be kept as short and clean as possible. Use of a nail brush should be encouraged. Nail varnish must not be used during food handling work. It hides any dirt harboured beneath finger nails, and it may flake off into food.

Ornaments should not be worn on the hands. Wedding rings are usually permissible, but jewelled rings are not suitable. Watches, bracelets and bangles should not be worn. They tend to harbour skin bacteria and they may fall off into the food.

Question
Why are wedding rings permissible, while jewelled ones are not?

> Wedding rings are usually plain gold bands, which offer minimal opportunity for bacterial growth, while jewelled rings have a space behind each stone, where food can lodge and bacteria grow. Also, wedding rings are worn permanently and may be much more difficult to remove.

Even with the cleanest nails and hands, staff should handle foods as little as possible. Hands should be dry for touching food, as dry hands transfer fewer bacteria than wet ones. Cooked foods and items for chilled storage are particularly sensitive to contamination and should be handled least of all. Hands should be washed regularly with non-perfumed, anti-dermatitis, antibacterial liquid soap. Washing is required:

(i)   After using the lavatory;
(ii)   Before entering food preparation areas from the changing room or the street;
(iii) After handling raw or waste food; and
(iv)   Whenever staff pass from a 'dirty' area to a 'clean' area of the kitchen (see Chapter 5).

Pedal-operated taps and a disposable drying medium such as paper towels prevent recontamination after washing (see Chapter 6).

Skin diseases may cause serious food contamination. Even those not caused by bacteria (such as psoriasis or allergies) may produce weeping and flaking skin, providing a habitat for *Staphylococcus aureus*. Individuals suffering from severe allergies should seek other employment, particularly if the allergy is actually caused by a particular food. Cuts also harbour bacteria but are not likely to contaminate food during handling, provided proper precautions are taken. Cuts should be covered with a waterproof plaster (to keep fluids *in*, not out). Dressings should be blue, so that they can easily be seen if they fall off into food. In food production plants with magnetic monitors, dressings should incorporate a metal strip to make them easily detectable.

Septic cuts, whitlows and boils contain *pus*. This contains large numbers of live bacteria and is a serious contaminant. Plasters cannot be relied on to prevent pus getting into food. Individuals suffering from infections of this kind should be excluded from food handling until cleared by a doctor.

Other parts of the body

Forearms are almost as likely to touch food as are the hands themselves. Food handlers sometimes need to lift heavy items, meat carcasses for instance, on the *shoulders* where they may touch the *neck*. Ideally, all body parts should be prevented from coming into contact with food by suitable clothing. If this is not possible, neck, forearms and other parts should be subjected to the same hygiene standards as the hands.

Facial cosmetics may flake or powder into food. False eyelashes may fall off. Perfume may taint food or utensils, where the wearer has touched them. The same is true of scented soaps and hand creams. Cosmetics are often necessary for service staff but must be applied with taste and moderation. Food handlers must not wear cosmetics, perfume, after-shave or cologne while preparing open food.

Hair

Human hair generally carries *Staphylococcus aureus* from skin, and coliforms from the hands (via the faecal–oral route). These organisms may fall into open food on their own or may be carried on loose hairs or dandruff. Physical contamination (the classic 'hair in my soup') and biological contamination can occur at the same time. Hair ornaments, combs and hair-grips may also fall into the food. Hair should be washed regularly and a hat should always be worn while handling food. Hair-nets should be worn underneath hats if the hair is long. Hair ornaments should not be worn, and grips or combs for keeping hair in place must be kept under hair-nets. Food handlers should never scratch their heads while working. Combing and adjusting hair should be restricted to rest rooms and toilet areas. Dandruff is often unavoidable but can generally be kept out of food by wearing the proper head covering. Individuals with head sores or scalp disease should not be permitted to handle food.

Nose, mouth and ears

The nose, mouth and ears are permanently warm, permanently moist, food-rich havens for bacterial growth. *Staphylococcus aureus* and coliforms are the commonest, but carrier individuals may also harbour *Salmonella* or *Campylobacter* species. Bacteria may be transferred to food by coughing, sneezing, spitting and by hand contact (e.g. picking the ears or nose). Physical contamination may occur from ornaments such as ear-rings falling into food.

Food handlers must not spit, or indulge in habits, such as taking snuff, which may make them cough or sneeze. Sufferers from tuberculosis (TB), bronchitis, colds or flu should be excluded from handling food for the same reason. Habits which involve hand-to-mouth contact should particularly be avoided. These include smoking, chewing gum, and eating while working. Food handlers must not pick at their nose, ears or teeth while working or dip their fingers into food to taste it. Nor should they lick their fingers to wet them before opening polythene bags or picking up greaseproof paper. Food handlers should only blow their nose in rest-rooms or toilet areas. Disposable paper tissue should be used and the hands washed afterwards.

Eyes have a sparse bacterial population, compared to the nose, mouth and ears. However, bacteria can multiply if eyes are irritated, inflamed or infected. Food handlers should not use eye cosmetics at work and should avoid rubbing the eyes. Those with irritated, weeping or discharging eyes should not be permitted to handle food.

General illness

The Food Hygiene (General) Regulations (1970) prohibit individuals suffering from *Salmonella* or *Staphylococcus* infections, or dysentery, from handling food. To these diseases should be added tuberculosis and infections by *Campylobacter*, *Giardia* and *Cryptosporidium* species. These are easily passed from person to person and can probably also be transferred via food. In addition, the Salmonella Subcommittee of the PHLS (1983) recommends exclusion of food handlers suffering from rotavirus enteritis, hepatitis A, threadworm (*Oxyuris vermicularis*) and pork tapeworm (*Taenia solium*). Clearance criteria are shown in Table 7.1.

Individuals showing symptoms of infection should be excluded from food handling work. They should see a doctor as soon as possible and where appropriate they should submit faecal samples for analysis.

Table 7.1   Clearance Criteria for Exclusion Infections

Organism	Clearance criteria
Typhoid/paratyphoid	At least twelve negative faeces specimens spread over six months
Shigella sp. (dysentery)	Negative faeces specimens for three consecutive days
Salmonella sp. (other than typhoid/paratyphoid)	Negative faeces specimens for three consecutive days
Escherichia coli (as acute/chronic gastroenteritis)	Negative faeces specimens for three consecutive days
Staphylococcus aureus	Septic lesion cleared and healed
Rotavirus (viral gastroenteritis)	Seven days after recovery
Hepatitis A	Seven days after the onset of jaundice
Threadworm (*Oxyuris vermicularis*)	Until treated
Pork tapeworm (*Taenia solium*)	Until treated

Source: PHLS Salmonella Subcommittee (1983)

Question

What are the likely symptoms of typhoid, paratyphoid, *Oxyuris vermicularis* and *Taenia solium*?

Typhoid and paratyphoid both begin with vomiting, diarrhoea and/or abdominal pain and there is high fever. Threadworms appear as tiny, waving threads in the faeces. Pork tapeworm releases flat, white, egg-filled body segments about the size of postage stamps, which can be seen in the faeces. Individuals with any suspect symptoms should be referred immediately to a doctor for confirmation of their condition. If the cause of illness is confirmed it should be notified to the Medical Officer of Health for the district. He/she can be reached through the local Environmental Health Department, who should also be notified. Sufferers should refrain from working with food until officially cleared by the Public Health Laboratory or by their doctor. General practitioners should be made aware of the health requirements of food handlers and of the recommended clearance criteria for communicable infections.

Protective clothing

Outdoor shoes and clothing commonly carry dust, dirt, bacteria and parasite eggs (from dog faeces and soil) from the street. Indoor garments carry the detritus of day-to-day human activity: human and animal hairs, cigarette ash, spilt food and other residues, loose fibres and buttons. In order to ensure that none of these contaminate food during handling, outdoor clothing should be removed and replaced with hygienic work-wear. A plentiful supply of protective clothing should be available, so that operatives may change regularly and are always clean and smart. Lockers should be clean and dry. Protective clothing should not be taken home for washing, or laundered with other clothing. A laundry service can be used, or special on-site facilities provided (ABLCRS, 1987). Food handlers' work clothing should be sterilized by boiling at each wash and must therefore be of a robust fabric such as cotton. Work-wear should particularly include the following: overalls, aprons, head-coverings, gloves and shoes or boots.

Overalls should cover day-clothes completely so that no sleeves or petticoats protrude. For example, shirt sleeves worn under shortsleeved overalls must be short, or securely rolled. Overalls should be light in colour, preferably white, to show up stains. White fabric is usually also more robust in the wash. Garments must not have loose fibres or tatters of fabric. Any worn or torn items should be discarded. Work clothing should be smart, as this improves employee morale and helps increase the confidence of customers. *Fastenings* are generally a problem. Velcro and zip-fastenings have the least potential for falling off into food. However, they wear out quickly with constant laundering. Press studs last longer and are satisfactory if firmly welded to the garment. Buttons come loose more easily than studs but may be easier to detect if they fall off into food.

Aprons should be worn as well as overalls for very dirty tasks or for jobs where any contamination might be critical. Like other work-wear, aprons should be light in colour and, ideally, waterproof. Disposable aprons are very effective, provided they are of stout plastic which will not tear or tatter during use. They should be pale blue, rather than white or colourless. Non-disposable aprons should be cleaned and disinfected after each use. They must therefore be of a resistant material which will withstand such treatment.

Question
Why should disposable items be pale blue?

It is difficult to keep track of numbers of disposable items to discover whether any have been lost. Disposable garments are usually more delicate than reusable ones and may tatter or tear, particularly around the fastenings. Whole items and parts of items are therefore more likely to get into food during processing. If they do, pale blue materials are more easy to see and remove than clear or white ones.

Head coverings include hair-nets and hats. *Hair-nets* should be of stretchy material to hold hair firmly. The mesh must be small enough to prevent ornaments and grips from falling out. Nets should be white, so as not to conceal stains and must be easy to wash and sterilize without the elastic perishing. The hair-net rule should be applied equally to all males and females whose hair hangs about the nape of the neck. *Hats* should completely cover the head. In particular no hair should protrude in a fringe or quiff at the front. Hats must be supplied in all appropriate sizes and fits. They should effectively prevent scratching and be of robust, white, washable material. Ideally hats should not require starching. However, smartness is one of the most important and encouraging qualities in headgear. Starching is permissible if it is necessary for improving appearance and morale.

Gloves of rubber or plastic may be required for operations which are wet, dirty or involve harsh chemicals. Handling of very hot or cold items (e.g. in frozen storage) may require fabric or leather gloves.

Gloves in general should be light in colour and easy to clean, launder or sterilize. Disposable gloves should be pale blue to prevent them from falling unnoticed into food. Talc provided for lubricating rubber and plastic gloves must not be perfumed. All gloves should be stored in a clean, dry, dust-free place, checked regularly, and all worn/torn pairs discarded.

Footwear should be provided for food handlers, because street shoes may carry dirt, dog faeces or other contaminants. Street shoes may also slip or let in water and provide little protection from falling objects. Work shoes should be robust, with welded uppers and steel toecaps and should be waterproof and comfortable to wear. They should not be worn outside the food processing area. Facilities for cleaning, disinfecting and storing footwear should be provided. Rubber or plastic *boots* should be worn in wet and dirty areas, such as waste collection points. Boots must be easy to clean and disinfect, i.e. light (preferably white) in colour and not fabric-lined. Boots should have anti-slip soles with a shallow tread so that they pick up the minimum of dirt.

Achieving staff hygiene standards

Ensuring that staff meet personal hygiene and health requirements depends on two things: the environment within which they must work and the quality of the staff themselves. From the food hygiene viewpoint the quality of the working environment depends upon the physical resources provided, e.g. washing, toilets and protective clothing. These have already been discussed in this and the preceding chapters. The quality of staff depends upon their health, their hygiene and their habits. The quality of staff may be maintained by the effective selection, training, monitoring and motivation of personnel.

Monitoring health and hygiene

Staff should always be inspected before they start work. Inspection should cover cleanliness of hands and forearms, use of jewellery and cosmetics, correct protective clothing and signs of illness. Staff should also be asked about illness. There must be a just and accepted system for dealing with sick staff who are excluded from work. It may be possible to transfer them to other duties, at the same rate of pay. Alternatively they should be sent home. Food handlers excluded from work due to illness should not be dismissed or made to accept a lower rate of pay. As well as being unjust, this may encourage them to seek work with an employer who is not so fussy. Local authorities are empowered to forbid sick individuals from working as food handlers. They may also pay compensation to workers inconvenienced in this way. However, responsible management should regard excluded staff within their staff welfare policy and should themselves take responsibility for compensation.

Monitoring of staff should include detailed health records. These can be commenced when staff are inducted and should be updated at least yearly, for example at staff appraisal interviews. Records can integrate other hygiene aspects such as training, discussed later in this chapter.

Staff selection

The first step towards ensuring the quality of staff is selection. Procedures for staff selection and recruitment generally involve the following:

- Job analysis.
- Job description.
- Job (holder) specification.
- Advertisement.
- Application form.
- Short-listing.
- Testing.
- Interviewing.
- References.
- Medical examination.
- Contracts/papers.

All of these are relevant to food hygiene in some way. Health and hygiene requirements should be considered carefully at each stage of the selection process.

Job analysis

This involves breaking down the work into tasks and functions. It is relatively easy to identify the elements of food hygiene required by a food handler. These will include good personal hygiene, proper process control, clean-as-you-go responsibilities and perhaps some other deep-cleaning tasks.

Question
Does hygiene only concern those who prepare and cook food?

Hygiene should be carefully identified in the job analyses of all food handlers, including waiters and bar staff. In addition, a number of jobs have an impact upon food hygiene besides those of food handlers. **Supervisors** must be able to demonstrate personal and other aspects of hygiene. **Managers** must be able to make decisions about premises, plant/equipment, personnel and processes, based on hygiene considerations. **Personnel officers** must be able to co-ordinate the selection and training of hygiene-oriented staff. **Maintenance workers** and **engineers** must be able to make adjustments and repairs without jeopardizing the hygiene of food operations.

Job description

The information obtained from job analysis is used to prepare a detailed list of the tasks, functions and responsibilities. Hygiene points noted in the job analysis should be included in the job description.

Study example 7.1

A *task* is a fixed, specified element of a job. A *function* usually involves carrying out a number of more or less specified tasks. A *responsibility* implies that the job holder has some freedom to decide what to do and how it should be done.

1. Which types or grades of job description are likely to be expressed mainly in terms of tasks?... in terms of functions?... in terms of responsibilities?
2. Classify the following as task, function or responsibility:
   (a) 'Ensure that company hygiene policy is adhered to with regard to equipment.'
   (b) 'Clean mincing machine daily.'
   (c) 'Ensure cleanliness of equipment.'
3. Write down one task, one function and one responsibility, each dealing with the maintenance/hygiene of premises, which might appear on a catering manager's job description.

Table 7.2 Job holder specification: hygiene characteristics for food handlers

Characteristics	Essential	Desirable
Physical appearance	Clean, neat, healthy	– –
Age	over 16	over 18 (permitted to clean prescribed dangerous machines)
Attainments	Basic Food Hygiene Certificateor (IEHO) or equivalent	Intermediate Food Hygiene Certificate, equivalent
Personality	Considerate, careful of detail	– –

Job specification

The next step is to decide what characteristics will be needed by applicants for the job defined in the job description. The job specification (more correctly called the job holder specification) lists these selection criteria. It is usual to group characteristics as 'essential' or 'desirable'. Areas of interest include physical characteristics, age, experience, attainments and personality. Hygiene characteristics for food handlers are shown in Table 7.2.

Medical requirements can also be included in the job specification. For instance it can be specified that the job holder should not be a *Salmonella* carrier. However, applicants should also be required to undergo a medical examination.

Advertisement

A hygiene qualification such as the IEHO Basic Food Hygiene Certificate should be included in the job specification. It should also be stipulated in the job advertisement. Advertisements should mention that food hygiene is a part of the job, and offer a reasonable rate of pay to attract a good quality of applicant.

Application form

Application forms should permit applicants to present their personal characteristics in a way that can be matched to the job specification. Forms should therefore have space and prompt lines for hygiene qualifications and medical details. However considerable detail is usually needed and it may be more practical to issue a separate medical questionnaire. An example of such a questionnaire is shown in Figure 7.1. Its function is to identify whether the applicant:

- Is a carrier of pathogenic organisms (*Salmonella typhi*, *Salmonella paratyphi*, *Shigella*, *Mycobacterium tuberculosis* or parasites).
- Has a chronic coughing illness.
- May have been exposed to pathogens and become a carrier.
- May have a residual infection from a recent illness.
- May have acquired a latent illness abroad.

Medical report forms should also require the name and address of the applicant's general practitioner and a signed, dated declaration.

Figure 7.1   Medical report form for food handlers

A   Have you had any of the illnesses listed below?

Illness	No	Yes	Details if 'yes'	
			When	Where (hospital/doctor)
Dysentery	[ ]	[ ]	....	....
Typhoid fever	[ ]	[ ]	....	....
Paratyphoid fever	[ ]	[ ]	....	....
Tuberculosis (TB)	[ ]	[ ]	....	....
Bronchitis/recurrent cough, asthma	[ ]	[ ]	....	....
Parasitic infection (e.g. worms)	[ ]	[ ]	....	....

B   Have any of your close family or friends suffered from the diseases listed above*?

Yes   [ ]   No   [ ]

Details, if 'yes' - ....
Name of illness: ....
Date and place ....
....
....

C   During the last two years have you had any of the illnesses listed below*

Illness	No	Yes
Vomiting, diarrhoea	[ ]	[ ]
Allergies or skin rash	[ ]	[ ]
Recurrent boils	[ ]	[ ]
Discharge from: nose	[ ]	[ ]
eyes	[ ]	[ ]
ears	[ ]	[ ]
other parts of the body	[ ]	[ ]

please specify ....

*Please consult your doctor before completing this if there is any doubt.

D   Please give details of any other illness or disability which may affect your work as a food handler

....
....
....
....

E   **Have you been abroad during the last two years?...yes [ ]   no [ ]**

Destination...
....

Duration ....

F   **Give the name and address of the doctor with whom you are registered.**

....
....
....

G   **I declare that the above details are correct to the best of my knowledge. If necessary I will agree to submit any specimens requested by the medical authorities for sampling.**

Signed_____ Date_____

Question

Is there a difference between being a pathogen carrier and having a latent illness?

Pathogen carriers differ from latent illness sufferers in that they are not likely to have symptoms of the illness. They have usually developed immunity through a subclinical infection. On the other hand, a latent illness may just be in its incubation period and could show symptoms at any time.

Forms should be printed in simple, straightforward language. If it is impossible to avoid complicated medical terms, the form should refer applicants to their GP, who can explain the questions and has access to their medical history.

Short-listing, testing and interviewing

Short-listing involves comparing different candidates' application details with the jobholder specification. Candidates with hygiene qualifications are to be preferred. Previous employment should also be considered. It may have been with a firm that has an excellent food hygiene reputation. Alternatively the individual may be out of work because the previous employer's premises are under a Closure Order. Previous employers' reputations need not necessarily reflect an applicants attitude; the duration of the previous employment may not have been long. However there certainly is a correlation between employer's attitudes to hygiene and the proportion of their staff with hygiene qualifications.

Testing of food handlers is not usual at interview, but it can be used to discover the level of an applicant's food hygiene knowledge. Multiple-choice or short-answer questions such as those used in the IEHO Basic Food Hygiene Certificate examination are suitable. Role-play situations may also be used to assess attitudes to hygiene.

Interviews should be well-prepared and should allow adequate time to ask questions concerning food hygiene knowledge and motivation. However, much important visual information is available at interview. *Candidate report forms* should be used to assess interviewees and must have adequate space for noting:

- Cleanliness, neatness and tidiness; for instance, clean, polished shoes often indicate a tidy attitude and an attention to detail. In particular, hands should be clean, with short, unvarnished nails.
- Bitten nails are evidence of constant hand-to-mouth contact.
- Apparent health; there should be no obvious signs of illness such as coughing or skin infections.
- Signs of heavy smoking – nicotine-stained fingers indicate poor personal hygiene as well as proneness to coughing and respiratory disease.
- Jewellery and cosmetics should be worn in moderation and tend to reflect the wearer's attitude to cleanliness.

References

Employees' behaviour and attitudes towards hygiene may not be specifically mentioned in previous employers' references. Nor can failure to mention them be taken as damning evidence on the basis of 'reading between the lines'. A better approach is to use standardized reference forms which draw out comments on all aspects, including food hygiene.

Medical examination

Successful job applicants should provide samples of faeces, and these should be analyzed for *Salmonella*, *Shigella* and evidence of parasites. Applicants should also have a chest X-ray to check for tuberculosis scars on the lungs. The medical examination is an alternative opportunity to complete a medical report form. If there is any doubt about any of the points on the form, the examining doctor can send for the applicant's medical notes.

Contracts and other documents

Issue and acceptance of a *letter of employment* constitutes a binding contract. At the same time, the employee should be sent:

1.   The company's hygiene policy.
2.   A statement of legal responsibility.

Hygiene policies are produced by many companies along the lines of, and often integrated with, health and safety policies. The latter are legally required under the Health and Safety at Work Act, 1974 (see Chapter 4). Hygiene policies usually contain a general policy statement requiring all employees to comply with the letter and spirit of the legislation. In addition, specific areas of concern may be listed. These are frequently identified under the general headings: plant, premises/equipment, personnel and process. Hygiene policies are discussed in greater detail in Chapter 9.

Statements of legal responsibility should quote or paraphrase the legislation which applies specifically to the hygiene and behaviour of food handlers. Under Section 29 of the Food Hygiene Regulations, 1970 employers commit an offence if they do not notify staff of their legal responsibilities. Statements of legal responsibility can be incorporated into company food hygiene policies. Staff should also be notified that breach of legal responsibility, and/or failure to abide by the company hygiene policy will result in disciplinary measures.

Question
What are the basic legal responsibilities of food handlers?

A statement of legal responsibility should inform staff that they must keep themselves and their clothing clean, cover cuts, avoid hand-to-mouth habits near food and notify the company if they contract prescribed diseases. Policies and statements of legal responsibility should be clearly written in simple English. They should describe employees' duties and responsibilities in an intelligible and practical way. Any threatened disciplinary action must actually take place. Otherwise the hygiene policy will have neither force nor credibility.

Summary – personnel selection

Do
- Include food hygiene components in job analysis and description.
- Include food hygiene qualifications in job specifications and on application forms.
- Maintain up to date (and past) medical records.
- Notify staff of their legal obligations.

Do not
- Take 'short-cuts' with interviewing, or other aspects of the selection process.

Training and education

Training is probably as important as selection for ensuring high quality staff. From the food hygiene point of view, staff should be trained to:

(i)   Keep themselves clean by proper personal hygiene;
(ii)   Keep foods clean and safe by avoiding cross-contamination;
(iii) Carry out food handling operations properly so that bacterial growth is minimized; and
(iv)   Work as a team with others.

Training means preparing individuals to do a job. It involves breaking the job down into component tasks. Workers are then taught to do each specific task. Often this just involves *psychomotor skills* (i.e. physical skills such as applying the correct pressure in rolling out pastry). Food hygiene aspects can be built into such training, in the form of particular movements or procedures. These will become virtually automatic and therefore effective, but the trainee will not have learned much transferable knowledge in the process.

Education strictly means providing knowledge, attitudes and skills which are complementary to jobs and tasks. In theory these do not need to be specific to any particular task or even to the job as a whole. Thus food hygiene education could be construed merely as studying bacterial structure, habitats and so on.

Practical food hygiene 'training' is neither pure training nor pure education, but has to lie somewhere between the two. Food handlers seldom have a single repetitive task to do, as do production-line workers.

Furthermore the range of tasks and the nature of each vary at different establishments, This affects training and particularly food hygiene training, which must be highly transferable within the range of tasks (Pope, 1974).

Teaching and learning

Successful training must result in *learning*. This depends on communication between the trainer and trainee, on the trainee's own efforts and on the skills and personal qualities of the trainer.

Communication is most effective if it uses several channels. Kubias (1982) gives the following estimates for communicated and practical learning. Trainees remember:

- 10% of what they read.
- 20% of what they hear.
- 30% of what they see.
- 50% of what they hear and see.
- 70% of what they say.
- 90% of what they say as they do a task.

The use of more senses (smell and touch for instance) can still further increase learning.

Trainees' own efforts can be channelled by building practical work into the training programmes. This is easier with job-specific training, aimed at mastery of a particular physical operation. Many practical, job-specific training programmes break down tasks into their elements. Trainees first learn to describe each element of the task and then to do it. Finally they perform the whole task, at the same time describing what they are doing.

Question
How precise do you think Kubias estimates for the % retention of learning actually are?

Measurement of learning is notoriously imprecise. A lot depends upon the type of assessment used, and how soon the measurement is made after the learning event. Some subjects are learned less efficiently and less permanently than others and of course different indviduals will learn at different rates. However there is no doubt that a combined use of telling and showing is more effective than just telling. Most effective of all is to have the trainees perform and simultaneously describe their actions.

Personal qualities of the trainer

The effective trainer should have good communication skills and a thorough grasp of the material to be taught. Ability to relate to the trainees and to understand their needs and interests is also very important. These qualities should enable the trainer to:

(i)   Set learning objectives for the trainees;
(ii)   Present materials in a clear, comprehensive way;
(iii) Ensure trainees' interest; and
(iv)   Reassure trainees of their ability to learn.

There is some argument whether good trainers are 'born or made'. However, it is generally recognized that experience and education can improve the effectiveness of all trainers.

Training strategies

In **trainer-centred** approaches the trainer communicates knowledge by means of lecturing, demonstrating, audio-visual aids etc. Trainees are not called upon to do more than attend and perhaps take notes. Some trainer-centred work is nearly always necessary to introduce a topic or to present essential information. However, learning is not very efficient unless lectures are supported with practical work by the trainees themselves.

Trainees can generally be assumed to have an attention span of 10–20 minutes. In practice this means that different individuals remember different 10–20 minute portions of a long lecture session. The meaning of a carefully structured sequence may be lost completely. Unfortunately, most of us came away from school or college with the idea that we learned what we learned from teacher-centred classes. We tend to forget all the coaching, question-and-answer and self-instruction that went into our education. Inexperienced, untrained trainers often rely heavily upon formal teaching, and trainees' learning suffers as a result.

A **trainee-centred** style involves activity on the part of the learner. This activity may be practical, written, oral or some combination of these three. It is most effective when trainees are required to think about what they are doing, or to accept some measure of responsibility for it.

Study example 7.2

Khimji (1986) describes training sessions in which the employees set up an experiment to compare the numbers of bacterial colonies from meat broth stored in a fridge, in the kitchen and in a *bain-marie*. The trainees evaluated the results and, through open questions, established the principle that the time and temperature of storage affects bacterial growth. This learning was reinforced by the trainees' ability to relate the principle to their work. Khimji's approach represents a trainee-centred style with elements of both education and training.

1. Why is it a trainee-centred style?
2. How could the same point be taught in a trainer-centred manner?
3. What elements of (a) pure 'training' and (b) pure 'education' are present?
4. How can the trainees use this principle in their work?
5. Undoubtedly learning in this way is effective. What disadvantages does the technique have?

The training cycle

Organizing and administering training consists of five stages:

- Assess training needs.
- Set objectives.
- Plan the training.
- Deliver.
- Evaluate.

Evaluation should relate back to the objectives and also forward, towards assessing future training needs. Thus the training process should be an ongoing cycle, as shown in Figure 7.2.

Assessing training needs

Three factors should be taken into account when considering training needs. External factors, requirements of the job and the requirements of individuals.

Figure 7.2   The training cycle

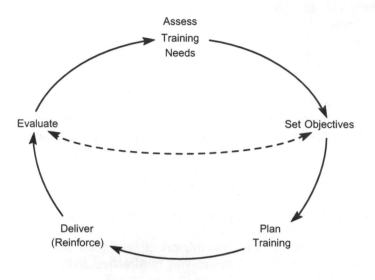

External factors include pressures from outside the company: legal and political pressures. For example, it is a legal requirement to provide food hygiene training for personnel who are directly responsible for handling food. Companies should also have a policy for ensuring that engineers who deal with food machinery are also trained. Food hygiene should also be integrated with other relevant areas covered by training policies, such as total quality management or customer-care schemes.

Job needs differ, depending on the process and the product. For example the production of ready-to-eat meals for chilled storage requires a higher level of hygiene awareness than normal, cook–serve restaurant work. Conveyor-belt production systems tend to require very specific task-oriented hygiene training. For most work however, non-specific, trans-ferable training is preferable. A need for training may become apparent from a fall in hygiene standards, noted by management through inspection checklists (see Chapter 5). Alternatively a critical inspection and Environmental Health Officer's report may pinpoint a need to update or consolidate training.

Individual training needs may be indicated by a general fall in the quality of recruited staff, due to demographic or other changes. They may be assessed by examining personnel records or by issuing a questionnaire. It may also be important to ensure that staff are capable of carrying out written instructions. The content of job cards may not be instantly clear to some individuals. Others may hide the fact that they cannot read, or cannot understand English. Low morale following the introduction of a new process may show a need for training, probably including hygiene. Training needs will also be identified during annual staff appraisal sessions, when staff should be encouraged to upgrade their food hygiene qualifications. There should be a general policy encouraging staff to attain the highest level of food hygiene training that they are able.

Setting objectives

Objectives should be based on identified training needs. They should be aimed at an identifiable, preferably measurable, end product. Thus objectives should specify the qualifications which staff will gain. Alternatively they may consist of practical outcomes: better hygiene standards reported by the checklist system, or more favourable Environmental Health Department reports. Achievement of measurable objectives is very good for morale. Objectives such as 'to improve morale' are unclear, unachievable and unlikely to have the desired effect. The objective '80% of personnel certificated by the end of the programme' is much better. Objectives should be set with subsequent evaluation in mind and any evaluation of training must take account of the original objectives.

Question
What is the relationship between objectives and evaluation?

Objectives set out to achieve a particular outcome. The function of evaluation is to check whether the outcome stated in the objectives has been achieved.

Planning the training

A training scheme has five aspects which require planning. These are:

(i)   Personnel scheduling;
(ii)   Type of training;
(iii)   Location of training;
(iv)   The trainer; and
(v)   The training programme.

Personnel scheduling involves co-ordinating who will be trained, and when. Training may remove workers from the job at irregular times, requiring changes of shift. Advanced courses require longer periods of study and tend to cause more disruption. Therefore very careful records and schedules must be kept in order to ensure that all staff achieve the maximum level of hygiene training.

Type of training may be on-the-job or off-the-job. On-job training is carried out actually at the workplace. It is usually assessed by a supervisor, by a training officer or by out-reach college staff, using a competence check-list. Food hygiene is an element of the nationally-validated on-job Caterbase programme. What is learned is immediately relevant to the job and reinforces company food hygiene policy. Learning is enhanced in the practical environment. On-job training is very good for staff induction and also for training in simple, repetitive techniques. However, the trainee/trainer ratio is low, so costs are high. Supervisors and training officers must be specially trained, and there is little opportunity to discuss theoretical issues or ask questions. Off-the-job training in the classroom is mostly used for food hygiene training programmes. Economical trainee/trainer ratios can be achieved and specialist trainers such as Environmental Health Officers may be used. There are opportunities to discuss the subject and to ask questions. Off-job training is potentially more flexible and transferable because it is not integrated with any specific task. However, trainees have to learn how to apply their new knowledge to their workplace, which is a disadvantage. Off-job training may not be an effective induction, if trainees are not familiar with the situation in which the food hygiene knowledge will be used. Induction training has to be very practically oriented in order to make it seem relevant.

Location of training may be on-the-job or in a classroom. Large organizations may find it most convenient to arrange for training on site. Off-job training requires a room large enough to comfortably hold about twenty trainees. This is the maximum which will permit individual attention, discussion or question-and-answer sessions. If there are not enough trainees from the large organization to make up a viable class, staff from smaller, neighbouring establishments can be invited. Alternatively classes may be held at the local Environmental Health Department offices or at a local college.

The trainer's job is not merely to inform or to communicate, but to *manage learning*. Thus an effective trainer, like an effective manager should be:

- Confident; and
- Competent.

Confidence depends mainly upon having a thorough grounding in the subject. This inspires confidence in the student and gives training sessions depth and credibility. Trainers should also have sufficient background knowledge to answer questions and offer reasoned arguments. The Institute of Environmental Health Officers requires that trainers for the Basic Food Hygiene Certificate have at least reached the level of the Advanced Certificate. Trainers for Intermediate and Advanced Certificate levels should have a degree or diploma in an appropriate subject.

Competence involves an understanding of educational principles. Trainers should have undergone a period of training covering the nature of learning, different styles of teaching, training aids etc. Ideal qualifications in this respect are the ***Diploma*** or ***Certificate in Education***, validated by the Council for National Academic Awards (CNAA) and by several universities. They usually involve one year's full-time or two years' part-time study. The City and Guilds of London Institute ***(CGLI) 730 Teacher's Certificate*** is offered by many centres as a one-year part-time course. The minimum qualification for group, off the-job training is the ***Training Diploma*** or ***Institute of Training and Development (ITD) Membership***. The Training Diploma can be built up in stages by means of short courses with the following titles:

- Training Practice and Assessment (5 day).
- Training Techniques Development (2 day).
- Managing the Training Function (3 day).

Programmes are offered by the Hotel and Catering Training Company (HCTC). Parallel courses are offered by the ITD and other bodies.

Planning the Training Programme involves deciding the content and the teaching/learning strategy. A training programme requires:

(i) A syllabus;
(ii) A scheme of work; and
(iii) Session plans.

A syllabus should contain practical food hygiene knowledge required by employees to do the job (Morrison and Carter, 1975). The IEHO, RSH and RIPHH offer a number of accredited food hygiene syllabuses, at several levels as shown in Table 7.3. These are nationally recognized and there is a degree of parity between the levels.

Table 7.3   Accredited off-job hygiene courses

	Minimum hours of study	Course work	Written exam(s) (hrs)	Oral exam
Institute of Environmental Health Officers (IEHO) Basic Course in Food Hygiene	6	×	1	×
IEHO Intermediate Certificate Course in Food Hygiene	18	×	2	×
IEHO Advanced Food Hygiene Certificate	36	√	3	√
Royal Institute of Public Health & Hygiene (RIPPH) Primary Certificate in Hygiene for Food Handlers	7	×	1	×
RIPPH Certificate in Food Hygiene and the Handling of Food	16	×	2	√
RIPPH Diploma in Food Hygiene	42	×	4	√
RIPPH Diploma in Hygiene Management (supplement to Cert. in FH + HF above)	×	√	×	×
Royal Society of Health (RSH) Certificate in the Hygiene of Food Retailing and Catering	22	×	1	√

Course content

Basic courses – bacteriology, food poisoning, prevention of contamination, pest control, cleaning etc.

Intermediate courses – more detailed microbiology, law, food preservation etc.

Advanced courses – training of food handlers, design of premises, equipment, management techniques.

Question
What is meant by 'parity between the levels'?

> All three bodies, the IEHO, RSH and RIPHH, offer basic, intermediate and advanced level courses. These qualifications are not identical, but the three levels can be taken as roughly equivalent in terms of what is learned.

Food hygiene is also included in catering courses such as **City and Guilds 706**. **Caterbase units**, designed for on-job training, contain a food hygiene component, accredited by the National Council for Vocational Qualifications (NCVQ). The general use of accredited syllabuses makes it easier to gauge the training level of new personnel. Choice of syllabus should take previous levels of training into account. Knowledge and skills are not learned or upgraded if they seem repetitive. However, staff will not learn if they are presented with new, apparently incomprehensible material. Syllabuses specify the topics to be covered and the way in which they are assessed. They usually give guidelines about teaching time and may suggest teaching methods. The order in which syllabuses are organized is frequently unhelpful in terms of learning. A scheme of work should be produced as part of the planning, to translate the syllabus into a more appropriate form.

A scheme of work should organize the topics of the syllabus so that they are presented in a way that assists learning. In practice this means progression:

- From the simple to the complex;
- From the practical to the theoretical; and
- From the familiar to the unfamiliar.

For example, the syllabus for basic level courses generally contains: Basic microbiology; Food poisoning; Prevention of contamination; Personal hygiene; Cleaning and disinfection; Premises, equipment, pest control; and Legislation.

Structures, growth requirements and binary fission of bacteria are theoretical, unfamiliar aspects. On the other hand, legal requirements will have been notified to food handlers with their contracts of employment. Thus one way to restructure the syllabus might be to begin with legislation, working from this to general hygiene and basic microbiology. The exact order is a matter of personal preference and also depends on the way each training section is structured. The scheme of work should specify the topics dealt with at each session (week by week and day by day). It may also provide some idea of the training strategies (lectures, discussion sessions or workshops) and training aids used (handouts, or audio-visual equipment). It may be useful to have the scheme typed and give out copies to trainees, together with a reading list and information sheets in a 'trainees' pack'. This will help them organize their background reading, notes and examination revision. It also inspires confidence and helps them to take the training programme seriously. An example of a scheme of work is shown in Figure 7.3.

Figure 7.3   Scheme of work for food hygiene training

Structure:	Six one-hour classroom-based sessions
Week No.	**Content/activities**
1	Laws affecting food handlers. Introductory discussion. Analysis of handouts.
2	Bacteria. Structure, requirements for growth, habitats. Completing handouts from OHP etc. class discussion.
3	Food poisoning – species, symptoms. Film, completion of questionnaires.
4	Preventing contamination and growth. Discussion, workshops/plenary. Items for code of practice.
5	Personal hygiene. Discussion, workshops/plenary. Items for code of practice.
6	Cleaning + disinfection. Workshops/plenary. Assemble code of practice. Revision.

Session plans should be produced for each training session, showing how the material allocated in the scheme of work is to be taught. The session should be divided up into a series of episodes and the plan should specify trainer and trainee activities for each of these episodes. Periods of formal teaching should be short: not more than 10–20 minutes, and should be interspersed with reinforcing activity by the trainees. A sample session plan is shown in Figure 7.4.

Figure 7.4   Session plan for food hygiene training

Objectives:

By the end of this session, trainees will be able to:

identify contamination/cross contamination routes and bacterial growth opportunity

relate contamination and growth to their own food handling practice

codify good food handling practice, in terms of bacterial contamination and growth

Plan:

5 minutes: Revise sources of contamination, from weeks 2 and 3 (Question/Answer)

5 minutes: Outline contamination routes, cross contamination, etc.

10 minutes: Discussion of routes present at trainees workplaces

5 minutes: Revise bacterial reproduction and growth requirement, from week 2 (Question/Answer)

10 minutes: Trainees identify common opportunities where bacterial growth may occour, at theit workplace – discussion

5 minutes: Issue and introduce handout on common contamination and growth opportunities in food preparation

10 minutes: Divide group into teams of three or four. Each team to brainstorm and identify aspects of good practice (for a code of practice) in:
                 handling raw foods
                 storing raw foods
                 handling cooked foods
                 storing cooked foods

10 minutes: Plenary session in which teams report back, their ideas are briefly discussed and recorded and the session summed up

Question

What is 'formal teaching' and why should these episodes be short?

In this context the term 'formal teaching' refers to lecturing, demonstration or presentation by the trainer. It must not exceed the trainees' attention span (20 minutes maximum).

Delivering training

Training 'delivery' may simply involve sending scheduled staff on courses offered by outside bodies. Courses delivered in-house however, should be carefully programmed and scheduled. Classroom sessions should involve extensive use of overhead projectors, videos and other visual aids. Trainees should be provided with course brochures, schemes of work and other handouts. Input by the trainer should be interspersed with activity by the trainees. Question and answer sessions should be used, where the trainer *poses* a question, *pauses* to allow the class time to think, then *pounces* on one (named) individual. Trainers should aim at interesting, well modulated presentation. They should be smartly dressed with a sympathetic, friendly manner. Annoying habits, like beginning each sentence with the same word: 'Well...' should be avoided.

Learning is easier for trainees if the material is presented logically, with each topic leading naturally into the next. Training sessions should be introduced with a welcome and should end with a summary of the session's learning and a friendly dismissal. Food hygiene topics are taught (but not necessarily learned) on several catering courses and trainees may feel they have covered the material before. Training may seem less repetitious if it is given a 'company' slant: 'This is the way we do it here'. *Reinforcement* of training can take several forms. *Retraining* may involve repeating some or all of the syllabus, in greater detail, or in a more job-specific way. *Discussion groups* may be used to translate information learned on a course into workplace terms. They may also provide useful suggestions about hygiene for the company. *Quality circles* are a type of discussion group aimed at identifying good practice and promoting quality. Discussion groups should be well prepared and well managed so that they do not wander off the subject. Food hygiene can be one of the areas considered in company-wide 'total quality' or 'customer care' programmes. It should be seen as applying to managers, engineers and other personnel as well as to food handlers. Food hygiene training may also be reinforced by *staff awareness schemes*, with notices, posters or badges.

Evaluation

The first priority is to evaluate the achievement of objectives. For example, evaluation of the objective 'to obtain certification for 85% of the food handlers during the training period' means comparing the actual certification rate with the original goal of 85%. It is usually also possible to comment on apparent, but not necessarily measurable aspects, such as improvements in general hygiene or staff morale. Evaluation should also consider the course itself. The trainees and trainer can be invited to comment on the teaching/learning and assessment strategies used. Numbers of applicants, participants, drop-outs, examination successes and failures should be recorded. The course should be reviewed and modified at each cycle.

Question
Why are both 'applicants' and 'participants' listed?

Not all of the applicants will necessarily come forward for the course, but their number provides an indication of the numbers originally interested, and perhaps of problems which prevented them attending.

Summary – training

Do
- Aim to train all those involved with food: food handlers, supervisors, managers, maintenance personnel etc.
- Aim to train all staff to their maximum ability and potential.
- Aim training at learning, rather than at teaching.
- Use accredited syllabuses.
- Use confident, competent trainers.
- Reinforce training.
- Evaluate training.

Do not
- Use long lecture or 'chalk and talk' sessions.

Motivating staff

Training will ensure that staff have adequate knowledge and skill to deal with food hygiene matters. Whether they apply that knowledge and skill depends upon their attitude. Training may improve staff attitudes but it cannot be relied upon to do so. A conscious programme of motivation at the workplace is much more effective in this respect (see, for example, White, 1974). Motivation should aim at changing the **culture** of an organization i.e. the attitudes held in common by the employees. Group pressures will then be exerted on individuals who fail to behave in the accepted, hygienic way.

A useful way of describing the motivational needs of individuals is that of Adair (1968), shown diagrammatically in Figure 7.5. Employees have **task needs**, **group needs** and **individual needs** and the job of an effective motivator is to make sure that all these needs are satisfied, and balance them so that positive attitudes are produced.

Figure 7.5   Three components of motivation

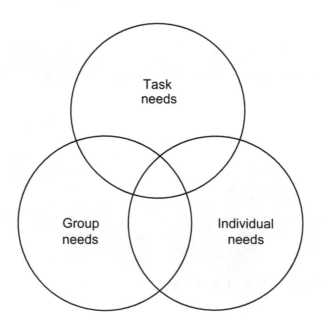

Source: Adair (1968).

Task needs

Employees must be supplied with the correct *equipment* for the job. Utensils, machines and storage equipment actually used in the production of food should be efficient, non-contaminating and cleanable. Equipment for cleaning and for personal hygiene must be of the most hygienic quality: e.g. anti-bacterial soap dispensers, towel dispensers, pedal-operated taps etc. In particular there must be no conflict between the tools and equipment available and the employees' training. Staff soon develop a 'why bother' attitude if, for example, they are taught the dangers of wooden chopping boards, but still use them at work. The same applies to protective clothing, which must be clean, smart and in good supply. Boots and gloves should be available for dirty work, with facilities for cleaning, disinfecting, drying and storage.

Jobs should be well-defined and clearly communicated. *Specified tasks* are easier to achieve and hence more motivating. An advantage of job cards is that they specify precisely what is to be done. Clear instructions for both food preparation and hygiene operations will help to motivate staff. Tasks should be broken down into components wherever possible. This makes them easier to comprehend and they can be tackled in stages. Job instructions which first require the individual to analyze the task tend to demotivate; so do large, seemingly unachievable tasks. Jobs should be well-scheduled, with adequate time allowances. Individuals who fail to meet time allowances should be trained and encouraged rather than simply disciplined.

Task outcomes should be easy to demonstrate and measure. For example, there should be clear criteria of cleanliness on job cards for hygiene tasks. Assessment checklists should specify standards in such a way that no doubt can arise whether they have achieved. Achievement of clearly set objectives is a strong motivator.

Group needs

Employees need to feel that they are working in a team which has common values and attitudes. Managers and supervisors should aim to build the team around them, not to be outside it. They can strongly influence food hygiene attitudes if they lead by example. For instance, managers should have at least as much food hygiene training as their staff. They should always wear specified protective clothing when they enter food production areas. Under no circumstances should they break any of the rules of hygiene behaviour.

Groups may be made more cohesive if they are allowed to discuss hygiene aspects and to make recommendations. Paid time should be allowed for this activity. This emphasizes the relevance to work and the importance of the activity to the manager. Discussion groups should be carefully focused, otherwise they will wander off the subject. This can be done by giving the group a particular goal such as defining hygiene standards, or producing hygiene awareness materials.

Codes of practice may be produced by a group to apply to all hygiene aspects of their work. A code of practice is a simple set of hygiene instructions for all to follow. In effect it is a written declaration of the group culture. Codes formulated by workers for their own particular situation have the greatest motivating value. The code should be engraved onto rigid plastic and firmly fixed to the wall. Papers or cards may tatter or come loose.

Competition between groups helps to improve their cohesiveness and focus their attitudes. Clean-as-you-go systems, which make departments responsible for the hygiene of communal equipment can be used as a basis for competitions. However, there must be an unequivocal system for scoring points. Winning departments may be rewarded with badges, specially designated work-wear (e.g. with coloured collars or pockets) or trophies. Trophies should be held in a conspicuous place with a notice indicating the current winners. Competition with other establishments is possible through good hygiene awards offered by local Environmental Health Departments. Success tends to consolidate the whole workforce into a single team, producing strong motivation.

Individual needs

Individuals are best motivated by means of the 'three Rs': *reward*, *recognition* and *responsibility*.

Reward means pay, gifts, perquisites or improved conditions. It is commonly supposed that pay is the most important motivator. However, tangible rewards are probably the least effective way of promoting food hygiene. It is seldom possible to define the reward criteria sufficiently objectively. Jealousy tends to break out among those who have been rewarded and those who feel they have an equal claim. This may destroy group morale and motivation. Rewards generally tend to demotivate if they acknowledge the individual at the expense of the group.

Recognition on an individual basis is more effective than a reward. The process of recognition can be shared with the group, for instance with certificates, badges or praise, bestowed during a group meeting. Recognition is not as tangible or as vital to well-being as reward. Therefore it is less open to jealousy, though rivalry between individuals may still disrupt group cohesiveness. Objective assessment of individual food hygiene contributions is always a problem.

Responsibility can be conferred by designating individual workers as 'food hygiene officers' on a permanent or rotating basis. Food hygiene officers may be freed from some of their normal duties or may accept the role in addition to their usual work. Individual responsibility means extra work and is therefore not a strong motive for jealousy. Nor does it require very precise measurement of individuals' food hygiene contributions. If the food hygiene officer is elected, rather than appointed, he or she will act as a focus, binding rather than weakening the group.

Study example 7.3

Maslow's pyramid, shown in Figure 7.6 (on page 262), places human needs in a hierarchy. Individuals first seek to fulfil the needs at the base of the pyramid, then move up towards the apex.

Exercise
Group the three Rs described above into Maslow's categories.

Summary – Motivation

Do
- Provide correct materials, equipment, clothing etc.
- Communicate and schedule tasks.
- Identify clear, objective goals wherever possible.
- Aim to promote a group culture aimed at food hygiene.
- Lead by example.
- Acknowledge individuals by conferring responsibility or by recognition.

Do not
- Emphasize individual, at the expense of group performance.
- Encourage jealousy by giving material rewards for subjectively assessed achievement.

Figure 7.6   Maslow's Pyramid: the hierarchy of human needs

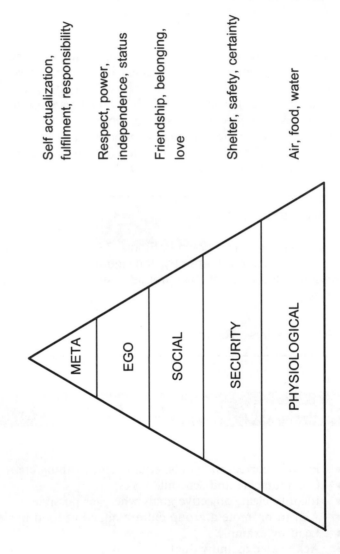

META — Self actualization, fulfilment, responsibility

EGO — Respect, power, independence, status

SOCIAL — Friendship, belonging, love

SECURITY — Shelter, safety, certainty

PHYSIOLOGICAL — Air, food, water

8 Food Hygiene and Process Management

Objectives

To identify the legal obligations of a food production manager with regard to the food production/service process. To discuss the principles and practice underlying analysis, planning and design of the production service process to ensure food hygiene and customer safety.

Introduction

There is more to food hygiene than the cleanliness of premises, plant, equipment and personnel. Food handling *processes* must also be controlled in order to ensure the safety of food produced. Process hygiene aims at:

- Minimizing contamination, by controlling the passage of food through the process.
- Preventing the growth of bacteria, by controlling the way food is stored and held.
- Destroying pathogens, by controlling the cooking process.

The Food Hygiene (General) Regulations 1970 make provision for process hygiene in two main ways. *Regulation 9* seeks to prevent food contamination as follows:

- Unfit food must be kept separate from food intended for human consumption.
- Open food must not be placed lower than 18 inches from the ground in forecourts or yards.
- Animal food must not be kept in food rooms unless in a suitable container.
- Open food must be protected from risk of contamination during delivery or sale.

Regulation 27 seeks to control the growth of bacteria during storage. It identifies two classes of high-risk foods and sets out maximum holding temperatures as follows:

- Storage at 5°C or below: cut, soft cheeses; chilled cooked items to be eaten cold; cured meat and fish (if not aseptically packed).
- Storage at 8°C or below: whole soft cheeses; chilled cooked items intended for reheating; yoghurts; salads; pies and sandwiches.

Alternatively, foods at risk may be held above 63°C or served within two hours. Two degrees' (± 2°C) variation is permitted during the transport of chilled foods.

Table 8.1   Factors contributing to outbreaks of food-borne illness in the UK and USA

Factor	% cases UK**	% cases USA*
Preparation too far in advance (G)	60.6	21
Storage at room temperature (G)	39.6	–
Inadequate cooling (G)	31.9	46
Inadequate reheating (D)	28.7	12
Contaminated processed food (C) (not canned)	19.1	5
Undercooking (D)	15.4	–
Inadequate thawing (D)	6.1	–
Cross contamination (C)	5.9	7
Improper warm holding (G)	5.7	16
Infected food handlers (C)	5.2	20
Use of left-overs (G)	4.8	4
Raw food consumed (C)	4.4	11
Extra large quantities prepared (G)	3.1	–
Contaminated canned food:		
(a) freshly opened (C)	2.8	–
(b) not freshly opened (G)	0.9	–
(c) not known (C/G)	0.7	–
Inadequate cleaning of equipment (C)	–	7
Inadequate cooking or processing (D)	–	16

* 1152 cases 1961–76 (Bryan, 1978)
** 1044 cases 1970–79 (Roberts, 1982)

Source: Bryan (1978) and Roberts (1982).

Because of their general nature the Regulations can make only minimal stipulations about the control of bacterial contamination, growth and survival. No provisions are made for the adequate destruction of bacteria. Effective process management involves much more precise control. This is achieved by analyzing the process in detail and setting up systems to ensure that it operates correctly.

Table 8.1 lists factors responsible for outbreaks of food-borne illness in the UK and USA. The letters C, G and D in the table refer to *contamination*, *growth* and *destruction* of bacteria, respectively. Table 8.2 shows the relative importance of these three processes. Bacterial growth is the most important cause of food-borne illness in both countries. Thus storage, holding and transport of food are probably the most important areas from the point of view of process hygiene. However, contamination routes and inadequate destruction of bacteria are clearly significant and cannot be neglected.

Table 8.2   Relative importance of bacterial contamination, growth and destruction events in food-borne illness outbreaks

Problem	UK		USA	
	no items	%* cases	no items	%* cases
Contamination	6	39	5	50
Growth	8	147.3	4	87
Destruction	3	50.2	2	28

* These figures are simply obtained by adding the percentages given in Table 8.1. Many items are counted under more than one heading, so that these percentages do not add up to 100.

Source: Data extracted from Table 8.1, opposite.

Question

Why is the emphasis on contamination and destruction different in the two studies?

Results of the two studies are different, partly because of statistical variation, partly due to the way the data was gathered, and partly because practices are different in the UK and USA. The main point is that bacterial growth during holding and storage seems to cause more outbreaks than any of the other factors.

The microbiological quality of catered food depends on the extent of bacterial contamination, growth and survival within the production process. A primary responsibility of the food premises manager is therefore to ensure the hygiene of the process. This chapter describes how this may be achieved, using the following steps:

1. Defining the system.
2. Planning the menu.
3. Planning the production process.

Defining the system

The first step in identifying and solving process hygiene problems is to define the production process. Systems theory offers the most helpful basis for classifying catering operations. It enables inputs, outputs and subsystems to be identified and simply represented, giving a clear overview of the process. Contamination vectors can be identified among the raw materials used, some of which are not 'raw' at all. A clear representation of the system should indicate storage, preparation, cooking and holding operations, all of which affect food hygiene.

Definition of the system boundary may enable the manager's legal responsibilities to be identified by considering whether these are inside or outside the production/service system. For example, warranty obligations of suppliers, or opportunities for product abuse by customers may be identified.

Dwyer *et al.* (1977) use a modified systems approach to classify US food service facilities. It was originally developed for assessing energy use, but is also appropriate for food hygiene management. The systems features identified by Dwyer are shown in Table 8.3.

Inputs and subsystems can be interlinked using a classification developed by Paulus (1978). Inputs, intermediates and outputs are designated as *ready to prepare* (RP), *ready to cook* (RC), *ready to regenerate* (RR), *ready to serve* (RS), or *ready to eat* (RE). Together, Dwyer's and Paulus's techniques provide a simple way of describing any food production/service operation. Figure 8.1 uses this approach to represent a food production/service system (the area within the rectangular boundary). The system has a variety of inputs, representing all of Paulus's processing stages. Some of the intermediates are frozen and some chilled, but the only type of output shown is ready-to-eat food. This is by no means the only possibility. Catering outlets may retail foods in any state. For example, fish and chip shops sometimes sell raw fish as well as the cooked product. Other units may sell ready-to-cook or ready-to-regenerate products.

Table 8.3   Systems features of catering classification

Systems Feature	Description
Input (procurement)	Continuum of 'raw' material, ranging from unprocessed to completely processed
Subsystems (processing)	Production, hot/ chilled/frozen storage, reheating, portioning
Output (distribution)	Transport to retail outlets, to satellite kitchens, direct to consumers

Source: After Dwyer *et al.* (1977).

Figure 8.1   Systems model describing a food production process

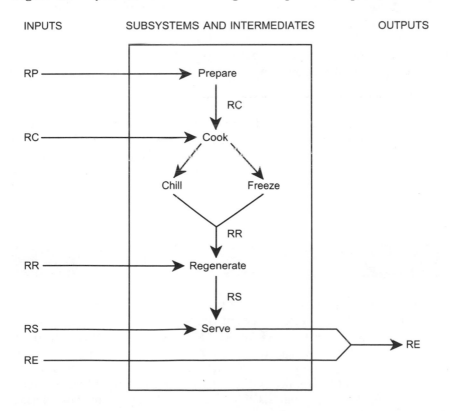

Study example 8.1.

The catering manager at a large car factory buys in a wide range of foods, varying from completely raw to direct retail items. Most of the food produced is consumed immediately in the staff restaurant.

  However, the unit also sells sandwiches which can be taken back to the workplace. In addition it operates vending machines throughout the factory, which supply drinks and microwavable meals.

1. Taking this factory catering unit as an example of a production/service system, identify two examples each of the five classes of system input: ready to prepare, ready to cook, ready to regenerate, ready to serve and ready to eat.
2. Identify one example each of the five classes of system intermediate.
3. How many classes of system output are there? Give examples.
4. Draw a systems diagram linking inputs, subsystems and outputs.
5. Several locations are possible for the system boundary, depending on what is sold through the vending machines and who is responsible for these machines. Explain this.

  The systems approach provides an overview of the production/service process. The next step is to look at the process in more detail. It is best to approach this by first studying the menu, which has an important influence over the types of raw materials used and the way they must be treated. Planning the menu, or style of menu, is thus the essential first step to a detailed plan of the process.

Planning the menu

Menu analysis usually concentrates upon the popularity and profitability of menu items. Analysis techniques of this kind may be applied to menus three or four times per year. (Hayes and Huffman, 1985). However, there is a danger that profitability may become the overwhelming consideration in menu design. This is particularly likely if a revenue-maximizing formula is frequently applied. Other aspects, such as food hygiene, may be overlooked in the analysis. This may be avoided by considering hygiene and safety aspects in a separate menu review, additional to reviews aimed at marketing or efficiency. Menus influence the hygiene and safety of food production directly or indirectly, through the:

- Number of items.
- Type of items.
- Equipment required.
- Daily sequence.
- Volume of production.

Number of items

Menus frequently contain more items than necessary. An overloaded menu may stretch staff skills, reducing their ability to cope. As a result less care may be taken in handling food, resulting in bacterial contamination, growth or survival. Over-production of menu items may result in the retention of a large number of foods in small quantities. This overloads storage space and hinders the orderly stock rotation of raw materials and cooked foods. Inadequate stock rotation and control may result in spoiled, contaminated raw materials entering the production process. Stores personnel may be overworked, so that spoilage is not noticed. The more menu items, the more complex the process and the more difficult it is for the manager to control hygiene and safety standards. Planning the menu must involve conscious decisions about the number of items. Reducing the number of menu items may also reduce costs, by reducing stock levels and helping to control over-production.

Question
What factors tend to increase menu size?

It may be necessary to respond to competition by offering customers a wider choice. Adaptation in a declining market may involve catering to a wider range of market sectors. An alternative strategy in such a situation is new product development. All of these strategies tend to increase the number of products on the menu.

Type of items

As was discussed in Chapter 3, some raw materials are more likely to contain biological or chemical contaminants than others. For example, raw chicken is more likely to carry *Salmonella* than other raw meats. In general, raw ingredients are more likely to contaminate other foods than are processed ones. Menu design offers the opportunity to minimize the number of contaminated ingredients. For instance, in theory the substitution of red meat for chicken should reduce the likelihood of *Salmonella* entering the premises. Unfortunately this would increase costs for a minimal microbiological benefit. However, it is sometimes possible to use prepacked or processed ingredients instead of raw ones. Substitution of this kind must not impair quality or reduce customer satisfaction. The former is an offence under the Food Safety Act, 1990. The latter is harmful from a marketing point of view. Another approach may be to change from large to small purchase packs. This may be particularly appropriate with high-cost ingredients such as meats. It might be tempting on cost grounds to keep large packs which have partially spoiled, where small ones would be discarded. Use of small, portion-controlled packs of steak, for example, can be designed into the process at the menu-planning stage.

Equipment required

Many kitchens acquire their equipment in an *ad hoc* fashion over several years. Frequently there is a mismatch in capacity between different processing stages. For instance, a boiler may produce three or four times the amount of cooked potato that a mixer can mash at one time. Cooked potato must then wait in bulk while smaller batches are mashed. Delays before and after mashing offer opportunities for contamination and for bacterial growth. Process mismatch may become a serious problem if the finished product is to be kept for some time, or chilled or frozen and regenerated before serving. Menu design should anticipate potential process mismatch. Volume of cooked product likely to be needed should be considered at the outset and output adjusted to the available equipment. Alternatively, new equipment should be planned to cope with the new output required. This is particularly important with foods containing meat, fish or dairy products. The most serious process mismatches are those involving hot- or cold-holding equipment. Serious bacterial growth may occur if space in *bain-maries*, hot cabinets, refrigerators etc. is inadequate.

Daily sequence

Some items are too costly to throw away at the end of the working day. Often they can be used up satisfactorily the following day provided that the menu is planned to allow for this possibility. Bryan and McKinley

(1979) report that where roast beef from the previous day was incorporated into stroganoff or curry, the product remained microbiologically safe. Surviving bacteria are killed by the next day's cooking, provided joints of beef are quickly chilled at the end of the day and are kept adequately refrigerated. However, large food items such as roasts cool slowly unless a blast chiller is used. Bacteria can then multiply during the slow cooling itself and in subsequent cold-holding, reheating and hot-holding. Menu design requires clear decisions from the manager about what can or cannot be kept and these must be communicated to kitchen staff.

Volume of production

Volume of production should be within the output capacity of the kitchen, equipment and staff. Otherwise excessive production demands may stretch equipment, manpower and working space to the limit. Human error due to stress and fatigue may result in unhygienic practices or careless time/temperature control. In addition, processing and storage equipment may be overloaded. Lack of adequately sized equipment may result in multiple batches of food being processed, with long delays during which the food is at risk. Stock rotation, storage, processing efficiency and the hot- and cold-holding of foods may all be adversely affected. Production volume is a particular problem at peak periods such as Christmas, at banquets and on special occasions. There is a tendency to oblige customers and to compete for business by stretching production capacity to its limit. In fact outbreaks of food-borne illness, particularly of those involving *Salmonella* are reportedly more common at banquets than at other times (Roberts 1982, Munce, 1981). Menus for banquets and festive occasions should be carefully planned within production limits. They should avoid raw materials known to be contaminants, or at least control their use as far as possible. For example, whole roast turkey may have to be produced the day before it is required, because of limitations of staff shifts/cooking times. This is not practicable on food hygiene grounds unless:

(i)   Rapid chilling equipment is available;
(ii) There is adequate refrigerator space for overnight cold storage;
(iii) The turkeys can be reheated right through to at least 72°C before serving; and
(iv) There is adequate refrigerator space for defrosting the frozen birds.

If these facilities are not available, smaller birds such as chickens, which can be cooked and served the same day, should be used instead.

Even if capacity is not exceeded in any one service period, problems may result from consistently working to the limit. Busy periods may not leave adequate time for thorough cleaning and disinfection. Storage capacity tends to fill up with over-produced items unless there is a scrupulous attitude to housekeeping. Shift work makes it difficult to ensure that stored, over-produced foods are rotated or discarded. It is very difficult to know the limit of production exactly. This is particularly true where there is an extensive menu and different items make different demands on equipment. Best practice is to design kitchen and equipment slightly larger than is necessary for the maximum output likely to be required. It is then always possible to work within the physical limits of capacity. In any case the manager must estimate the maximum acceptable production level and ensure that it is never exceeded.

Question
On what basis could such a decision be made?

Such a calculation can be made by starting with the capacity of the available equipment and working out the number of covers which can be produced. From this it is possible to estimate a realistic seating capacity which will not overload the facilities.

Planning the production process

When the menu has been considered, the process itself can be planned. Four main stages are involved:

- Analyzing the process.
- Eliminating or minimizing contact of contaminants with cooked food.
- Eliminating or minimizing bacterial growth opportunities.
- Ensuring the destruction of microorganisms, parasites and toxins.

Analyzing the process

Process analysis should take into account everything that happens to food from its purchase as a raw material to the time it is sold. In the case of retail or vended items the caterer may wish to know what happens after the food is sold (consumer abuse of the product can sometimes occur). Food hygiene problems may occur during delays in the production process and during hot- or cold-holding prior to service. The objectives of process analysis are as follows:

- To identify all the individual process operations.
- To classify the operations in terms of the hygiene problems they might cause.
- To rationalize hygiene aspects.
- To eliminate all avoidable hygiene problems.

The usual way to analyze processes is by *flowcharting*. The ideal flowchart should possess three characteristics. It should show the *sequence* of events, so that causes and effects become visible. It should show the *spatial layout*, i.e. it should be superimposable upon a kitchen plan, so that contacts between contaminants and cooked foods can be identified. It should also indicate **time delays** and any possible *time/temperature* problems. Various styles of flowchart can be used, but in general no single style adequately shows all these characteristics. It is often desirable to use more than one of the following charting techniques.

Box style flowchart

In a 'box' style flowchart, the process operations are drawn as boxes, linked by arrows. An example of this type of chart is shown in Figure 8.2.

Figure 8.2 'Box' style flowchart for preparing and roasting a frozen beef joint

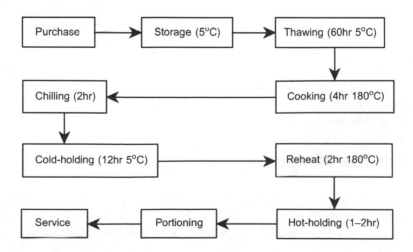

In its most basic form the chart only shows a sequence of events. However, other information can be incorporated into it. For example, boxes which represent particular contamination or time/temperature problems can be marked. It is also possible to include symbols for the equipment which is used, and for delays in the process. However, the main advantage of a box flowchart is its simplicity. Adding symbols may be confusing. In the confines of the box the symbols may become illegibly small. Box flowcharts cannot be used to show the actual movement of food items about the kitchen. Therefore contamination pathways involving contact between raw and cooked foods may not be revealed by this type of chart.

ASME symbols

ASME symbols (developed by the *American Society of Mechanical Engineers*) are an alternative way of representing process operations (Addison, 1971). They were originally developed for flowcharting manufacturing processes, but can also be used to chart the flow of paperwork or other processes in the hospitality industry. Figure 8.3 shows a chart of a food production process. ASME symbols have the advantage that delays and storage operations are quickly recognizable. This makes them appropriate for analyzing food hygiene problems. Like the box flowcharts, ASME symbols cannot be used to show up unsuspected contact between cooked and raw food during transit in the kitchen.

Avery diagram

Avery (1974) has developed a system of flowcharting which can be superimposed on an outline kitchen plan. The format, shown in Figure 8.4 uses differentiated arrows to show flow of food, food and dishes, waste etc. This is therefore a very powerful analytical technique. Cross-contamination routes are clearly indicated because it is relatively easy to identify contaminants. Flow-lines showing the interaction between contaminants and foods at risk can be drawn on a scale plan of the production area.

Paulus diagram

Paulus's (1978) classification of foods (mentioned earlier in this chapter) provides another way to flowchart processes. This approach uses five categories of food undergoing processing i.e. ready-to-prepare, ready-to-

Figure 8.3   ASME flowchart for preparing and roasting a frozen beef joint

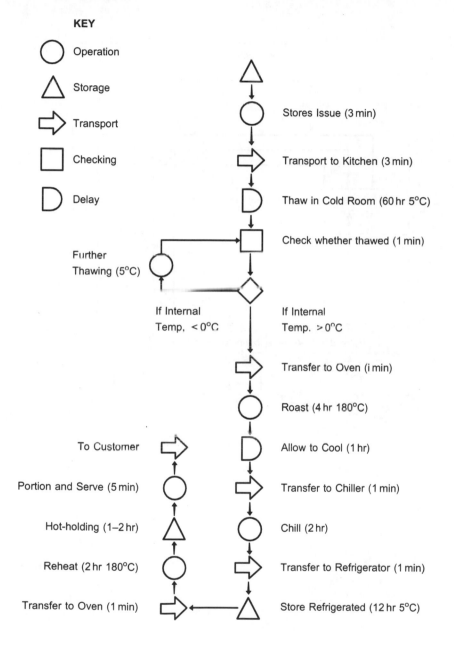

Figure 8.4 Avery diagram of food production flow

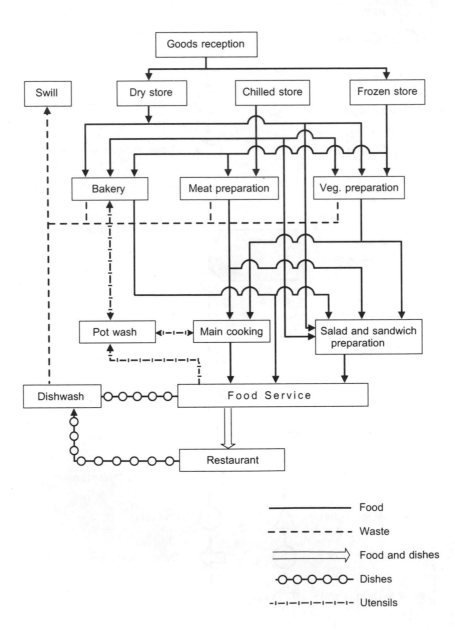

Source: Milson and Kirk (1979).

cook, ready-to-heat/regenerate, ready-to-serve and ready-to-eat. Thus it is possible to divide food production into successive stages, linked by labelled arrows. This is a helpful way to represent systems (see Figure 8.1, p. 267). Paulus diagrams have the potential to reveal cross-contamination by showing contact between processed foods, intermediates and cooked foods. However the example shown in the figure does not present much detail and it may become very complex if it attempts to do so. Diagrams of the type shown are difficult to superimpose on a kitchen plan, making spatial representation hard to achieve.

Black and white reproduction limits the detail that can be shown here. Using coloured felt pens it is possible to clearly indicate the flow of cooked and raw foods. For example, five different coloured pens can be used to correspond with Paulus's five 'ready-to' categories of food. This may be particularly useful in food hygiene terms, as many ready-to-prepare or ready-to-cook items may be serious contaminants of ready-to-regenerate or ready-to-eat foods. Using colour codes rather than symbols permits charts to be superimposed upon an actual kitchen plan. Alternatively the progress of particular contaminants such as raw poultry can be highlighted. Avery's system is also helpful for showing the flow of waste, dirty dishes and other potential sources of contamination. Using these techniques production activities may be directly related to systems theory. At the same time contamination risks can be effectively revealed.

It is often helpful to use different flowcharting styles to identify all the risks in a given process. Boxes or ASME symbols are useful for identifying sequence and timing. However contamination pathways can often only be analyzed with a spatial flowchart (i.e. one which can be superimposed upon a kitchen plan). The best technique to use for this purpose is a modified Avery or Paulus diagram as described above.

Process flow should take into account the clean and dirty areas and work flow patterns discussed in Chapter 5. An extensive menu makes the job more difficult, which is why menu analysis should be undertaken before the process itself is studied. Analysis then allows the individual operations which make up a process to be identified and classified. The process can then be rationalized by eliminating unnecessary operations, particularly those involving contamination and time/temperature risks.

Question
How does this relate to the growth and destruction of bacteria?

Time/temperature risks are of two types. Too much time between 5–63°C permits bacterial growth. Too little cooking time or an inadequate temperature may mean inadequate destruction of bacteria.

Study example 8.2

A pub kitchen buys frozen multi-portion trays of lasagne. These are stored an average of 3 days in the freezer before use. They are then transferred to the refrigerator overnight to thaw, and remain there between 12 and 36 hours (the unit works Monday–Saturday). Before cooking, the trays are removed to position A (Figure 8.5, opposite) on the preparation table, where they stay for an average time of 30 minutes. They are then baked for 40 minutes at 210°C. Finally the trays of lasagne are removed from the oven to position B on the preparation table. When they have cooled for 5 minutes they are divided into portions with a knife. Still in the tray they are transferred to a heated cabinet on the assembly and service counter. They remain here for 5–60 minutes waiting for a customer. The lasagne is then plated with salad and served.

1. Produce an ASME flow chart showing the progress of the lasagne from purchase to sale. What does the chart tell you about possible bacterial growth?
2. Use coloured pens to show the Paulus classifications as the lasagne passes through the kitchen (Figure 8.5). What does this chart tell you about possible contamination?

Avoiding contamination

Food flow diagrams like those of Avery show up the distances travelled by foods during preparation. These distances should be shortened as much as possible. In addition, all points where raw food, dirty dishes or waste cross the path of cooked foods should be eliminated. Mutual storage points (e.g. the same cold store for raw and cooked food) must also be eliminated or carefully controlled (i.e. by ensuring that raw and cooked foods are kept separate, or raw stored below cooked). Equipment can frequently carry contamination. If it is possible to avoid using the same slicer, mincer or table for both raw and cooked food, this should be done. Otherwise foolproof cleaning systems must be devised. Equipment such as chopping boards and knives should be colour-coded, as described in Chapter 6. Contamination via the hands of kitchen staff is greatly reduced by effective personal hygiene. This can be achieved by training, inspection and motivation, as discussed in Chapter 7. Flow diagrams will indicate transfer of staff and materials between clean and dirty work-centres in the production area. Such routes should be restricted by means of physical barriers, i.e. walls or screens, as described in Chapter 5. Hand

Figure 8.5   Kitchen plan for Study example 8.2

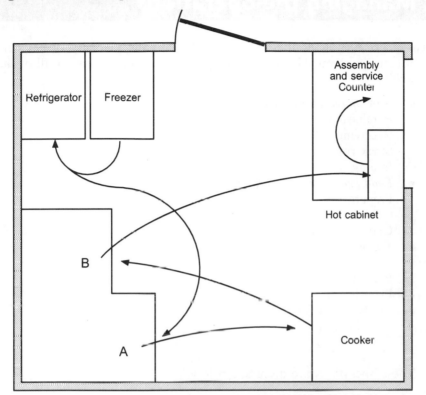

basins with instructions to wash should be located where staff are to pass
barriers from 'dirty' to 'clean' kitchen areas.

Avoiding storage and holding risks

Preparing food too far in advance is the single main cause of poisoning
from catered food, causing over 60% of known incidents. Delays in the
process can be identified using an ASME style flowchart. They must be
eliminated as far as possible by carefully scheduling and planning
production. For scheduled cold storage there must be adequate blast
chilling and refrigerator facilities. Proper planning will remove many
unnecessary food hygiene risks. However, the most carefully planned
menu and production processes may still cause outbreaks of food-borne
illness. The only way to ensure complete food safety is by careful day-to-
day management of the process operations themselves.

Managing the operations

An earlier section of this chapter dealt with the diversity of catering production systems. However, most processes contain some or all of the following:

- *Raw materials operations*:
  Purchasing
  Receiving
  Stock rotation
  Issuing
- *Food processing operations*:
  Preparation
  Cooking
  Chilling and freezing
- *Plating/Service operations*:
  Hot-holding
  Portioning
  Plate layout
- *Product handling*:
  Cold-holding
  Transport

These operations are discussed below.

Purchasing

Suppliers should be selected on a similar basis to that used for contract services (see Chapter 5). Criteria for choice include price, quality, reliability and frequency of deliveries. The criteria should be organized in order of priority and used to produce a *supplier specification*. This forms the basis for selecting the most suitable supplier. Product quality, efficiency and hygiene must be given due consideration. Selection based on price alone is hardly ever adequate. Ideally, the manager should also visit suppliers' premises to check hygiene conditions there. If this is not possible, other customers, or the local Environmental Health Department should be contacted. The latter will generally be able to comment on the hygiene and quality of products such as meats and bread.

Raw material quality should be specified before purchases are made. A *purchase specification* should be produced, containing the following:

- Name of the raw material.
- Photograph showing its appearance.

- Quality designation or product type,
  e.g. fresh, frozen, UHT, canned etc.
- Level of preparation, e.g. trimming of meat, boning of fish etc.
- Size/process level, e.g. whether whole, chopped, chipped etc.
- Weight.
- Packaging.

Most of these aspects have some impact upon food hygiene and this should be taken into account when producing the specification.

The purchase specification should be agreed with the supplier when the contract is drawn up. Another important aspect to consider may be the way the ingredients will be delivered. For instance, meat should be transferred directly to the cold store and bread trays should not be stacked on the ground.

Receiving

Incoming goods should be inspected carefully to make sure that they correspond to the purchase specification. This is particularly important when a new supplier is used, as quality from a less reputable supplier may deteriorate, once he is sure he has secured the business. Designated, trained raw material inspectors should be used, even if this is only a secondary function in an individual job description.

There should be a manual, based on the purchasing specification, clearly stating what the inspector is to look for. A comparison photograph of the product should also be available. Acceptance/rejection criteria should be clearly laid down. Authorized inspection staff must be on hand whenever deliveries are expected. A clear procedure should be laid down for goods rejection, i.e. paperwork for recording the event and for obtaining a credit note. Accepted goods should be labelled or tagged and stored immediately. Tags or labels should bear the date of receipt, and a 'use by' date. Packaging of incoming goods should be checked before the food is physically located behind the last received items. Storage must be at the appropriate temperature for the commodity and comply with the law.

Question
What are the legal restrictions on storage?

The Food Hygiene (General) Regulations, 1970 divide high-risk foods into two groups, which should be stored below 5°C, or below 8°C respectively. Safe storage temperatures for commodities were discussed in more detail in Chapter 3.

Stock rotation

Food stocks should be held for the minimum possible length of time. Any deterioration must be quickly identified and dealt with. Most effective stock rotation systems use the FIFO (first in, first out) principle. Incoming items are dated and physically placed behind older stock, so that rotation occurs naturally. Regular stock inspections should examine the smell, colour and general appearance of raw materials. Frozen items should be checked for 'freezer-burn' and cans for blowing (see Chapter 3). If deterioration is noticed there must be clear report system so that sensitive items such as meats can be discarded. Management must be prepared to admit and accept wastage. If this is not budgeted there will be a tendency to use spoiled ingredients. Stores procedures should be well documented, with clear codes and job cards. There should be records showing stock levels, as well as details of rejected or waste foods. Documentation enables quick investigation and review of the system if there are problems such as excessive wastage.

Issuing

Ingredients should be issued in strict FIFO order. Both the issuer and the user should have some way of reporting any deterioration. Some operations use daily issue report sheets to summarize food costs and these may also be used to document deterioration and wastage. Alternatively separate quality reports may be attached to the issue report sheets if deterioration is noticed. Quality reports should show the name of the ingredient and state what was wrong with it. They should also indicate whether the raw material was actually used. Unused ingredients should be kept for inspection. Raw material wastage is a problem because it may disguise fraud and pilfering. Incidents involving costly food ingredients must be investigated carefully. At the same time there must be sufficient wastage allowance, otherwise staff may be under pressure to use spoiled or unnecessarily contaminated raw materials.

Preparation

If purchasing, storage and issue are well managed, raw foods are not likely to spoil between delivery and use. Preparation areas of kitchens are not usually as contaminated as the raw foods themselves (Mendes *et al.*, 1978). Thus further contamination of raw materials at this stage is unlikely. However, processed foods are at risk in preparation areas. For instance, can-openers can be dangerously contaminated so that cans are infected with bacteria the moment they are opened. Cans and other sterile packaging should be opened with hygienic equipment in a separate area, away from raw food-stuffs. Preparation areas should be designated as 'dirty' areas (see Chapter 5) as they are a potential site for the contamination of cooked foods.

Food can deteriorate between preparation and use so it is important that preparation is not scheduled too far in advance. Particular care should be taken with thawing frozen foods. Thawing should always be carried out in a refrigerator. Otherwise the surface of the food may warm up sufficiently for bacteria to proliferate there, even though the centre of the food is not yet thawed. A special refrigerator should be provided if thawing is required on a regular basis. However thawing takes much longer in the refrigerator than at room temperature. It is essential that times and procedures are adequately laid down and that the long delays required for refrigerator defrosting are taken into account for each menu item. Standard thawing procedures can be printed on job cards. They should specify thawing times, unwrapping procedure and precautions to be taken with drip or thawing liquid. For instance, contaminated containers must be sterilized and surfaces disinfected. As an alternative to special thawing job instructions, preparation such as thawing can be regarded as an integral part of the production process. Thawing instructions will then be incorporated into standard recipes rather than being 'processes' in their own right.

Cooking

Cooking processes should be carefully monitored. Bacteria may survive in the food if times or temperatures are inadequately controlled. Kitchen staff should be issued with digital probe thermometers such as that shown in Figure 8.6 on page 284.

Temperatures should be measured at the **geometric centre** of large items such as roasts (see Figure 8.7 on page 285). It is also very important to check temperatures of reheated dishes containing meat or poultry. The materials of some utensils may contaminate food with chemical poisons. For instance, copper or aluminium from cook-ware may dissolve in the cooking liquor of acid foods (see Chapter 1).

Incorrect cooking will spoil food quality as well as jeopardizing safety. Controlling cooking means drawing up standard recipes which clearly define the materials and methods used. Standard recipes should specify:

(i)   The name of the dish or menu item;
(ii)   Ingredients;
(iii) Quantities;
(iv)   Equipment to be used;

(v)   Methods;
(vi)   Hygiene requirements;
(vii) Cooking time; and
(viii) Yield.

Modern ovens have integral probe thermometers. These should be used wherever possible to monitor time/temperature relationships during cooking. Times and desired food temperatures should appear on standard recipes and other documentation so that temperature-monitoring equipment is properly used. Microwave ovens may be a particular problem due to uneven distribution of the electric field within the cabinet, and of heat within the food (see Chapter 3). Sensitive preparation methods such as the thawing of frozen meat, poultry or fish should be included in standard recipes, as mentioned in the previous section. If thawing has to be scheduled days in advance, this fact should be noted

Figure 8.6   Digital probe thermometers

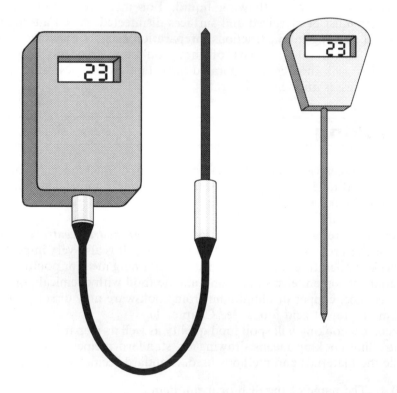

The thermometers are inexpensive, yet strongly built to withstand vigorous use. The clear, readable display gives accurate temperatures between −5°C and 120°C. Probes are of robust, food grade stainless steel.

on the recipe, as well as the actual cooking times required. A standard recipe is a very powerful management tool. It can be used to control issues of materials, costs and quality as well as food safety. Some restaurant chains, particularly in the fast food sector, use centralized recipe standardization to ensure consistency of quality from outlet to outlet. Standardization of recipes is equally beneficial for ensuring quality at a single outlet from day to day. Chefs should be encouraged to produce and update their own standard recipe cards. This not only gives better control over the process but also ensures continuity when staff changes occur. The number of recipes required depends on the number of menu items. A policy of using only standard recipes tends to control the number of items and to rationalize production. Standard recipes should contain food hygiene notes wherever possible. This helps to reinforce the food safety message to staff.

Figure 8.7   Geometric centre of an irregularly shaped object

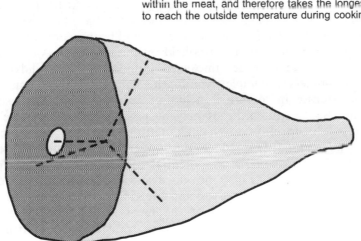

The geometric centre is at the deepest mean point within the meat, and therefore takes the longest time to reach the outside temperature during cooking.

Question
What sort of notes are required?

Standard recipes for operations requiring much handling of food should stress personal hygiene. Critical storage and cooking procedures should have clearly stated times and temperatures which must be adhered to. Particular care should be specified with high-risk foods.

Hot-holding

Incorrect hot-holding of foods is one of the commonest bacterial growth opportunities. Food must remain above 63°C at all times right through to its centre, in order to prevent bacterial growth and spore germination. Hot holding temperatures must therefore be clearly specified and regularly checked. The only way this can be adequately accomplished is to issue staff with digital probe thermometers, as described in the previous section. Meats, fish, sauces and rice are particularly at risk from incorrect hot-holding. Regular checks should be made of items:

- In *bain-maries*.
- On hot tables.
- In hot cabinets.
- Under infra-red lamps.
- Over flames.

Instructions for checking temperatures can be kept next to the equipment or included in the standard recipe. There should be a system for discarding items which are known or suspected to have been below 63°C for more than 30 minutes. Temperatures should be measured at the likely coolest point e.g. the top of roasts held on the hot table. Any part of a container of sauce or other thickened liquids (or semi-solids) which cannot be immersed completely into the *bain-marie* is at risk. Some items deteriorate in texture if held hot for too long. For example hollandaise sauce will curdle. It may be possible to prepare one large batch, divide it up into convenient quantities and chill these for later reheating as required. This reduces the danger that any batch will remain too long in the *bain-marie*. A potential difficulty with digital probe thermometers is that they may introduce surface bacteria into the centre of thick items such as meat (Bryan and McKinley, 1979). This cannot be avoided and is not a problem if the meat is handled quickly and correctly. However, the probes may also transfer bacteria from one food to another, possibly resulting in serious contamination. There should be a specified sterilizing procedure for probes, e.g. they should be kept in a chemical sterilant, removed and rinsed just before use. Staff should be trained in the correct use and sterilization of thermometers. Foods in hot-holding should be rotated on a FIFO basis like raw materials.

Some foods are allowed to stand and cool slightly between cooking and hot-holding. Occasionally production may exceed hot-holding capacity, although careful planning and scheduling should avoid this. There should be a stated policy that no food is allowed to remain at room temperature for more than two hours. After that time the item must be blast-chilled, transferred to hot-holding or thrown away.

Testing

The appearance, odour, texture and flavour of food are together called the *organoleptic* qualities. Organoleptic testing is a neglected area in catering, but very important. In addition to assuring the general quality of food before service, it can also help in detecting suspect items and preventing food-borne illness. Customers may not notice what they are eating in a restaurant situation. Dim lighting, social stimulation, music and wine all compete with the sense of taste, and contaminated food may be eaten unnoticed. Kitchen staff, on the other hand, are able to taste food and to assess its quality in good light and a business-like environment. Suspect items can be noticed and dealt with before there is a problem. Tasting/testing conditions and practice should be set out in detail in a manual. There should be a tasting area in the kitchen, well lit and as far as possible away from the smell of cooking food. Only designated staff should be allowed to taste. Utensils for tasting should be sterilized by immersion in boiling water or a non-tainting sterilant before and after use. A different utensil should be used to sample each food. It is essential to have an established procedure for samples which have to be rejected. This should always involve a report form and, as with raw materials, a wastage allowance should be budgeted. Whilst it is usually necessary to investigate rejects and wastage, individuals who spot problems should be praised or rewarded, rather than penalized. In addition, it may be necessary to retain food samples for subsequent inspection by the manager or the public analyst. Samples must be covered and kept refrigerated, away from foods destined for sale. Flavour and colour changes do not always indicate contamination. Sometimes such foods may be usable, and it may be a good idea to ask the advice of the local Environmental Health Department. Some establishments monitor food quality on a regular basis at the point of service, including both organoleptic assessment and temperature measurement. Testing cannot reliably identify all contamination hazards. Only microbiological analysis in the laboratory can do this adequately, and the information is always produced too late to be useful. However, systematic food tasting can certainly identify gross contamination and quality problems. Customers will doubtless still complain from time to time, and there should be an effective system of complaint response. Food tasting and complaint response procedures are not substitutes for one another, but it is to be hoped that adequate tasting will reduce the number of complaints.

Portioning and plate layout

Presentation and portion size may be included on the standard recipe. Alternatively, separate plate layout specifications can be used. In the case of cold items the 'standard recipe' itself may be little more than an assembly/plate layout specification. This should contain the following:

- The name of the menu item.
- Ingredients.
- Instructions.
- Photograph of the finished item.
- Food hygiene notes.

Ingredients may be raw items such as salad vegetables, or cooked foods, or a mixture of both.

Question

When might an assembly specification contain only cooked foods?

> Assembly or plate layout specifications are mostly relevant to cold foods. However, they can also be used for plating cooked meals if a particular standard or style of presentation is required.

Food hygiene notes on plate layout specifications should seek to prevent contamination. For instance, it should be specified that cold meats are only handled with tongs. An important problem with cold plate assembly is that handling may contaminate the components with harmful bacteria from skin or from previously handled raw ingredients. Subsequent careless storage may allow the bacteria to multiply. Items such as sandwiches are particularly at risk because they involve considerable handling, and meats and other ingredients are in thin pieces (Snyder, 1986). Plate layout instructions for cold goods should emphasize personal hygiene, the minimum of handling and particular care with cold cooked meats, poultry and fish. Plates, containers, cutlery etc. used in portioning and arranging such foods must be scrupulously clean. Assembly specifications should also contain instructions for rapid chilling and cold holding of the plated food if necessary. Scheduling should be so organized that no cold, cooked meat, poultry, fish, egg or rice dishes remain at room temperature for more than 2 hours.

Cold-holding

Rapid chilling and cold-holding of prepared foods may be an integral part of the process, as in cook–chill or cook–freeze systems. Alternatively, chilling and refrigeration may be required on a casual basis, for instance with over-produced items, and may simply indicate poor scheduling. Production flow should be reviewed and modified if there is much unscheduled cold storage. It monopolizes valuable storage space and interferes with the orderly use of prepared foods. Both of these events may lead to incidents of food-bone illness. During chilling, food items should not take more than four hours to fall below 4°C, right through to the centre. This often necessitates the use of a blast-chiller. It is helpful to check the temperatures of foods during standing, chilling and storage. However, this may be impossible with wrapped items; the best that can be done is to monitor the temperature inside the refrigerator cabinet.

Scheduled chilling and cold-storage operations should be documented using job cards, if the latter are not already incorporated in standard recipes or plate layout specifications. Staff should be trained to keep strictly to time/temperature criteria. It may be possible to put a supervisor in charge if the operation is a large one. Casual storage of over-produced items is much more of a problem. Time/temperature standards and procedure can be included in the food hygiene notes on standard recipes. For instance, recipes for sensitive left-over items such as large pieces of roast meat should contain chilling and cold-holding procedures in case of over-production.

Foods intended for lengthy cold-holding before serving (e.g. cook–chill products) should be produced with particular care. Contamination must be eliminated and time/temperature criteria scrupulously maintained. The objective is to keep bacterial counts so low in the product that there is no risk to the consumer, even if some growth occurs during storage. The production process is thus 'microbiologically engineered' for food safety. However, some bacteria always survive and spoilage will eventually occur, even though all pathogens have been destroyed. Stock-rotation and management are particularly important in such operations. Storage and transport temperatures must be maintained at the constant, correct level. This is a very different situation from that of over-produced, left-over foods. These have not generally received any special hygiene care and are probably slightly contaminated so they cannot be held safely for long. A good general rule is to ensure that all such foods are used or discarded within 24 hours. Items should be clearly labelled, with dated sticky labels. Newly-wrapped, labelled foods should be placed at the back of the refrigerator so that older stock is automatically taken first.

Transport

Prepared foods must frequently be moved from one place to another before use. Transport may involve a relatively long distance by van, or short distances by trolley. In either case contamination and bacterial growth can occur. Points to note are:

(a)   Choice of vehicle.
(b)   Loading/unloading.

The vehicle must be appropriate for the operation. It must be clean and well maintained. It should also be efficiently refrigerated if goods are to remain in transit more than a total of 30 minutes. Temperature checks should be made at least during loading/unloading. On long journeys the temperature should be read and logged at regular intervals on the driver's job record sheet. In large vehicles foods must be carefully stacked and secured. Vehicles must not be so small that several trips are necessary; this makes loading and unloading unnecessarily complicated. Regular, scheduled transporting is usually only associated with cook–chill or cook–freeze operations. A 'cold chain' should operate, in which food is never out of cold storage for more than a few minutes. Vehicles should to be able to back right up to the cold store door and load or unload directly. Trolleys can be used to transport food along corridors to stores, but such routes must be kept as short as possible. Long routes increase opportunities for contamination, cleaning and maintenance costs. Unless trolleys are refrigerated, times and temperatures may permit bacterial growth. Cold-chain procedures should be communicated to drivers and stores personnel in a manual. It is very important that staff fully understand the cold-chain philosophy and why it is required.

Question
How should this understanding be achieved?

There should be extensive food hygiene training, awareness programmes and discussion groups. However, it is equally important for management to set a good example, e.g. with hygienic dress and habits.

Casual transport of cooked foods may have to be used for occasional outside catering, for barbecues and marquee events and in emergency, when a kitchen fails. Often it may not be possible to obtain a refrigerated vehicle at short notice. An emergency situation can never be completely safe, but safety can be improved by adequately instructing staff. Foods must always be covered. The two-hour rule should apply, i.e. the time required for transporting and setting out the food should be no more than two hours before it is to be eaten. Routes for transporting cooked food must not be near stored rubbish or raw meat. Trays and food containers must not touch the ground during loading and unloading. A trestle should be available on which to stack trays etc. Vending machines which dispense chilled food are often located well away from the main cold store. This may make the use of a trolley unavoidable. Restocking schedules should be arranged so that foods remain at room temperature for the minimum of time. Trolleys should travel radially out and back from the store. Restocking rounds of several dining areas, which are usual for drinks vending machines, must be avoided with chilled foods. Temperatures in chilled display units and vending machines should be regularly checked and recorded. Where security is a problem it is essential that the person entrusted with the keys also has a digital thermometer so that monitoring is maintained. The temperature of the cabinet and of selected foods within it should be regularly measured and recorded. If there is an automatic temperature-recording device incorporated in the unit the information it contains must be regularly documented. It is also important that refrigerated machines are not turned off overnight. Robertson (1986) recommends correct labelling, stock rotation and adherence to sell-by dates for vending operations. This advice is equally applicable to chilled display units. Staff checking expired sell-by dates should examine for leakages or other damage to stock at the same time.

Study example 8.3

In the interests of productivity it is proposed to rationalize food production in a group of hotels. All but one of the hotel kitchens will be reduced in area and re-equipped with regeneration equipment. The remaining central kitchen will be reorganized to produce *sous vide* products. These will be used as the basis of à la carte and room service menus by the other units.

In the role of hygiene consultant explain to the directors of the hotel group the hygiene implications of the change. Consider particularly the following areas:

- Operational control procedures.
- Critical time/temperature events.
- Process monitoring.
- Transport and distribution.

You may wish to review the section in Chapter 3 which describes the *sous vide* process.

Summary – process management

Process hygiene aims to minimize bacterial contamination, growth and survival by careful planning and control. Menus should be planned first because the product mix defines the steps of the process. Planning the menu should consider food hygiene equally with marketing, productivity and profit. The following action is advised:

Do
- Restrict the number of items as much as possible.
- Minimize the number of raw materials which are known contaminants.
- Plan to use up, or discard, left-over items within 24 hours.
- Allow for wastage.
- Match sales volume to production capacity.

Do not
- Add new items without considering process control.
- Try to produce more covers than the kitchen was designed for.

Planning the process consists of identifying and rationalizing all the operations. Food hygiene should be considered along with cost, productivity and ergonomic factors.

Do
- Flowchart the process.
- Identify operations which may involve contamination or the proliferation or survival of bacteria.
- Shorten transport distances and keep flow lines of cooked and raw food apart.
- Remove delays as far as possible.

Do not
- Schedule food preparation in advance of the time it is needed.
- Use holding refrigerators for cooling large items or bulk quantities of food.

Process control involves detailed paperwork explaining to staff how the job is to be done, and monitoring that it has been done adequately. In controlling purchasing, receiving, stock handling and issuing:

Do
- Use a detailed inspect/accept/reject procedure.
- Date stock items and physically rotate them.

- Have an issue procedure which checks rotation.
- Use stock control paperwork to report spoilage problems.

In controlling preparation and cooking:

Do
- Use detailed job cards/standard recipes, including procedures and food hygiene notes.
- Issue digital thermometers and specify regular monitoring of temperatures and times.

In controlling portioning, holding and testing:

Do
- Include detailed hygiene notes in plate layout specifications.
- Specify tasting procedures, accept/reject criteria.
- Allow for wastage and encourage the reporting of problems.

9 Food Hygiene Strategy and Policy

Objectives

To identify possible operational strategies for the management of food hygiene. To examine different approaches to food hygiene policy and to discuss how these may be integrated with other organizational goals, to ensure product quality and customer safety.

Introduction

The food premises manager has three main policy objectives concerned with food hygiene:

(i)   To get the job done hygienically;
(ii) To satisfy legal requirements; and
(iii) To harmonize food hygiene policy with other goals.

Getting the job done hygienically means managing premises, plant/ equipment, personnel and process aspects effectively. The information presented in the preceding chapters indicates how this might be achieved. It has, however, been presented for some non-existent 'average' catering organization and must be organized and prioritized for use in any particular, real situation. The present chapter discusses how this may be done.

The Food Hygiene (General) Regulations, 1970 (Regulation 29) hold the manager of food premises responsible for any breach of the law. The Regulations also apply to managers who are not based on the premises. Under the Food Safety Act, 1990 (Section 36) directors and managers are responsible for infringements if consent, connivance or negligence can be proved.

Management can satisfy their obligations under the law to some extent by producing a written food hygiene policy and by ensuring that employees comply. This chapter examines some of the issues involved in food hygiene policy-making.

Food hygiene policies are unlikely to have effect if their objectives clash with other goals of the organization. This chapter examines several operational strategies for food production and service and identifies the advantages and disadvantages of each from the point of view of food hygiene.

The '4 Ps' Approach

Premises, *Plant/equipment*, *Personnel* and *Process* (the '4Ps') are a commonly used basis for organizing food hygiene programmes. The four aspects are mentioned in this order in the Food Hygiene (General) Regulations, 1970. They also tend to be the areas (and order) of interest of Environmental Health Officers' inspections. In catering it is quite natural to regard premises, plant/equipment, personnel and the process as separate operational areas to be managed. A programme designed on the '4Ps' basis seems logical and attractive, agreeing with the perceptions both of industry and of the enforcing authorities. In fact, though, the Food Hygiene Regulations are designed, not to ensure excellent, hygienic catering, but merely to give a minimum of protection to the public. They attempt to prevent bad practice by a process that is piecemeal rather than logical. For instance, the premises aspect of hygiene is dealt with first and in greatest detail by the Regulations. Yet it is the food production process which constitutes the greatest danger in terms of contamination, proliferation and survival of bacteria.

A more appropriate order for the '4Ps' might be process, personnel, plant/equipment and premises. But even this is an inadequate approach. The '4Ps' (in whatever order) do not apply directly to any one catering operation.

In the late 1960s an alternative system of food hygiene management was developed, known by the initials HACCP. This concentrates on hazards and risks in the food production process. These risks stem from the hygiene of the personnel, plant/equipment and premises directly involved in the process. Interrelationships between the '4Ps' are therefore dealt with naturally and their relevance to the food production process is emphasized. Each hygiene aspect is also dealt with in proportion to its importance.

Question
Which 'interrelationships between the '4Ps' are meant?

An example of an issue which bears on several of the '4Ps' is the introduction of digital probe thermometers (plant/equipment), described in Chapter 8. This would also have implications for training (personnel) and for amending job or recipe cards (process).

HACCP

HACCP (the acronym is pronounced 'hassop'), stands for Hazard Analysis and Critical Control Points. It represents a completely new approach to food hygiene management because the HACCP system:

- Covers all the hygiene areas, i.e. premises, plant/equipment, personnel and process in a systematic way, so that no essentials are left out.
- Emphasizes the direct relationship between hygiene and product safety.

The HACCP system and concept were developed in the USA by NASA, the Pillsbury Company and the USA Army Natick Research Laboratories. It is particularly important to ensure the microbiological quality of space-flight meals (Heidelbaugh, *et al.*, 1973). They have to be reheated in the reduced pressure of a space capsule, where water boils at well below 100°C. Bacteria may not be killed at these lowered temperatures as they would be during normal cooking. At the same time, preventing food poisoning is crucial. An outbreak in a space capsule might impair astronauts' faculties and critically endanger them. Bauman (1974) describes how HACCP assures zero defects in product quality: i.e. all meals can be guaranteed free of contamination, without the need to analyze every one. Subsequently the HACCP system has been used for quality assurance in a range of industrial food processing operations. It is the method recommended and used by the US Food and Drugs Administration (Kauffman, 1974). HACCP has also been applied to large scale catering systems (Silverman, 1982). US health inspectors encourage its use by chefs and restaurateurs (Riggs, 1986). The WHO (1982) recommends the HACCP method of food hygiene management in all food processing operations.

Hazard analysis

The terms hazard and risk have acquired very specific meanings in cause-and-effect studies of disasters (e.g. Gorbell, 1982; and Ozog and Bendixen, 1987) Definitions of these terms can be adapted for the catering industry as follows. In food safety terms a *hazard* is defined as: An object or material which has the potential ability to cause harm, because it contains contaminating micro-organisms, toxins, chemical poisons, or foreign bodies. On the other hand, the definition of a *risk* is: The probability that a hazard will actually cause harm, combined with the magnitude of the harm caused. (i.e. in food hygiene terms it is the likelihood that the contaminant will pass through the process to the finished product. Lethal hazards such as botulin toxin represent a higher risk level).

Examples of hazards and risks are shown in Table 9.1. Vectors of food-borne illness (discussed in Chapter 1) are all hazards. *High-risk foods* (high-protein, high A_w, high pH) are also hazards, because bacteria may grow in them and generate contamination.

Table 9.1 Hazards, risks and critical operations

Hazard Source	Risk if not Controlled	Examples of Critical Operations
Ingredients	Contamination Growth	Purchase Inspection Receipt Storage Stock Rotation Transport
Intermediates and Products	Contamination Growth Survival	Preparation Cooking Hot- or cold-holding, Transport
Personnel	Contamination Growth Survival	Induction Training Hand washing Clothing Health Behaviour
Plant/Equipment	Contamination Growth (e.g. holding equipment)	Cleaning Disinfection Maintenance Pest control Monitoring
Premises/ Environment	Contamination	Cleaning Disinfection Maintenance Pest control Ventilation/air supply

Source: Derived from Sheard (1988) and Bobeng and David (1978a/b).

Hazard analysis, the first step in a HACCP programme, has the following goals:

(i)   Identify hazards;
(ii) Classify hazards by considering the potential harm they might cause; and
(iii) Rationalize and eliminate hazards as far as possible.

Identifying and classifying hazards

The objective of this exercise is to prepare an inventory of everything that could cause contamination of the final product. Hazards are found throughout the process, so a careful and thorough study should be made, including:

- Food ingredients, intermediates and products.
- Personnel.
- Plant/equipment.
- Premises.

Food ingredients, intermediates and products

The most suitable system of classifying foods is that developed by the US National Academy of Science (NAS, 1969). This is based on three hazard factors, which may be present in food products:

(a)   The foodstuff contains a 'sensitive' ingredient or ingredients which can be assumed to be a potential source of contamination under normal circumstances, i.e. the food is likely to contain pathogens, toxins or physical contamination.
(b)   The foodstuff contains an ingredient which has not undergone a controlled processing step that destroys harmful bacteria, i.e. at least one component has not been heat-treated.
(c)   There is substantial potential for microbiological growth during abuse in distribution or handling, that could render the product harmful when used or consumed, i.e. the food will support the growth of pathogens.

Foods can then be classified into four ingredient hazard categories, as follows:

Category I: A special category of non-sterile products designed for consumption by infants, the aged or the infirm.

Category II: Food products which contain all three hazard factors; (a, b and c) these are rated + + +, meaning:
- Contains a sensitive ingredient (a); and
- Not been pasteurized or heat-treated (b); and
- Able to support microbial growth (c).

Category III: Food products contain any two of the three factors: these would be rated 0 + +, + 0 +, or + + 0, meaning, respectively:
- Is not likely to contain bacteria or a toxin (a); or
- Has been pasteurized or heat-treated (b); or
- Is not able to support microbial growth (c).

Category IV: Food products contain only one of the three factors: these would be rated 0 0 +, 0 + 0, or + 0 0.

Category V: Food products which contain none of the three factors, and are therefore rated 0 0 0.

These food hazard categories are further illustrated and summarized in Table 9.2 overleaf.

Question

How would these categories be used to rate dried red kidney beans, rare beef, boiled rice, well-roasted pork?

> Red kidney beans are category III (+ + 0). They contain a natural toxin and have not been heat processed. Microorganisms are not likely to grow under most storage conditions. Rare beef and boiled rice are both category II (+ + +). They originally contained harmful bacteria which were not destroyed during processing, and the product can support microbial growth. Well-roasted pork is category III (+ 0 +). It originally contained contamination which has been destroyed during cooking. The cooked product is susceptible to microbial growth.

The severity of food-borne hazards can be assessed using the US National Research Council (NRC, 1985) classification:

Severe hazards: *Clostridium botulinum, Shigella, Vibrio cholerae, Brucella, Mycobacterium bovis,* Hepatitis A virus, fish toxins (ciguatera), shellfish toxins (saxitoxin), aflatoxin (and some other fungal poisons) and the *Salmonella* organisms responsible for the most severe diseases (*S. typhi, S. paratyphi, S. sendai* and *S. cholerae-suis*).

**Table 9.2   Food hazard classification using the NAS (1969) System:
Summary**

Category	Criterion	Food designation
Category I		Foods intended for infants, invalids or the aged
		Example: dried baby milk
Category II	+ + +	Initially contains viable bacteria Not heat-treated Will support bacterial growth
		Example: raw chicken
Category III	0 + +	Does not initially contain viable bacteria Not heat-treated Will support bacterial growth
		Example: fresh fruit
Category III (alternative)	+ 0 +	Initially contains viable bacteria Heat-treated Will support bacterial growth
		Example: pasteurized ham
Category III (alternative)	+ + 0	Initially contains viable bacteria Not heat-treated Will not support bacterial growth
		Example: uncooked raw rice
Category IV	0 0 +	Does not initially contain viable bacteria Heat-treated Will support bacterial growth
		Example: canned fruit
Category IV (alternative)	0 + 0	Does not initially contain viable bacteria Not heat-treated Will not support bacterial growth
		Example: dried fruit
Category IV (alternative)	+ 0 0	Initially contains viable bacteria Heat-treated Will not support bacterial growth
		Example: 'quick-cook' (parboiled) rice

Category IV	0	Does not initially contain viable bacteria
	0	Heat-treated
	0	Will not support bacterial growth
		Example: granulated sugar

Moderate hazards with potentially extensive spread: The other *Salmonella* species, *Escherichia coli* and *Streptococcus pyogenes* (food-borne scarlet fever).

Moderate hazards with limited spread: *Staphylococcus aureus*, *Clostridium perfringens*, *Bacillus* species, *Vibrio parahaemolyticus*, *Yersinia enterocolitica*, *Campylobacter* species, *Trichinella spiralis*, histamine, haemagglutinins.

Listeria monocytogenes is not listed in the NRC reference above, but should be classified as a severe hazard.

Personnel hazards

Personnel are a contamination hazard at all times. However, the hazard input can be reduced by identifying and eventually eliminating any of the following:

- Dirty, unwashed, contaminated hands or arms.
- Dirty, unlaundered or contaminated outer clothing.
- Any nose, throat or gastro-enteritic infection.
- Any skin infection, sepsis or allergy.
- Individuals who persist in some unacceptable, unhygienic practice.

Plant/equipment hazards

Plant/equipment items can potentially contaminate any food with which they come into contact. Hazard analysis should therefore identify the likelihood that a particular article will come into contact with food. The likely contamination of equipment items should also be considered, by classifying them as follows:

- Items which can be cleaned and sterilized after use.
- Items about which there is always some doubt as to whether they are completely clean and sterile.
- Items which are always or nearly always dangerously contaminated.

Tools, utensils and other small equipment mostly comes into the first category. Large plant and equipment may be more difficult to sterilize, particularly machines designed for continuous operation (see Chapter 6). Quite common items such as wooden chopping-blocks may come into the last category. Hazard analysis should try to assess the risk from such items and the necessity of having them at all.

Hazard analysis of premises

Premises may present three main classes of avoidable hazard:

- Pests.
- Dirt, dust or contaminated water coming into contact with food.
- Foreign matter, flaking paint etc.

The hazard analysis should pay particular attention to these, but should also note any other hazards associated with the operation.

Rationalization of hazards

Once the hazards within a process have been identified, an inventory should be drawn up. This should list:

(i)   The hazards;
(ii) Where they are located etc.; and
(iii) Their severity.

The severity of food hazards should be assessed using the US National Research Council (NRC, 1985) classification described above. Avoidable hazards associated with personnel, plant/equipment or premises should also be regarded as unacceptable. Rationalization consists of considering each hazard in the inventory and asking whether it could be removed or reduced.

Rationalization of *ingredient* hazards should concentrate on the most harmful categories. Menu analysis and planning can be used as a basis for this rationalization, as described in Chapter 8. However, removal of hazards does not necessarily mean changing the menu. For instance, raw eggs must be considered a category II hazard. They can generally be replaced with pasteurized egg – a category III hazard. This is particularly appropriate in items such as sauces and desserts, which may not undergo thorough cooking due to texture stability problems. Pre-processed ingredients are generally safer than raw ones, provided the processing has been adequately controlled. Managers are advised to insert clauses about bacterial content into purchase specifications for processed foodstuffs. Ideally suppliers' premises should be visited and examined to ensure that processing is being adequately carried out.

Management of *personnel* contamination hazards is best achieved by the following:

- Providing hand washing and toilet facilities.
- Regular inspection.
- Benevolent staff sickness policy.
- Detailed hygiene and job training.
- Motivation.

All these aspects of managing kitchen staff were discussed in Chapter 7.

Plant/equipment contamination hazards can be reduced by careful selection, regular cleaning and maintenance, as described in Chapter 6.

Hazardous aspects of *premises* can be managed by effective:

- Kitchen design.
- Cleaning.
- Maintenance.
- Pest control.

Detailed discussion of these areas may be found in Chapter 5.

Residual hazards

No matter how much care is taken identifying and rationalizing hazards, some will always remain. Very few ingredients can be produced in a sterile condition. Often it will be preferable on quality grounds not to use sterilized ingredients. Personnel will still carry bacteria, even though properly scrubbed and dressed. Microorganisms are in the air and in even the cleanest water supply. Hazards can be restricted but never entirely eliminated.

Question
What are the major unavoidable hazards in the commercial kitchen?

> Raw animal foods, particularly raw meat and poultry, constitute a major food hygiene hazard which can never be completely eliminated.

It is therefore necessary to control the food production process, so that the *risks* that hazards will cause harm are eliminated. The HACCP system achieves this by identifying the points in the system at which hazards are likely to cause harm. These 'critical control points' are rigorously monitored in order to reduce or eliminate the risk.

Critical control points

Critical control points (*CCPs*) are defined as: Subsystems within the food production/service process for which loss of control would result in an unacceptable risk of food-borne illness. Usually CCPs are the points at which residual, unavoidable hazards enter the system and become risks. These typical critical operations are shown in Table 9.1 (see page 299), together with their associated hazards and risks. CCPs are not identical with process operations. Any given process operation may have one or more CCPs associated with it, for example hygiene of personnel or equipment. Analysis of critical control points in a food production system consists of four main stages:

1. Analyzing the process to identify all the operations.
2. Identifying the critical operations within the process, and of the CCPs associated with them.
3. Setting appropriate standards for ensuring safety at the CCPs.
4. Establishing effective checking, monitoring and documentation.

Analyzing the process

Chapter 8 described a number of techniques which may be used in process analysis. The sequence, timing and locations of operations should all be identified, using one or more of these techniques. However, when all aspects of the process have been studied a simple sequence chart (box chart) should be produced, as shown in Figure 9.1. This should indicate:

(i)   Temperatures of processing/storage;
(ii) Times of processing/storage;
(iii) Likely contamination routes; and
(iv) Likely bacterial growth opportunities.

Figure 9.1 Typical CCP analysis for production of roast chicken

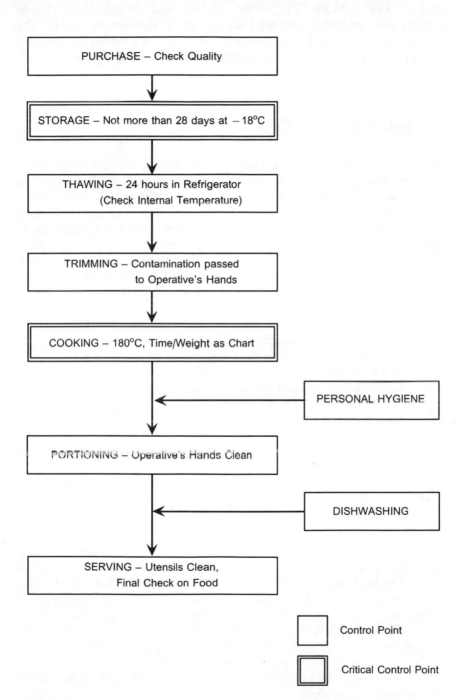

The clumsy notes shown in the figure can be partly replaced with symbols. For instance 'TT 30:180' can be used to indicate a critical cooking step involving time/temperature of 30 minutes at 180°C. The hazard inventory should be consulted in order to identify all possible contamination from personnel, plant/equipment and premises.

Identifying CCPs

Each process stage should be examined by asking the Question 'What would be the result of losing control of the process at this point?' A critical control point is one for which loss of control would bring unacceptable consequences. In Figure 9.1 incorrect thawing, cooking at less than 180°C, or misreading the cooking time from the weight chart may permit survival of *Salmonella* organisms in the chicken. Other critical operations shown in the chart are portioning, personal hygiene of employees and the cleaning of equipment. The following six aspects should be particularly examined in the search for CCPs:

(i)   Time available for microbial growth and proliferation;
(ii)   Temperature of storage, holding and processing;
(iii) Critical controls on the microbiological population such as pH or A_w;
(iv)   Employee personal hygiene;
(v)   Hygiene of plant and equipment; and
(vi)   Hygiene of premises.

Setting safety standards

A CCP can only be controlled if there are clear safety standards. The most important and easily applied standards are usually time/temperature measurements. Cooking conditions for meat and poultry should be adjusted so that the geometric centres of items reach at least 75°C. This corresponds to a near 10,000-fold reduction in *Salmonella* numbers over 4 minutes (calculated from the D and z values given in Chapter 2). With most cooking methods the maximum temperature, once reached, will be held longer than 4 minutes. On the other hand, spores of organisms such as *Clostridium perfringens* generally survive temperatures below 100°C. Therefore subsequent hot-holding, chilling and cold-holding should be very carefully controlled.

Question
What may happen if chilling and cold-holding are not controlled?

Clostridium perfringens spores are shocked into early germination by heating. They will germinate readily if the food temperature drops below 63°C and can multiply successfully at temperatures as high as 55°C.

Hot-holding should be at 65°C or above. This provides for ±2°C variance due to draughts etc. Chilling should be as rapid as possible; no item should take longer than 4 hours to fall below 4°C (Snyder, 1986). Thick cooked items such as roasts are at greater risk if boned and rolled or if the interior has been punctured with tenderizer syringes or thermometer probes. Cold-holding should be at 5°C to allow for possible fluctuation of the refrigerator cabinet. The temperature should not fall below 0°C. Freezing causes problems of inadequate regeneration, as well as deterioration of the product.

Safety standards of clothing and hygiene should be set for employees. Cleanliness standards for premises, plant and equipment should be defined as objectively as possible. A manual should be produced which sets out the standards and how they are to be monitored.

Checking and monitoring

Constant monitoring and control of CCPs is very important. Staff should be trained to use digital probe thermometers for measuring temperatures at the surfaces and geometrical centres of food items. Standards of staff dress and personal hygiene should be checked before shifts. Hand hygiene should be monitored where staff are likely to carry cross-contamination to a sensitive product. Standards of premises/plant hygiene and of pest control should also be regularly monitored. For most purposes, visual inspection is adequate for routine monitoring of hygiene standards. However, in the initial CCP analysis, contamination should be assessed using microbiological assay techniques. Test materials are available, such as the bacterial contact slides from Tillomed Laboratories. These give quick results and can be used by supervisors, little training being necessary. Microbial testing should be carried out routinely, once a month. For particularly sensitive products (cook–chill for invalids etc.) it may be advisable to check hygiene standards daily in this way.

There should be a report system so that CCP failure can be recognized in time to check, and if necessary reject the batch of finished product. Such systems will usually depend upon effective documentation of critical control points.

Documentation

The importance of documentation in operations management has been stressed throughout this book. Under the HACCP system critical control points must be adequately documented. This will generally mean:

- Instructions to staff (i.e. job cards) on how each operation should be carried out.
- Written standards for time/temperature control, hygiene, clothing etc.
- Instructions to supervisors etc. requiring regular inspections, temperature checks etc.
- A report system for communicating failures and faults to management.

Besides documentation for the actual food production process, there should be carefully documented hygiene procedures. Personnel, equipment and premises hygiene represent important critical control points affecting most process operations. A staff manual should specify hand-washing techniques and standards of clothing. Materials, methods and standards for cleaning equipment and premises must similarly be specified using job cards, as discussed in Chapters 5 and 6. In addition there should be specified procedures for checking, maintaining and reporting the operation of hot- and cold-holding equipment.

Pest control is also usually a critical control point and should be carefully documented and monitored. The best criterion for control is the actual number of pests which can be detected in traps. Failing this, the frequency with which bait is applied (in a specified manner), or the frequency of visits by a reliable contractor may suffice.

Supervisors should be provided with manuals detailing inspection procedures for all aspects of personnel, equipment or premises hygiene for which they are responsible. These must specify standards such as time and temperature measurements, clothing and hygiene standards. Instructions should also give the frequency with which inspection or checking should be carried out. Corrective action should also be specified in case of CCP failure.

Study example 9.1

Production of red kidney bean salad illustrates the application of HACCP in a simple way. Of the ingredients:

dried red kidney beans
fresh celery

fresh onions
green peppers
dessert apples
vinegar
olive oil
salt, pepper

only the dried red kidney beans represent a serious hazard, provided the salad is not intended for long, chilled storage. The kidney beans must be cooked at 98°C or above for at least ten minutes to destroy the haemagglutinin (see Chapter 3, page 82). Cooking the beans is a critical control point, because loss of time/temperature control can result in an unacceptable risk. Customers might be very ill or even die as a result of ingesting haemagglutinin. However, in practical terms, red kidney beans need to be simmered for two hours, or pressure-cooked for 40 minutes to make them palatable. No other stages of the process need be considered CCPs if the salad is to be served the day it is prepared.

1. Draw a simple, box-style flowchart showing the production of red bean salad. Indicate the CCP mentioned above.
2. Are there any other control points in the diagram which might be important, if not critical?
3. Are there any possible critical control points which are not stages of the process itself?
4. Two minimum standards could be set out for cooking the beans. What are they?
5. Is it necessary to use dried red beans in the process at all? What might be the alternatives?
6. How would the flowchart and the critical control points in the process change if the salad was to be held chilled for three days before serving?

Training

To ensure that manuals, job cards and other documentation are properly used by staff it is essential to have an adequate training programme. Introduction of a HACCP programme of hygiene management also means that several aspects of staff behaviour and hygiene will be identified as critical control points. Training programmes should include on-job, task-specific training for:

(i)   Understanding and execution of job card instructions/proce-dures;
(ii)   Understanding and application of control standards (time/tem-perature, hygiene criteria etc.); and
(iii) use of report systems and documentation.

Off-job, general hygiene training is important for:

(i)   Appreciating hazards, risks and critical control points;
(ii)   Understanding the need for hygiene; and
(iii) Awareness of possible problems.

Other Applications of HACCP

Large-scale production

HACCP is particularly suitable for production-line work and large-scale food processing, where there are relatively few product lines and output is high. Capital outlay for controls such as automatic time/temperature recording and rapid bacteriological analysis is justifiable. Products from such systems are often intended for retail consumption and need a long shelf life. Opportunities for spoilage and consumer abuse are consider-able, so the product must embody a high level of safety when it leaves the factory.

For such processes, computer models are available which can calculate and evaluate food safety risks. Such programs are based on a technique known as *fault-tree analysis*. Fault-trees are diagrams which show the relationships between effects and all their probable causes. A generalized example of a fault-tree for food output is shown in Figure 9.2. This shows the effect (food product contamination) and all possible causes:

- Contact with bacterial contaminants.
- Contact with foreign bodies or chemical contaminants.
- Time/temperature relationships, permitting bacterial prolifera-tion.
- Time/temperature relationships permitting bacterial survival.

Figure 9.2 Fault-tree analysis of food contamination

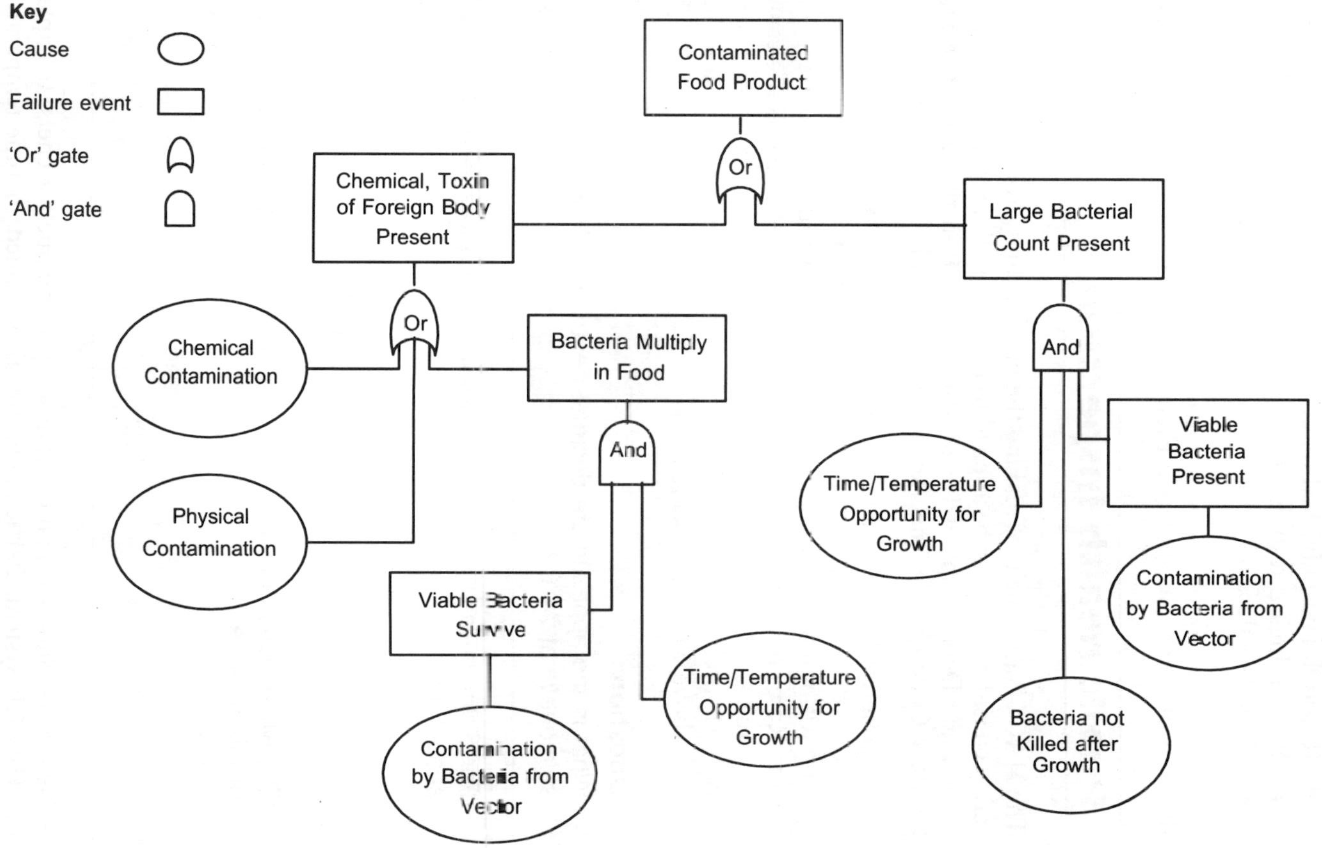

Probabilities of contamination, growth and survival processes are obtained from:

- Research and published data.
- Bacteriological testing on site.
- D and z values for various species and environments.

This data is fed into the computer and are used to calculate which of the 'and/or events', as shown in Figure 9.2, are most likely to take place.

Public health inspection

The HACCP approach, of making the product and process the first food safety consideration, can be applied to public health inspection. The New York State Department of Health uses HACCP in this way. The State Sanitary Code specifies time/temperature controls as follows:

(i)   High risk food held in the range 7–60°C for more than two hours must not be sold for human consumption;

(ii)   All poultry must reach an internal temperature of 74°C;

(iii) Rare roast beef must reach at least 55°C at the geometric centre; and

(iv)   All precooked chilled foods must be heated to 74°C and held above 60°C until served.

Question

What is the approximate decimal destruction time (D) of *salmonella* at 74°C?

For *Salmonella* D_{60} is approximately 4 min and z = 4°C, D_{72} should therefore be

$$\frac{4 \text{ min}}{1000} \quad \text{or} \quad \frac{240 \text{ sec}}{1000}$$

D_{74} will be less than this. It can be calculated at about one third of this time i.e.:

$$\frac{72 \text{ sec}}{1000}$$

New York State runs an educational programme for chefs, to explain the HACCP system. Participants are also trained in time/temperature control and shown how and when to monitor the temperatures in poultry and meat during cooking, chilling and storage. Reporting and documentation are encouraged. A good account of an inspection system based upon HACCP is given by Bryan (1981).

Quality, health and safety

HACCP is usually described as a microbiological quality assurance system. However, the concepts of 'hazard' and critical control point need not be restricted to microbiological quality. The system is equally suited to controlling contamination by chemicals or toxins (see Study example 9.1, for example). It even has potential for assuring flavour, aroma and texture, provided that hazards and CCPs are redefined. Many of these overlap with microbiological safety. Holding food hot for an excessively long time, for example, may endanger both quality aspects. More often a delicate 'balancing act' is needed between safety and customer acceptability. Such a balance is best achieved by careful control, standardization and documentation: all essential to an effective HACCP programme.

Hazard and risk analysis are not unique to HACCP. These techniques have been adapted from studies of fire outbreaks, explosions and other failure disasters. Their use is equally appropriate for identifying general health and safety problems. Using similar techniques throughout an operation reduces the need for training and reinforces the hygiene/safety message to staff.

Summary – how to implement HACCP

1. Identify ingredient hazards and classify them using the NAS system. Rationalize and eliminate where possible.
2. Draw up a flowchart for each process which uses one or more major ingredient hazards. It should indicate any process stages which could be critical to safety. Rationalize and eliminate these if possible.
3. Identify all critical control points concerned with the hygiene of personnel, plant/equipment or premises.
4. Specify safety standards for all CCPs.
5. Write process instructions for all operations, whether critical or not. Instructions for CCPs must specify standards.
6. Produce a manual (or job cards etc.) for the hygiene of personnel, plant/equipment and premises, specifying standards.

7. Instigate programmes of staff induction, training and retraining, using the specially produced manuals and process instructions.
8. Write a manual or checklist for supervisors to inspect and check each of the critical control points. Make sure that there are clear instructions of the procedure to follow if a fault is discovered.
9. Make occasional inspections at irregular intervals, using the manual or checklist, to act as a control audit.

Food hygiene policies

A food hygiene policy usually has two aims. It should communicate the intentions of management to the staff. It can also demonstrate management's good intentions in hygiene matters, i.e. that any infringement was not made with their consent or connivance. A food hygiene policy usually takes the form of a general policy statement followed by a list of responsibilities and a code of practice.

The *general policy statement* sets out the intentions of senior management regarding food hygiene. For example:

> *PQR Hospitality Ltd policy is to comply with the letter and spirit of the Food Safety Act, 1990, the Food Hygiene Regulations, 1970 and other relevant legislation, and to regard these provisions as minimum requirements. The highest hygiene standards will be maintained, to ensure our customers are served safe, wholesome food.*

> *We believe that it is essential for success that everyone accepts the personal responsibilities detailed in this policy and that there is active co-operation between management and workforce in promoting hygiene throughout the company.*

The *list of responsibilities* indicates who in the organization is responsible for what. For example:

Managing Director should uphold the Group Hygiene Policy by:

(a) Ensuring that adequate local Food Hygiene policies are set up in all areas under his control.
(b) Delegating to Regional Operations Directors the responsibility for overall control and administration of Food Hygiene Policy throughout their designated areas of operations.
(c) Regularly reviewing with Regional Operation's Directors the implementation of Food Hygiene Policies and Procedure to ensure that they are effective.

Regional Operations Director is responsible for:

(a) Ensuring that local Food Hygiene Policies are implemented in all units under his/her control.

(b) Ensuring that all unit managers have been given clear responsibilities with regard to Food Hygiene management. Such responsibilities must be confirmed in writing to the individuals concerned.

(c) Regularly reviewing with unit managers the operation of food hygiene policies, to ensure that they are effective.

Unit Manager is responsible for:

(a) Assessing all food handling activities in his/her unit, formulating and publishing codes of practice where necessary.

(b) Ensuring the cleaning and maintenance of premises, plant and equipment.

(c) Identifying the training needs of supervisors and employees under his/her control. Ensuring that hygiene training is carried out and that records are kept.

The food hygiene policy may also contain an organization chart, such as that shown in Figure 9.3. This shows who is responsible to whom within the organization. The policy will also specify responsibilities of supervisors and employees. Since the latter are engaged in a variety of tasks the list of hygiene responsibilities tends to remain rather general in scope. For example:

Employees are responsible for

(a) Observing company policy and codes of practice relating to:
  (i) Work practices;
  (ii) Their personal health and hygiene;
  (iii) Protective clothing; and
  (iv) Any premises, plant or equipment used by them in the course of their work.

(b) Participating in hygiene training exercises as arranged by management.

(c) Bringing to management notice any way of eliminating hazards and risks to food safety.

(d) Co-operating with management and seeking hygiene information if they are uncertain.

Codes of practice are lists of instructions which ought, if followed, to ensure hygiene working of the process. The more specific the code, the more effective it usually is. Often several codes of practice are required,

318

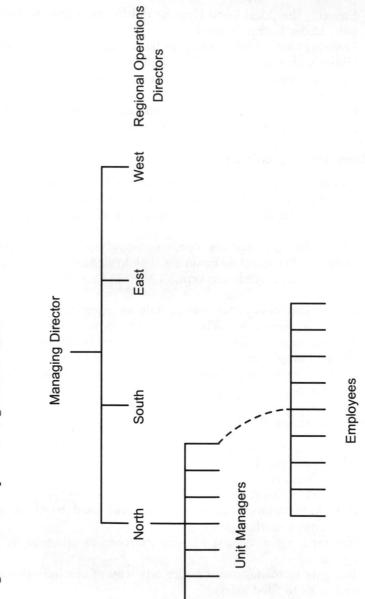

Figure 9.3   Example of an organization chart

each relating to a different aspect of the operation. An organization with a diverse range of outlets, for instance large and small hotels, or theme restaurants of different styles, can only have a generalized group code of practice. Such companies therefore often make unit managers responsible for formulating their own codes (see above under the responsibilities listed for 'Unit Manager').

However, Company Head Offices often issue generalized codes of hygiene practice which can be given to staff at their induction. For instance:

No smoking...
Smoking is strictly forbidden in any rooms where there is open food. This also applies to snuff and chewing tobacco!
Before you start work...
Always wash your hands
Always wear clean whites, overall or apron.
Keep your hair clean, tidy and well covered.
Coughs and sneezes...
Tell your supervisor if you are ill.
Keep coughing and sneezing well away from open food
Always use a tissue or handkerchief.
Never spit in a food area.
Hands...
Wash hands regularly, and ALWAYS after using the toilet.
Keep fingernails short, clean and without varnish.
Don't wear ornaments, rings with stones, or impractical bangles.
Keep cuts covered with a clean, waterproof dressing.
Tell your supervisor if you have a boil, sore or septic spot on your hands or fingers.
Food handling...
Keep raw and cooked goods apart.
Only use scrupulously clean equipment and containers.
Serve food as soon as you can after cooking.
Never let cooked meats, fish or eggs stand at room temperature for more than one hour.
Use the correct refrigerator: raw or cooked, 5°C or 8°C.
If you are ill...
particularly with vomiting, diarrhoea, fever or discharge from nose or ears:
See your doctor at once.
Tell your supervisor or your manager what is wrong with you.
Get a 'signing-off' certificate from your doctor before you come back to work. Show it to your supervisor or manager.
Remember: Our health and our customers' health go hand in hand!

There is no legal requirement for managers to have a written food hygiene policy, and a considerable amount of time and money is involved in the production of such a document. For this reason companies often prefer to include food hygiene with other health and safety objectives. Under the Health and Safety at Work Act, 1974 all employers of five or more persons must have a written health and safety policy and must publicize it to their employees. Advantages of incorporating food hygiene into the health and safety policy are:

(i)   Directors' legal responsibilities are more fully discharged;
(ii) Several policies can be communicated to employees in one, less confusing package;
(iii) Training and induction requirements associated with various legislation can be identified more easily; and
(iv) The enforcing authority in all cases is the local authority, who may be easier to satisfy if all policy documents can be presented together.

Whether incorporated with health and safety or not, food hygiene policies have a tendency to demotivate staff. They are usually drawn up in a format similar to that of the law, because this is the most convenient way for a manager to produce a policy. Like the law they tend to represent hygiene (and health and safety) as action taken in order to avert penalties. Such negative aspects of a job are not likely to receive much enthusiasm or even attention, unless an EHO inspection threatens. Furthermore the penalties for non-compliance do not come from the customer, from fellow workers, or even from the manager. Consequences of poor hygiene come from the local Environmental Health Department, or perhaps from a diligent Technical Services Department at Head Office. Thus hygiene policies contain a hidden message that their content is unimportant or even irrelevant to food handling activities. It is not surprising that policies are quickly taken for granted or disregarded. Nevertheless, food hygiene policies are important. They codify good practice and express the good intentions of management. In order to ensure that food hygiene standards are maintained, it is necessary to have some kind of implementation strategy which reinforces the policy statement.

Summary – food hygiene policy

Functions: A written food hygiene policy is not required by law but it does serve to communicate managements' intentions and to satisfy a legal responsibility.

Structure: A food hygiene policy usually consists of a statement of intent or of management philosophy, a list assigning responsibilities and a code of practice.

Availability: At least an abridged version of the policy should be given to all staff during their induction training.

Alternatives: Food hygiene can be included in the health and safety policy, which is required by law for any operation employing five or more persons.

Study example 9.2

1. Write a statement of intent for a health and safety policy for PQR Hospitality Ltd. Use the example given above as a model.
2. PQR operates hotels and restaurants. Suggest four sections which will be needed in the health and safety policy, other than food hygiene. Refer to Chapter 4 if necessary.
3. List the likely food hygiene responsibilities of:
   a food and beverage manager;
   a chef; and
   a kitchen porter.
4. Write a code of practice for waste disposal in the kitchen.

Strategy and food hygiene

Business strategy by nature centres around the main objectives of an organization, such as making a product, making a profit or keeping within a budget. Hygiene is not a primary objective. In the short term it may be in conflict with the main business goals because it requires inputs of money and time which are not perceived as productive. However, more sophisticated strategies aim at long-time survival and growth of the business. These goals can only be achieved if quality and productivity are ensured, both of which have implications for food hygiene management.

Quality strategies

Broadly speaking there are three possible quality management strategies:

1. Quality control (QC)
2. Quality assurance (QA)
3. Total quality management (TQM)

Quality control involves checking the quality of each batch of product as it is produced. Effective QC relies on an ability to stockpile goods while they are checked, before sale. It is therefore largely irrelevant to the food service industry, where the product is sold instantly and is highly perishable. Food tasting and visual inspection are practicable, but quality control cannot assure hygiene or food safety. Microbiological checking of individual batches of food takes several days, by which time the food is useless.

Quality assurance includes all activities and functions concerned with attaining quality. For instance the quality of chips depends upon:

- The dimensions to which they are cut.
- The style of cutting ('crinkle cut' etc).
- Storage times and conditions after cutting (whether 'whitener' is used, and how much).
- Temperature of cooking.
- Time of cooking.
- Average hot-holding time.

A quality assurance programme must consider all these aspects. Regular checking of the product is also necessary to ensure that the programme is working. Thus QA usually retains an element of quality control.

HACCP is a quality assurance system directed at microbiological quality. It relies on monitoring times, temperatures and hygiene criteria (the CCPs) rather than bacteriological assay which would take too long to be practical. Thus the QA approach is particularly suitable for ensuring microbiological quality. It is also possible, as discussed earlier, to extend the HACCP approach to cover other quality aspects of food.

Quality assurance strategies can be applied to service as well as to production. The elements of reception and food service can be analyzed in a similar way to that shown above for the preparation of chips. Employees' attention can then be focused on the problems and solutions of successful service. This approach is the basis of most customer care programmes. Quality assurance strategies can thus be used to link all the quality aspects of food production and service. This results in a general increase in staff morale. In particular, the hygiene aspects of food production and service are viewed in a new, positive way. Their relevance to customer satisfaction and to staff professionalism is underlined.

Total quality management aims at making quality the responsibility of all employees, throughout the company. The original, Japanese concept was that everyone should be a quality controller. Statistical quality control techniques were taught to all personnel so that there was almost no chance of quality deficiencies going unnoticed. As discussed above, quality *control* is not really applicable to industries with highly perishable products. Therefore TQM in service industries such as catering involves widespread quality awareness training of personnel. This is quite a different approach from production line QA and particularly HACCP, which are primarily directed at setting up systems. The two techniques can be regarded as compatible if QA is primarily directed at production and quality awareness at service.

Productivity strategies

Food hygiene management reflects the way an operation is managed as a whole. Therefore strategies which seek to improve operational efficiency or productivity tend to have a profound effect on hygiene and the microbiological quality of the food produced. There are three main strategic approaches for improving productivity:

1.   Systematization.
2.   Reorganization.
3.   Mechanization.

Systematization aims at control by monitoring what is used and what is produced. Amounts and quality of raw materials used, yields, portion sizes and the product quality are specified. Processes are carefully analyzed and documented. The aim is to minimize waste of materials and effort. Well-run systems generally assure quality and hygiene.

Question
Surely there is a conflict between maximizing output and maintaining quality?

> There is always a potential conflict between quality and productivity. However a well-run system enables the relationship between quality and productivity to be clearly identified, monitored and if necessary corrected.

Reorganization means changing the system so that operatives have less to do for a given output. This reduces the labour input and increases productivity. One way to do this is to change spatial layout. For instance, tables and service stations in a restaurant can be relocated so that service staff do not have so far to walk. Conveyor-belt food preparation and dish assembly reduce the labour content of food production. Such techniques usually result in improved hygiene. Work-flow lines can be rationalized, reducing cross-contamination. Training is easier for the simplified, repetitive actions and can incorporate elements of job-specific food hygiene.

Food service can also be reorganized so that the customer takes over some of the functions of the waiter. This occurs, for example, in cafeteria-style operations. Fondue and 'hot-rock' cookery make it possible for customers to actually cook their own food. Such approaches tend to detract from food hygiene because the opportunities for consumer abuse are increased.

Another reorganization strategy is to separate food production from service. Thus food can be produced centrally, chilled or frozen and then regenerated at the service station. Centralized production can be systematized to a high degree; economies of scale mean that a HACCP system can be implemented in great detail in order to assure bacteriological quality.

Mechanization means the increased use of equipment instead of manual labour. Production becomes more capital-intensive and less labour-intensive and thus labour productivity increases. The trend is towards:

- More machines.
- Continuous, rather than batch processes.
- Self-cleaning, rather than manually cleaned equipment.

All these tend to compromise food hygiene considerations. Machines may be difficult and labour-intensive to clean unless well-designed. Continuous equipment may be more prone to uncleanable internal 'dead spaces' than batch operated units. Self-cleaning relies heavily on the competence of the designer, if it is to be as efficient as manual cleaning. Thus in general the increased use of machines requires greater control of hygiene matters by the manager. Often this can be achieved by increased systematization of the process.

Study example 9.3

Productivity strategies like those described above have been extensively used by the retail industry, for example by grocery supermarket chains such as Sainsbury and Tesco.

1. Which productivity strategies have been used to develop the supermarket from the original shopkeeper-service type of outlet?
2. What mechanization is employed at check-out tills?
3. Is any systematization obvious in modern supermarkets?
4. Which of the trends described above is reversed by the advent of in-store bakeries?

Summary – strategy and food hygiene

Of three possible quality strategies considered:

- Quality control is inappropriate for food hygiene management.
- Total quality management is relevant but concentrates upon personnel aspects rather than systems aspects of quality.
- Quality assurance is appropriate for all aspects of food production and service, including food hygiene management.

Of three productivity strategies considered:

- Systematization is likely to underpin all aspects of food hygiene.
- Reorganization will generally improve food hygiene management, except where increased self-service may result in consumer abuse of the product.
- Mechanization tends to oppose food hygiene interests unless designers specifically concentrate on this aspect.
- Mechanization requires increased management control, which is best achieved by systematization.

Answers to Study Examples

Chapter 1   Food Hygiene and General Health

Example 1.1
1. Faeces samples from the guests contained live *Salmonella* bacteria.
2. Starter and turkey.
3. The turkey, because the dose was greater.
4. The turkey was not adequately cooked.

Example 1.2
1. From the environment.
2. During the first day after the can opener was used.
3. While the meat was standing in the bowl at room temperature i.e. between 10.00 am and 6.00 pm.
4. Food left in opened cans may pick up harmful levels of tin contamination.

Example 1.3
1. (i)   Distinctively coloured powder (or liquid) cleaning products (available from several manufacturers).
   (ii) By clearly labelling containers.
2. (i)   By issuing clear instructions for use with cleaning products.
   (ii) By standardizing applicators/containers (this passage refers to spray bottles).
   (iii) By training employees.
3. (i)   Saucepans (and consequently food) may be contaminated if not rinsed.
   (ii) Food residues in the pans may inactivate the disinfectant in the sanitizer.
4. (i)   Some fabrics inactivate disinfectants.
   (ii) Organic matter inactivates disinfectants.

Chapter 2   Food-borne Illness, Microorganisms and Parasites

Example 2.1
1. Typhoid fever, paratyphoid fever and dysentery.
2. *Salmonella typhi and Shigella sonnei.*
3. Botulism in food poisoning, listeriosis in food-borne diseases.

Example 2.2

1. D value = the time taken, in minutes, for a bacterial population to fall to 10% of its original value at a given temperature.
   z value = the temperature rise in degrees Celsius which will reduce the D value to 10% of its original value.
2. Those containing sugar and fat.
3. *Streptococcus faecalis.*
4. 70°C, because a 10°C rise causes a ten-fold reduction of the D value: D_{60} = 5 minutes, so D_{70} = 0.5 minute.
5. (a) Viruses are potentially more infective than bacteria.
   (b) Ice cream contains much sugar and fat.

Example 2.3

Infective	Toxic
Salmonella sp.	*C. perfringens*
Campylobacter sp.	*S. aureus*
V. parahaemolyticus	*Bacillus* spp.
E. coli	*C. botulinum*
S. zooepidemicus	Mould species
Shigella sonnei	
Listeria monocytogenes	
Yersinia enterocolitica	
Aeromonas hydrophila	
Brucella spp.	
Viruses	
Protozoa	
Roundworms	
Flatworms	

Chapter 3   Food Commodities, Food Processing and Cooking

Example 3.1

1. (i) Choking or asphyxiating while lying down.
   (ii) Dying in a fire.
   (iii) Being robbed.
2. (i) Rare roast venison may contain pathogenic bacteria. (e.g. of tuberculosis), or parasites.
   (ii) Raw oysters may contain pathogenic viruses, bacteria from sewage, or saxitoxin.
3. (i) Select reputable dealers and specify quality.

(ii)   Examine for quality.
(iii) Store the foods properly.
4. (i)   Check goods on delivery.
    (ii)   Store commodities correctly.
    (iii) Prepare and cook commodities correctly.

Example 3.2
1. + 0 +.
2. 0 0 +.
3. + + 0.
4. + + 0.
5. + 0 +.

Example 3.3
1. On the surface.
2. They will be spread from the surface into the interior, i.e. to all newly-cut surfaces.
3. By conduction.
4. Because the centre of rare beef is deliberately undercooked and unlikely to reach a high enough temperature for long enough to kill them.
5. Because the surviving bacteria may multiply to dangerous numbers in the meat.

Chapter 4   Food Hygiene and the Law

Example 4.1
1. The fly contravenes Section 14 and the botulin Section 7.
2. The fly is not of the substance, i.e. not an ingredient of soup.
3. For *Clostridium botulinum* to have grown the soup must have been stored for several days in anaerobic conditions, i.e. vacuum-packed or canned.
4. That the vacuum-packed or canned soup was bought from another company and that he had no way of knowing or suspecting that it was poisoned. There is no possible defence concerning the fly.
5. The soup must have been pre-prepared and therefore the word 'fresh' could be taken as misleading under Section 15 of the Act.

Example 4.2
1. Premises: Regs. 6, 8, 14, 15, 16, 17, 22, 23, 24, 25, 26, total 11.
2. Plant/equipment: Regs. 7, 18, 19, 20, 21, total 5.
    Personnel: Regs. 10, 11, 13, total 3.
    Process: Regs. 9, 12, 27, total 3.

3. The emphasis is strongly on Premises, with Plant/Equipment a poor second.
4. Premises are most likely to become and remain dirty due to neglect. They take a relatively long time to clean and may harbour pests. They are easier to inspect than other aspects.
5. The commonest cause of food poisoning is bacterial survival and growth due to poor time/temperature control. In order of decreasing probability this is likely to be caused by:
Process (most likely).
Personnel.
Plant/equipment.
Premises (least likely).

Example 4.3
1. The Offices Shops and Railway Premises Act, 1963; the Local Government (Miscellaneous Provisions) Act, 1976; and the Chronically Sick and Disabled Persons Act, 1970.
2. The Food Hygiene (General) Regulations, 1970, the Offices Shops and Railway Premises Sanitary Accommodation Regulations, 1960; the Washing Facilities Regulations, 1964; and the Sanitary Conveniences Regulations, 1964. The Building Regulations.
3. BS 6465 stipulates the provision of sanitary appliances in hotels and restaurants. It is commonly used as a guide by EHOs for judging compliance with the law.

Chapter 5 Food Hygiene and the Management of Premises

Example 5.1
1. Clean areas are cookers, salad preparation area, hot holding areas (*bain-maries* and hot plate servery).
2. **Strengths**: Stores are close to appropriate work areas. Flow is linear between raw food stores and servery.
Weaknesses: Transfer routes for raw and cooked foods must cross considerably during working. Waste foods have to be carried out through the whole kitchen, risking contamination.
Suggested improvements: Make a new exit through the wall to the waste collection area. Move freezers closer to storage rooms.
3. **Strengths**: The meat preparation area is isolated from the rest of the kitchen. So is the staff rest room.

Weaknesses: The vegetable preparation area is not separated from the kitchen. It is not clear where final food preparation should occur.

Suggested improvements: Meat and vegetable preparation areas should be brought closer together and partitioned from one another and from the rest of the kitchen. A final preparation area should be established. Work flow should be through the two partitioned areas.

4. *Strength*: Hand basins are available in the kitchen close to work surfaces and ovens.

Weakness: Basins are not located where staff enter from locker rooms or pass from dirty to clean areas.

Suggested improvement: Basins should be located wherever staff pass from one functional area to another. Notices above basins should be of rigid plastic and firmly attached to the wall.

Example 5.2

1. 'Complaint level' is the number of pests present necessary for customers to complain. 'Awareness level' is the number of pests present necessary for staff to notice them.
2. Pheromones are sex attractants which can be used to lure insects into traps. Just a few molecules represent an almost irresistible attraction.
3. Non-viable population means that numbers are not enough to sustain themselves by reproduction.
4. Pheromones may remove all members of one sex, so breeding cannot occur.
5. In theory sensitive detection is not needed for complete eradication. In practice the process cannot be monitored without such techniques.

Example 5.3

1. The standard is 'clean, dry and free from loose dirt, rubbish and food'.
2. (a)   Use of a hazard notice.
   (b)   Care with alkaline cleaning products.
3. There are many possibilities, for instance:
   (a)   The temperature of the water could be specified.
   (b)   The amount of cleaning powder.
   (c)   Specific procedure could be given for stains.
   (d)   Specific procedure could be given for corners, edges etc.
4. A blue powder cannot be mistaken for other products. It does not require dissolving or metering. It shows up if it accidentally gets into food or if it is not properly mopped up from the floor.
5. A powder gives poor coverage and contact, compared with a liquid or a dissolved chemical. It is usually expensive, compared with products which have to be dissolved.

Chapter 6   Food Hygiene and the Management of Plant and Equipment

Example 6.1
1. Pre-clean, main clean, rinse, disinfect and dry.
2. (c) is the pre-clean; (d) the main clean, rinse, disinfect and dry for the removable components; (e), (f) and (g) are the main clean, rinse, disinfect and dry stages for the machine body.
3. (a)   Unplug the machine.
   (b)   Dismantle the guard, blade and other moving parts.
   (c)   Soak detachable parts in hot water and sanitizer for five minutes.
   (d)   Meanwhile wipe over the body of the machine with sanitizer on a moist cloth.
   (e)   Dry with paper towels and reassemble.
   (f)   Check that the machine will run.
4. The machine should be kept in a clean, dry place at least 450 mm above ground, ideally it should be covered to exclude dust.

Example 6.2
1. (i)   Speed of dismantling/reassembly.
   (ii)   No need for tools when dismantling/reassembling.
   (iii)   Integral bolts etc., rather than removable ones.
   (iv)   All parts accessible to view.
   (v)   All parts accessible to brush or cloth.
   (vi)   No grooves or crevices in which food might lodge unnoticed.
   (vii)   Smooth external housing.
   (viii)   Glossy exterior finish.
2. (i)   Waterproof electrical components.
   (ii)   No sharp, projecting fixings.
   (iii)   Low voltage operation.
   (iv)   Adequate guard.
3. Blade – food grade stainless steel.
   Table – food grade stainless steel.
   Bearings – food grade nylon.
4. Pale blue, high gloss, thermoset enamel.

Example 6.3
1.
$$\frac{0.05 \times (450)^2 \times \sqrt{(400)} \times \sqrt[3]{(50)} \; m^2/hr}{1000}$$

$$= \frac{0.005 \times 202500 \times 20 \times 3.69}{1000}$$

$$= 747.2 \text{ m}^2/\text{hr}.$$

2.
$$\frac{0.05 \times (2 \times 300)^2 \times \sqrt{(300)} \times \sqrt[3]{(50)} \text{ m}^2/\text{hr}.}{1000}$$

$$= 1150.4 \text{ m}^2/\text{hr}.$$

3. Rotor size is the most important, because its value is squared in the equation, while speed is used as the square root.

4. Single rotor machine (a): $\dfrac{100 \times 60}{747.2} = 8.03$ min.

   Triple rotor machine (b): $\dfrac{100 \times 60}{1150.4} = 5.22$ min.

The operation could be part of the clean-as-you-go system as long as (a) the area could be completely closed off for that time and (b) the equipment could be set up and stored again within the total 15 minutes.

Chapter 7   Food Hygiene and the Management of Personnel

Example 7.1
1. Tasks: Operative's job, e.g. kitchen porter.
   Functions: Supervisor's job.
   Responsibilities: Manager's job.
   However, any level of job description may contain all three.
2. (a)   Responsibility (imagine the sentence beginning: 'Responsible for ensuring . . .').
   (b)   Task (clearly defined).
   (c)   Function (there will be at least as many tasks as types of equipment).
3. Task: 'Engage a maintenance contractor'.
   Function: 'Inspect the building for necessary repairs'.
   Responsibility: 'Ensure that the premises are kept hygienic and pest-free'.

Example 7.2
1. Because trainees are required to design and carry out experiments, i.e. they learn through actions.
2. By lecturing; by displaying overhead transparencies with tables of growth data, by showing slides of spoiled foods; or by a demonstration of growth in food stored at different temperatures.

3. Training: the work is carried out at the workplace which may make it seem directly relevant to the job.
    Education: an underlying, theoretical principle is being taught, which trainees can apply to a variety of situations.
4. By storing foods in the refrigerator rather than at room temperature; by holding food in *bain-maries* for the minimum time.
5. It is expensive of materials and time. Part of its effectiveness is due to a generous allowance of time for learning.

Example 7.3
Reward, with money, food, or even privileges, comes low in the pyramid, because these things satisfy *basic* needs (physiological or security needs).
Recognition satisfies *social* and *ego* needs (recognition, approval and respect).
Responsibility satisfies *ego/meta* needs (independence, responsibility and self-actualization).

Chapter 8   Food Hygiene and Process Management

Example 8.1
1. *System Inputs*
    RP Unpeeled potatoes, bone-in meat, frozen chickens.
    RC Peeled/ chopped vegetables, frozen burgers, filleted fish.
    RR Chilled, prepared meals, frozen plated items.
    RS Ice cream, bread, multi-portion chilled items.
    RE Fresh fruit, confectionery, ready-made sandwiches.
2. *System Intermediates*
    RC Peeled potatoes, thawed chicken.
    RR Chilled, prepared meats, frozen, plated items.
    RS Salads, multi-portion desserts.
    RE plated salads, cooked steaks.
3. *System Outputs* – depends on where the system boundary is drawn, but could include:
    RR Chilled vending items.
    RE Plated and other retail foods.
4. See figure SE.1 on page 334.
5. Vending machines for which the manager is responsible should be enclosed in the system. Sometimes the catering unit may provide meals through independently operated machines. In this case the unit is not responsible for any deterioration of the food and the machines should be considered as outside the system.

Figure SE.1   Systems diagram for study example 8.1

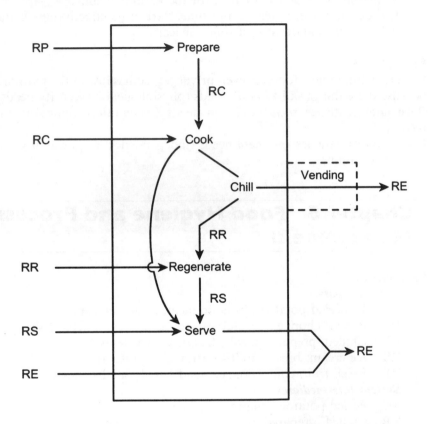

Example 8.2
1. See figure SE.2. The chart should show the long delays in the refrigerator and in the hot display cabinet. Both may permit bacterial growth. The delay in the hot cabinet is the more serious.
2. The chart shows potential cross-contamination of the cooked product on the preparation table. A chart of personnel movements showing hand washing may reveal further contamination routes.

Example 8.3
Operational control procedures are basic, or absent altogether, in much good quality restaurant production. A high output process will require

Figure SE.2   ASME flowchart for study example 8.2

◯	Delivery
⇨	To Freezer
△	Store Frozen (2 days)
⇨	To Refrigerator
D	Thaw (12–24 hr, 5°C)
D	Wait at A (30 min, room temp.)
⇨	To Oven
◯	Bake (40 min, 210°C)
⇨	Transfer to B
D	Allow to Cool (5 min0
◯	Divide into Portions
⇨	Transfer to Hot Cabinet
△	Wait for Customer (5–60 min, 65°C)
◯	Serve

much more detailed paperwork: specifications, schedules, job cards, codes of practice and documentation systems, along the lines discussed in this chapter.

Cooking, chilling, cold holding and regeneration are all critical time/ temperature events on which the safety and quality of the product depend. Criteria for timing and temperature monitoring must be set out on job cards. Staff must be trained in the new processes and issued with probe thermometers.

Time and temperatures for critical processes should be documented for each batch. pH should be measured and adjusted if it rises above 4.5. Samples of each batch should be retained for analysis.

Refrigerated vans will be needed for distribution. Loading bays and cold stores may need to be adapted, so that the chilled product is never at risk of warming during transit.

Chapter 9   Food Hygiene Strategy and Policy.

Example 9.1
1. See figure SE.3.
2. *Washing* the beans may be an opportunity to remove foreign matter such as stones. *Cooling* the beans should not take much more than 1 hour; in principle, *Clostridium perfringens* could grow, though this is not very likely.
3. Personal hygiene before mixing the salad may be important. So may the washing of utensils and the cleaning of the premises.
4. There could be a minimum temperature standard for simmering, e.g. 98°C, assuming a standard time of 2 hours. Alternatively, a minimum time standard of ten minutes could be set for pressure-cooking (which operates at about 115°C if correctly carried out).
5. No, canned red beans are available, which would eliminate the haemagglutinin hazard, the energy and the time required at one stroke.
6. It may be necessary to blanch the raw vegetables or adjust the pH of the salad to safeguard it during storage. Both of these steps would be CCPs. The cold storage step would also become a CCP, as excessive storage may be risky.

Example 9.2
1. The Directors of PQR regard the health and safety of their employees and customers as of paramount importance. All company employees are therefore required to abide at all times with the letter and spirit of the Health and Safety at Work Act, 1974 and its related legislation. (Examples or a full list of legislation may be given here.)
2. For example, first aid, safety signs, notifiable diseases, prescribed dangerous machines, boilers and pressure vessels, fire safety, etc.

Figure SE.3 CCP Analysis for Red Bean Salad for Study example 9.1

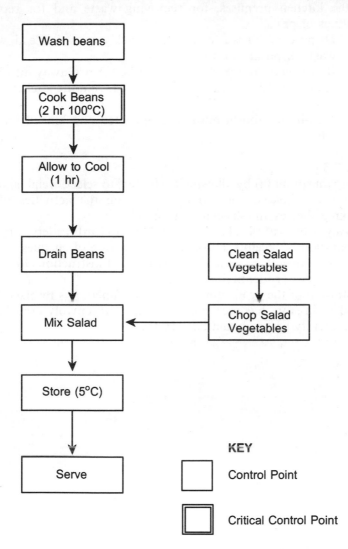

3. **Food and Beverage Manager**: overall responsibility for the hygiene of premises, plant and personnel; for pest control, staff induction and training etc.
    Chef: specific responsibility for ensuring the ensuring the cleanliness of plant and equipment, the cleanliness and fitness of individuals reporting for work, and the correct operation of the production process.

Kitchen porter: responsibility for ensuring the day-to-day cleanliness of the kitchen premises, for removing waste and for reporting sightings of pests.

4. (i)   Dispose of all waste food as quickly as possible down the waste disposal sink unit.

(ii)   Bones, cans and packaging must be thrown away into bins.

(iii) All non-food rubbish must be cleared from the kitchen twice a day.

(iv)   Non-food rubbish must be compacted and binned immediately.

Example 9.3

1. Reorganization: (a) by allowing customers to select, weigh and serve their own choices; and (b) by restricting the activities of staff stocking shelves and checking out goods.

2. Conveyor-belts at tills, bar-code readers, zip card readers, automatic preparation of receipts, automatic preparation of cheques.

3. Check-out operators sometimes have lists of instructions for dealing with cheques or identifying goods.

4. Separation of the production and service function is reversed by the trend to in-store bakeries. The latter are presumably used because good quality bread should be very fresh.

Glossary

Key

biol	biology
bldg	building, construction or services
chem	chemistry
cleaning	cleaning science or general hygiene
culin	culinary
eng	engineering
epidem	epidemiology: the study of disease
food tech	food technology
law	law
managmt	management
math	mathematics
med	medical
microbiol	microbiology
personnel	personnel management
pest con	pest control
phys	physics
toxicol	toxicology: the study of poisons

Abrasive *(cleaning)* Powdered substance with tiny, hard grains which is added to cleaning agents to enhance their scouring power.

Acid *(chem)* Substance which dissolves in water to give a sour-tasting, corrosive solution with a pH value less than 7.0.

Acute toxicity *(epidem)* Poisonous effect which develops rapidly after one or a few doses of a toxic substance.

Agar *(microbiol)* Inert extract of seaweed used to thicken broth, forming a gel on which microorganisms can be grown.

Alkali *(chem)* Substance with a pH value greater then 7.0, which, when dissolved in water, will neutralize acids.

Allergy *(biol)* Hypersensitivity to some substance, causing illness symptoms such as dermatitis, coughing etc.

Allergenic *(biol)* Capable of causing an allergy.

Alzheimer's disease *(epidem)* Disorder of the brain which leads to premature senility.

Ambient temperature *(phys)* Temperature of the surroundings, e.g. 'room temperature'.

Amphoteric *(chem)* Having both positive and negative electrical properties within the same atom or molecule.

Anaerobic respiration *(biol)* Process of energy production within a living organism without the use of oxygen.

Anionic *(chem)* Having a negative electrical charge within the atom or molecule.

Antibiotic *(microbiol)* Very specific antibacterial agent of complex chemical structure, usually produced by other microorganisms.

Anticoagulant *(med)* Drug which prevents the clotting of blood.

Antimony *(chem)* Heavy greyish metal similar to lead but more brittle.

Appeal *(law)* Resort to a higher authority to change a legal decision.

Architrave *(bldg)* Moulding around a window aperture or doorway, usually of wood.

Aseptic *(microbiol)* Free of bacteria and other microorganisms.

Asphalt *(bldg)* Black or coloured tarry substance made up of bitumen, sand and grit, used for surfacing roads and pedestrian areas.

Bactericide *(microbiol)* Chemical substance capable of killing bacterial cells; disinfectant.

Bacteristat *(microbiol)* Chemical substance capable of inhibiting bacterial growth; preservative.

Bain marie *(culin)* Device for holding food hot in containers immersed in heated water or steam.

Baiting *(pest con)* Use of poisoned bait to kill rodent or insect pests.

Bile duct *(biol)* Narrow tube which conducts bile from the gall bladder and liver into the small intestine.

Biological washing *(cleaning)* Textile washing which relies upon enzymes to dissolve protein binding dirt onto clothing.

Binary fission *(microbiol)* Reproductive process of bacteria in which each cell splits into two new organisms

Blanching *(food tech)* Heat processing of raw fruit and vegetables to destroy spoilage enzymes before freezing or canning.

Blast chilling/Blast freezing *(food tech)* Rapid cooling by means of a strong current of cold air directed over the food.

Botulism *(epidem)* Severe poisoning caused by botulin toxin, which is produced by *Clostridium botulinum* bacteria.

Bovine spongiform encephalopathy *(epidem)* Degenerative brain disease of cattle thought to be transmitted through cattle feed.

Breather pipe *(bldg)* Pipe rising from sewers which releases gases and prevents pressure building up.

BSE *(epidem)*, see **Bovine spongiform encephalopathy.**

Bush *(eng)* Metal tube or sleeve which acts as a bearing for a rotating shaft.

Cationic *(chem)* Having a positive electrical charge within the atom or molecule.

Cell *(microbiol)* Smallest unit of living matter capable of functioning independently.

Cell membrane *(microbiol)* Permeable, flexible skin surrounding the cell contents.

Cell wall *(microbiol)* Rigid, protective casing which encloses the cells of bacteria, fungi and higher plants.

Chronic toxicity *(epidem)* Poisonous effect which develops slowly over many years before symptoms are observed.

Cobalt-60 *(phys)* Radioactive isotope of cobalt which emits high-energy gamma rays. Used in radiotherapy and in the irradiation of foodstuffs.

Code of practice *(managmt)* Simplified set of rules or procedures which can be easily communicated to staff.

Colony *(microbiol)* Cluster or group of bacterial cells on an agar surface, formed from the reproduction of one original cell.

Conduction *(phys)* Process of heat transfer through a solid object, or from one solid to another.

Court of Record *(law)* Specially designated court of law in which discussions and decisions are recorded for future public reference.

Coving *(bldg)* Concave, curved (sometimes decorated) surface between the wall and ceiling or wall and floor of a room.

Cyst *(biol))* Protective, bladder-like membrane surrounding the larva of a worm or protozoon.

Cytoplasm *(microbiol)* Jelly-like contents of a cell, not including the nucleus.

Damp-proof course/Damp-proof membrane *(bldg)* Impermeable layer set into a wall to prevent damp rising up it by capillary action.

Dermatitis *(med)* Inflammation, reddening, encrustation etc. of the skin.

Detritus *(cleaning)* Loose dirt or waste matter.

Dichloromethane *(food tech, cleaning)* Solvent used for extracting caffeine from coffee. Also used for degreasing equipment and for removing fats, oils etc.

Diffuser *(bldg)* Translucent cover for diffusing the light from a fluorescent tube lamp.

Dinoflagellate *(biol)* Reddish coloured single-celled algae, some species of which produce powerful toxins.

D.p.c. *(bldg)* see **Damp-proof course.**

Emulsify *(phys)* Break up a fat or oil into small droplets and suspend it in water.

Endospore *(microbiol)* Bacterial spore formed inside the cell and released by rupture of the cell wall.

Enzymes *(biol)* Complex proteins produced by all living things, which catalyze biochemical reactions such as digestion.

Epoxy resin *(bldg)* Self-hardening resin based on the epoxide chemical group (a type of ether linkage). Very tough and resistant.

Ergonomics *(managmt)* Study of human efficiency in the working environment

Ergot *(toxicol)* Toxin produced by *Claviceps* fungi which are found as parasites of rye and rye grass.

Evaluation *(managmt)* Assessment of value, based on a logical process.

Exponential *(math)* (of a quantity) Doubling in a set interval or series.

Faeces *(biol)* Solid bodily waste of humans or animals.

Faecal–oral route *(epidem)* Infection route in which bacteria from faeces are transferred to the mouth.

Fluorescent lamp *(bldg)* Electric lamp, usually in the form of a tube, in which electrical energy is converted into visible light by fluorescent solid material.

Flux *(phys)* A flow, field or discharge, particularly of electromagnetic radiation such as light, microwaves etc.

Forced convection *(phys)* Heat transfer to or from a pumped current of liquid or gas.

Fungicide *(microbiol)* Chemical substance capable of killing fungi and moulds; disinfectant.

Fungistat *(microbiol) Chemical substance capable of inhibiting the growth of fungi and moulds; preservative.*

Galvanized metal *(chem)* Iron or steel which has been protected from corrosion by coating with zinc. The zinc preferentially corrodes, thus sparing the iron.

Gastro-enteritis *(epidem)* Inflammation of the intestine and/or the stomach, usually with sickness and diarrhoea.

Gland *(eng)* Sealing device to prevent lubricant passing through a bearing along a rotating shaft.

Granolithic flooring *(bldg)* Composite flooring material made of granite chippings and fine cement ground down to a smooth finish.

Growth medium *(microbiol)* Broth or agar jelly used to support the growth of microorganisms.

Haemagglutinin *(toxicol)* Complex protein toxin present in raw, dried beans, causing severe vomiting and illness when ingested.

Heat exchanger *(food tech)* Device for transferring heat from one liquid to another without allowing the two to mix.

Heavy metal *(chem)* Any metallic element which has a higher atomic number than iron. Salts of heavy metals are usually poisonous to humans.

Histamine *(biol/chem)* Chemical substance released in the body during allergic reactions, causing irritation, reddening of skin, palpitations etc.

Histidine *(biol/chem)* Amino acid present in all protein, but especially in the flesh of tuna and mackerel.

Hydrogen ion *(chem)* Positive particle formed by removing the electron from a hydrogen atom; hydrogen ions are released by acids and bound (neutralized) by alkalis.

Hygroscopic *(phys)* Capable of absorbing moisture from the air.

Infection *(med)* Invasion of the body or its organs by bacteria, parasites or other pathogenic organisms.

Infra-red *(phys)* Radiant heat with a wavelength greater than that of (visible) red light.

In situ *(Latin)* 'In place' e.g. in situ cleaning or maintenance is carried without removing a machine or its parts to another location.

Intoxication *(toxicol)* Poisoning of any sort.

Jaundice *(med)* Disease of the liver which causes yellowing of the skin, due to abnormally high levels of bile pigments in the blood.

Lactose *(chem)* The sugar present in milk. It is chemically similar to sucrose (cane sugar), but much less sweet to the taste.

Latent heat *(phys)* The energy which is required to produce a change of physical state, i.e. to convert ice to water or water to steam.

Larva *(biol)* Immature form of an insect or other lower form of life, which develops into the adult by metamorphosis.

Leptospirae *(microbiol)* Spiral bacteria which cause Weil's disease.

Listeriosis *(epidem)* Illness caused by *Listeria* bacteria.

Magnetron *(phys)* Device for producing microwaves by passing alternating current through a wire coil.

Mesophile *(microbiol)* Bacterium which grows best in the middle temperature range: 20–40°C.

Metmyoglobin *(food tech)* Brownish, oxidized form of myoglobin.

Mezzanine *(bldg)* Intermediate storey of a building, situated between two floors.

Microorganism *(microbiol)* Living organism of microscopic size, e.g. bacterium, yeast, virus etc.

Microaerobic *(microbiol)* (of bacteria) Requiring a small concentration of oxygen or air for growth.

Microwaves *(phys)* Electromagnetic radiation with a wavelength longer than infra-red but shorter than radio waves, used for cooking.

Modified atmosphere packaging *(food tech)* System of packaging food in a special mixture of gases which helps maintain the keeping quality.

Multiple-choice test *(personnel)* Test with several possible answers, from which the candidate must choose the correct one.

Mycelium *(biol)* Intertwined mass of filamentous cells making up the main body of a fungus or mould.

Mycotoxins *(toxicol)* Poisonous substances produced by fungi and moulds.

Myoglobin *(biol)* Red pigment of muscle tissue.

Nisin *(chem)* Natural antibiotic found in cheese, where it is produced during fermentation and maturation.

Nucleus *(microbiol)* Spherical or egg-shaped body within every living cell, which contains the cell's genetic material.

Nutrient *(microbiol)* Any substance capable of providing nourishment (e.g. to microorganisms).

Obstruction *(law)* The offence of hindering the detection or punishment of an(other) offence.

Oil-immersion lens *(microbiol)* Very high-resolution objective lens designed to be dipped into a drop of oil on the microscope slide and giving very high magnification.

Omnivore *(biol)* Animal which eats both animal and vegetable foods.

Organism *(biol)* Any living thing, including plants, animals, bacteria etc.

Organoleptic *(food tech)* Testing or sampling using the senses: taste, smell, sight etc.

Osmosis *(chem)* Migration of a solvent through a semi-permeable membrane from a less concentrated to a more concentrated solution.

Oxalic acid *(toxicol)* Natural toxic agent of rhubarb leaves and parts of certain other plants.

Oxidation *(chem)* Process of reaction with oxygen or an oxidizing agent.

Parasite *(biol)* Organism which depends upon a host organism for food, shelter etc. and thereby harms the host.

Pathogen *(microbiol)* Any organism capable of causing illness.

Phosgene *(chem)* Poisonous gas of formula $COCl_2$ used as a manufacturing intermediate and in chemical warfare.

pH Scale *(chem)* Measure of the hydrogen ion potential of a solution; values above pH 7.0 indicate alkalis, those below pH 7.0 acids.

Plasmid *(microbiol)* Portion of genetic material which can be passed from one bacterial cell to another, causing a mutation.

Plasticizer *(chem)* Oily substance added to rigid plastics, particularly PVC, to make them more supple.

Polyphenol oxidases *(biol)* Plant enzymes responsible for the browning of fruit and vegetables by catalyzing the reaction of their polyphenolic constituents with air.

Proliferation *(microbiol)* The rapid multiplication and growth of microorganisms.

Protozoa *(microbiol)* Comparatively large, single-celled organisms such as amoeba, paramecium etc.

Psychrotroph *(microbiol)* see **Psychrophile**.

Psychrophile *(microbiol)* Bacterium which grows best in the low temperature range: $-8°C$ to $+40°C$.

Public analyst *(chem)* Analytical chemist within a private practice to whom individuals, companies and local authorities can bring samples for analysis.

Pus *(med)* Thick, yellow or greenish liquid produced within a boil; contains bacteria, antibodies, breakdown products etc.

Real ale *(food tech)* Beer which undergoes secondary fermentation in the cask and is dispensed by hand pumping, rather than pressurized with carbon dioxide.

Red tide *(microbiol))* Reddening of sea water due to proliferation of dinoflagellates. Often associated with death of sea life due to dinoflagellate toxins.

Rennet *(food tech)* Enzyme extracted from the fourth stomach of a calf, used for clotting milk in junket and cheese manufacture.

Rising damp *(bldg)* Moisture drawn up through the masonry of a wall when the damp-proof course fails.

Role-play *(personnel)* Teaching method in which students act out situations and describe their behaviour and emotions.

Royal assent *(law)* Formal signing of a new Act of Parliament by the monarch, after which it becomes law.

St John's fire *(epidem)* Burning/tingling illness of the limbs caused by eating rye bread contaminated with ergot.

Sanitizer *(cleaning)* Any cleaning product which simultaneously disinfects.

Saponification *(chem)* Reaction of alkalis with fats or oils, forming soap.

Scarify *(cleaning)* To scratch off, break up or loosen stubborn dirt.

Semidisposable *(cleaning)* Capable of being used more than once before being discarded.

Sensible heat *(phys)* Heat content of an object which raises its temperature and can therefore be sensed (as opposed to latent heat).

Septic *(med)* Infected with bacteria to the point of producing pus.

Sequestering agent *(cleaning)* Chemical substance which adheres to calcium and magnesium ions in hard water, so that they do not interfere with the washing process.

Silt trap *(bldg)* Trap similar to a grease trap immersed in a drain below a vegetable peeler etc. to retain organic waste.

Skirting *(bldg)* Protective border of wood or tile fixed along the bottom of an interior wall.

Solar gain *(bldg)* Heat gain in a building due to sunlight entering (mostly) through the windows.

Sphincter *(biol)* Ring of muscle around an opening in the body, acting as a valve.

Statute *(law)* Any formal, written law.

Statutory implement *(law)* Usually applies to an item of secondary legislation, i.e. to Regulations or Orders drawn up by a Minister at the authorization of Parliament.

Sterilization *(food tech)* Complete destruction of all microorganisms, usually by heat.

Summary trial *(law)* Trial in a Magistrate's or Sheriff's Court.

Surface active agent *(cleaning)* Chemical substance capable of suspending dirt and reducing the surface tension of water.

Surfactant *(cleaning)* see **Surface active agent.**

Synergist *(chem)* Chemical which enhances the activity of another (e.g. a drug, detergent etc.) so that a mixture of the two is more potent than the same weight of either on its own.

Tanking *(bldg)* Moisture-proofing of a cellar by applying a water-repellent membrane to the outside or interior.

Tap proportioner *(cleaning)* Device which injects a controlled dose of cleaning agent into the water it dispenses.

Terrazzo *(bldg)* Composite flooring material made of marble chippings and fine cement ground down to a smooth finish

Thermophile *(microbiol)* Bacterium which grows best in the high temperature range: 35–80°C.

Thermoplastic *(chem)* (of synthetic resins) Capable of being softened and moulded into shape when heated.

Thermosetting *(chem)* (of synthetic resins) Set by heat into a rigid mass which cannot be softened or moulded on further heating.

Three-phase equipment *(eng)* Electrical equipment which uses more than one alternating 'live' supply so that a maximum of 415V is delivered to it rather than the 240V of any one 'live' phase.

Total viable count *(microbiol)* Total number of bacteria which can be grown from a sample or swab.

Toxicity *(epidem)* Potential of a poisonous substance to cause illness or death.

Toxin *(microbiol)* Poisonous substance (produced by a living organism).

Tungsten filament lamp *(bldg)* Electric light bulb, filled with low-pressure gas, containing a tungsten wire filament.

TVC *(microbiol)* see **Total viable count.**

Ultra-violet *(phys)* Electromagnetic radiation similar to visible light, but of shorter wavelength. Capable of destroying some air- and water-borne bacteria.

Vaporization *(phys)* Conversion from a liquid into a vapour.

Virion *(microbiol)* Single unit of a virus.

Virulence *(toxicol)* Potential of a pathogenic organism to cause an infection.

Viscera *(biol)* Intestines and other entrails of an animal.

Weevils *(biol)* Small beetle species which live and produce their young in stores of foodstuffs such as cereals.

Whitlow *(med)* Localized septic inflammation around a finger or toenail.

White metal *(eng)* Any of a number of metal alloys used in bearings and bushes.

Zoonosis *(med)* Disease which can be transmitted to humans from animals.

Bibliography

* All texts published in London unless shown otherwise.

ABLCRS (Association of British Laundry, Cleaning and Rental Services) (1987) 'Hygiene and clothing – the role of workwear in the food industry', *British Food Journal*, May/June, pp. 58–59.

Adair, J. (1968) *Training for Leadership*, Macdonald.

Addison, M. E. (1971) *Essentials of Organization and Methods*, Heinemann.

Allen, D. M. (1983) *Accommodation and Cleaning Services, vol. 1*, Hutchinson.

Anon. (1985) 'The Crown immunity debate', *Health and Safety Institute Bulletin*, 119, 5 Nov, pp. 10–11.

Anon (1986) 'Food epidemiology: gastro-intestinal infections 1977–1985', *Environmental Health*, 94, pp. 159–160.

Armstrong, R., Aveyard, J. and Pinegar, J. A. (1989) 'Listeria in cook–chill menu items', *Environmental Health*, 97(9) pp. 24–26.

Avery, A. C. (1973) 'Equipment arrangement for greater worker productivity' in *Increasing Productivity in Food Service*, Pedderson, R. B. *et al.* (eds) Boston: Cahners Books, pp. 57–87.

Avery, A. C. (1974) 'Development and evaluation of a hospital kitchen rehabilitation layout and design system', in *Food service trends*, C. E. Eschbach (ed.) Boston: Cahners Books.

Barrow, G. I. and Miller, D. C. (1976) '*Vibrio parahaemolyticus* and seafoods', in *Microbiology in Agriculture, Fisheries and Food*, Skinner, F. A. and Carr, J. G. (eds) Academic Press, pp. 181–195.

Bauman, H. (1974) 'The HACCP concept and microbiological hazard categories', *Food Technology* (September) pp. 30–34.

Beynon, A. K., Griffiths, L., Reeves, P. and Stewart, D. (1988) 'Game controls', *Environmental Health*, 96(7) pp. 14–15.

Blaser, M. J. (1982) '*Campylobacter jejuni* and food', *Food Technology*, 36(3) pp. 89–92.

Bobeng, B. J. and David, B. D. (1975) 'Identifying the electric field distribution in a microwave oven: a practical method for food service operations', *Microwave Energy Applications Newsletter*, 8(3), Nov/Dec.

Bobeng, B. J. and David, B. D. (1978a) 'HACCP models for quality control of entrée production in hospital food service systems I', *Journal of the American Dietetic Association* 73, pp. 524–529.

Bobeng, B. J. and David, B. D. (1978b) 'HACCP models for quality control of entree production in hospital food service systems II', *Journal of the American Dietetic Association* 73, pp. 530–535.

Bryan, F. L. (1978) 'Factors that contribute to outbreaks of foodborne disease', *Journal of Food Protection*, 41(10) pp. 816–827.

Bryan, F. L. (1979) 'Prevention of foodborne diseases in food service establishments', *Journal of Environmental Health*, 41, pp. 198–206.

Bryan, F. L. (1981) 'Hazard analysis of food service operations', *Food Technology*, February, pp. 78–87.

Bryan, F. L. (1988) 'Factors that contribute to outbreaks of food borne disease', *Journal of Food Protection*, 51, pp. 663–673.

Bryan, F. L. and McKinley, T. W (1979) 'Hazard analysis and control of roast beef preparation in food service establishments', *Journal of Food Protection*, 42, 4–18.

Bushell, R. J. (1979) 'Preventing the problem – a new look at building planned, preventive maintenance', *Institute of Building Information Service, Information Sheet no. 11*.

Chattopadhyay, B. and Teli, J. C. (1986) 'Bacterial contamination of spices', *Environmental Health*, 94(6) pp. 106–107.

CEC (Commission of the European Community) (1985) *Completion of the Internal Market: Community Legislation on Foodstuffs*, COM(86) 747 final, 23 December.

Clacherty, J. E., Stringer, S., Truscott, V. and Tebbutt, G. M. (1988) 'Study reveals problems with real-cream cakes', *Environmental Health*, 96(1) pp. 13–17 and 96(4) pp. 23–24.

Daniels, D. (1988) 'Sous vide and Capkold; two approaches to cooking under vacuum', *The Consultant*, Spring, pp. 26–28.

Dempster, J. F., Reid, S. N. and Cody, O. (1973) 'Sources of contamination of cooked, ready-to-eat, cured and uncured meats', *Journal of Hygiene (Cambridge)*, 71, pp. 815–823.

Denny, C. B., Humber, J. Y. and Bohrer, C. W. (1971) 'Effect of toxin concentration on the heat inactivation of staphylococcal enterotoxins in beef bouillon and phosphate buffer', *Applied Microbiology*, 21, pp. 1064–1073.

Dwyer, S. J., Unklesbay, K., Unklesbay, N. and Dunlop, C. (1977) *Identification of Major Areas Energy Utilization Within the Food Processing/Foodservice Industry, Research Report to the NSF*, NSFSIA 75–16222, Washington, D.C.

Eastwood, M. (1986) 'The developing role of the environmental health officer', *Environmental Health*, 94(8) pp. 215–219.

Edelmeyer, H. (1982) 'Amphotensides – how they kill and clean in the food factory', *Food Processing Industry*, August, pp. 17–18.

FMF (Food Manufacturers' Federation) and FMA (Food Machinery Association) (1970) *Report of the Joint Technical Committee on the Hygienic Design of Food Plant*.

Galbraith, N. S., Barrett, N. T. and Sockett, P. N. (1987) 'The changing pattern of food-borne disease in England and Wales', *Public Health*, 101, pp. 319–328.

Genigeorgis, C. and Riemann, H. (1979) 'Food processing and hygiene', in *Foodborne Infections and Intoxications*, Riemann, H. and Bryan, F. L. (eds) New York: Academic Press, pp. 613–713.

Gilbert, R. J. and Taylor, A. J. (1976) '*Bacillus cereus* food poisoning', in *Microbiology in Agriculture, Fisheries and Food*, Skinner, F. A. and Carr, J. G. (eds) Academic Press, London, pp. 197–250.

Gorbell, G. L. (1982) 'Loss prevention evaluations for chemical operations' in *Safety and Accident Prevention in Chemical Operations*, Fawcett, H. H. and Wood, W. S. (eds) New York: Wiley Interscience, pp. 711–738.

Grater, C. (1979) 'The caterer's requirement for food quality', in *Advances in Catering Technology*, Glew, G. (ed.) Applied Science Publishers, pp. 57–63.

Green, P. (1989) 'Food Hygiene – the missing directive', *British Food Journal*, 91(2) pp. 28–30.

Haberstroh, C. (1988) 'HACCP: making the system work', *Food Engineering*, August, pp. 70–80.

Harrington, J. R. (1981) *Hotel Management Accountancy and Control Systems*, Northwood, p.56.

Hayes, P. R. (1979) 'Hygiene and the design of equipment for the catering industry' in *Catering Equipment and Systems Design*, Glew, G. (ed.) Applied Science Publishers, pp. 109–132.

Hayes, D.K. and Huffman, L. (1985) 'Menu analysis: a better way', *Cornell Hotel and Restaurant Administration Quarterly*, February, pp. 64–70.

Heidelbaugh, N. D., Smith, M. C. and Rambaut, P. C. (1973) 'Food safety in NASA Nutrition Programs', *Journal of the American Veterinary Medical Association*, 163(9) pp. 1065–1070.

Hobbs, B. C. (1976) 'Microbiological hazards of international trade', in *Microbiology in Agriculture, Fisheries and Food*, Skinner, F. A. and Carr, J. G. (eds) Academic Press.

Holt, P. E. (1981) 'Role of Campylobacter spp. in human and animal disease: a review', *Journal of the Royal Society of Medicine*, 74(6) pp. 437–440.

Illuminating Engineering Society (1977) *The IES Code: Interior lighting*, IES.

Jacob, M. (1988) 'Regulation of water quality for the food industry', *British Food Journal*, 90(3) pp. 114–116.

Jarvis, B. (1976) 'Mycotoxins in Food', in *Microbiology in Agriculture, Fisheries Food*, Skinner, F. A. and Carr, J. G. (eds) Academic Press, pp. 251–267.

Jones, P. (1983) 'The restaurant – a place for quality control and product maintenance?', *International Journal of Hospitality Management*, 2(2) pp. 93–100.

Kauffman, F. L. (1974) 'How the FDA uses HACCP', *Food Technology*, September, pp. 51–52.

Khimji, P. L. (1986) The 'discovery learning' technique in food hygiene training', *Environmental Health*, 94(7) pp. 191–192.

King, C. A. (1984) 'Service-Oriented quality control' *Cornell Hotel and Restaurant Administration Quarterly*, November, pp. 92–98.

King, C. A. (1986) 'Service quality is different,' *The Consultant*, Winter, pp. 27–31.

Kotschevar, L. (1968) 'Some basic factors in food service planning', *Cornell Hotel and Restaurant Administration Quarterly*, May, pp. 104–113.

Kubias, F. O. (1982) 'Tools and techniques for chemical safety training', in *Safety and Accident Prevention in Chemical Operations*, Fawcett, H. H. and Wood, W. S. (eds) USA: Wiley Interscience, pp. 739–757.

Lacey, R. and Kerr, K. (1988) 'The enigma of food-borne listeriosis', *Environmental Health*, 96, (10) pp. 7–9.

Longree, K. and Armbruster, G. (1987) *Quantity Food Sanitation*, USA: Wiley Interscience.

McDowell, D. A., Hobson I., Strain, J. J. and Owens, J. J. (1986) 'Bacterial microflora of chill-stored beef carcasses', *Environmental Health*, 94(3) pp. 65–68.

Martin, C. A. and Clark, B. R. (1989) 'The use of production management techniques in the tourism industry', *4th Annual International Conference of the Operations Management Association*, University of Glasgow.

Melling, J. and Capel, B. J. (1978) 'Characteristics of *Bacillus cereus* emetic toxin', *FEMS Microbiology Letters*, 4, pp. 133–135.

Mendes, M. F. and Lynch, D. J. (1976) 'A bacteriological survey of washrooms and toilets', *Journal of Hygiene (Cambridge)*, 76, pp. 183–190.

Mendes, M. F. , Lynch, D. J. and Stanley, C. A. (1978) 'A bacteriological survey of kitchens', *Environmental Health*, 86(10) pp. 227–231.

Merricks, P. and Jones, P. (1986) *The management of catering operations*, Holt, Reinhart and Winston.

Miller, I. S., Botton, F. J. and Dawkins, H. C. (1986) 'An outbreak of campylobacter enteritis transmitted by puppies', *Environmental Health*, 94(1) pp. 11–14.

Milson, A. and Kirk, D. (1979) 'The caterer as a process engineer', in *Advances in catering technology*, Glew, G. (ed.) Applied Science Publishers, pp. 157–172.

Morrison, R. P. and Carter, R. R. (1975) 'Certification of Food Service managers – why and how?', *Journal of Milk Food Technology*, 38(3) pp. 176–181.

Munce, B. A. (1981) 'The role of the food service industry in the microbiological safety of food: a review', *Food Technology in Australia*, 33(7) July, pp. 326–331.

Munce, B. A. (1984) 'Hazard analysis and critical control points and the food service industry', *Food Technology in Australia*, 36(5) pp. 214–217 and 222.

Murphy, F. J. and Mepham, P. (1988) 'Microbial quality of ice cubes: a survey' *British Food Journal*, 90(3) pp. 120–122.

NAS (National Academy of Sciences) (1969) *Classification of Food Products according to Risk: An Evaluation of the Salmonella Problem*, USA: National Academy Press.

Noah, N. D., Bender, A. E., Reaidi, G. B. and Gilbert, R. J. (1980) 'Food poisoning from raw red kidney beans', *British Medical Journal*, 281, pp. 236–237.

North, R. (1987) 'Memorandum for producing clean kitchen machinery', *Environmental Health*, 95(1) pp. 23–27.

North, R. A. E. (1980) 'Food contact surface disinfectants: additional criteria for selection', *Environmental Health*, 88(1) pp. 10–14.

NRC (National Research Council) (1985) *An Evaluation of the role of microbiological criteria for foods and food ingredients*, National Academy Press, USA.

Olsvik, O. and Kupperud, G. (1982) 'Enterotoxin production in milk at 22°C and 4°C by *E. coli* and *Y. enterocolitica*', *Applied Environmental Microbiology*, 43, pp. 997–1000.

Ozog, H. and Bendixen, L. M. (1987) 'Hazard identification and quantification', *Chemical Engineering Progress*, April, pp. 55–64.

Paulus, K. (1978) 'Ready to serve foods: definitions, application and quality requirements', in *How Ready are Ready-to-serve Foods?* Paulus, K. (ed.) Basle: S. Karger.

Phillips, P. (1986) 'Pest control – an ecological approach', *Environmental Health*, 94(6) pp. 138–141.

PHLS Salmonella Subcommittee (1983) 'Recommendations on exclusion of food handlers', *Community Medicine*, 5, pp. 152–169.

Pope, H. H. (1974) 'How to develop an employee training system in food service organizations', in *Food Service Trends*, ed. Eschbach, C. E., Cahners Books, USA, pp. 90–95.

Power, V. F. and Collins, J. K. (1986) 'The production of microbiologically safe shellfish – lessons from the classification of shellfish at source', *Environmental Health*, 94(6) pp. 124–128.

Prescott, A. (1989) What's the harm in aluminium? *New Scientist*, no. 1648, 21 Jan, pp. 58–62.

Prugh, R. W. (1982) 'Practical application of fault-tree analysis', in *Safety and Accident Prevention in Chemical Operations*, H. H. Fawcett and, W. S. Wood (eds) USA: Wiley Interscience, pp. 789–805.

Reid, C. (1986) 'Bacterial quality of salad bar foods', *Environmental Health*, 94(5) pp. 91–94.

Riggs, S. (1986) 'Today's Food Safety Codes on trial', *Restaurants and Institutions*, 1 October, pp. 109–112.

Riordan, T. (1988) 'Investigation of outbreaks of winter vomiting disease', *Environmental Health*, 96(8) pp. 17–20.

Roberts, D. (1982) 'Factors contributing to outbreaks of food poisoning in England and Wales 1970–1979', *Journal of Hygiene (Cambridge)*, 89, pp. 491–498.

Roberts, D. (1988) 'Review of the Food Act', *British Food Journal*, 90(5) pp. 219–220.

Roberts, R. J. (1976) 'Bacterial diseases of farmed fishes', in *Microbiology in Agriculture, Fisheries and Food*, Skinner, F. A. and Carr, J. G. (eds) Academic Press.

Robertson, P. (1986) 'The modern drinks vending machine: a link in the food poisoning chain?, *Environmental Health*, 94, pp. 281–285.

Robinson, R. P. (1987) 'Ridding NHS hospitals of serious infestations', *Environmental Health*, 95(1) pp. 31–32.

Rock, R. and Warren, M. (1986) 'Trial summarily or on indictment', *Environmental Health*, 94(5) pp. 125–131.

Rose, J. B. (1988) 'Occurrence and significance of cryptosporidium in water', *Journal of the American Water Works Association*, 80(2) pp. 80–87.

Sheard, M. (1988) 'The application of HACCP in the UK catering industry', in *Hygiene Management in Catering: The Need for Change*, Light, N. (ed.) Conference proceedings, Dorset Institute, Poole, Dorset.

Silverman, G. (1982) 'Assuring the microbial quality of hospital patient feeding systems', in *Hospital Feeding Systems*, Washington, DC: National Academy Press.

Snyder, O. P. (1986) 'Microbiological quality assurance in food service operations', *Food Technology*, July, pp. 122–130.

Stewart, A. J. (1986) 'Kitchen design' *The Consultant*, Winter, pp. 43–44.

Sumner, J. L., Samaraweera, I., Jayaweera, V. and Fonseka, G. (1982) 'A survey of process hygiene in the Sri Lankan prawn industry', *Journal of the Science of Food and Agriculture* 33 pp. 802–808.

Taubert, C. A. (1982) 'Defining sanitation hazards and critical control points in foodservice operations', *Journal of Foodservice Systems*, 2, pp. 171–175.

Tebbutt, G. M. (1984) 'A microbiological study of various food premises, with an assessment of cleaning and disinfection practices', *Journal of Hygiene (Cambridge)*, 92, pp. 365–375.

Thomsett, C. E. (1986) 'Mussels from the Wash; pollution problems', *Environmental Health*, 94(7) pp. 169–172.

Turner, B. D. (1987) 'Forming a clearer view of L. bostrychophilus', *Environmental Health*, 95(5) pp. 9–13.

White, E. C. (1974) 'Motivation and productivity in middle management', in *Food service trends*, Eschbach, C. E. (ed.) New York: Cahners Books.

WHO (World Health Organization) (1977) *Food Hygiene in Catering Establishments: Legislation and Model Regulations*, WHO offset Publication No. 34, Geneva.

WHO (1982) *Report of the International Commission on Microbiological Specifications for Foods: The Hazards Analysis, Critical Control Point System in Food Hygiene*, WHO document no. VPH/82.37, Geneva.

Further reading

Food Hygiene and General Hygiene

Allen, D.M. (1983) *Accommodation and Cleaning Services, vols. 1 and 2*, Hutchinson.

Cornwell, P.B. (1973) *Pest Control in Buildings*, Hutchinson Benham, London.

Meehan, A.P. (1984) *Rats and Mice: Their Biology and Control*, Rentokil Library.

Food-borne Illness, Microorganisms and Parasites

Riemann, H. and Bryan, F.L. (eds) (1979) *Food-borne Infections and Intoxications*, New York: Academic Press.

Food Commodities, Food Processing and Cooking

Skinner, F.A. and Carr, J.G. (eds) (1976) *Microbiology in Agriculture, Fisheries and Food*, Academic Press, London.

Conning, D.M., Leigh, L. and Ricketts, B.D. (1988) *Food Fit to Eat*, Sphere Books

Food Hygiene and the Law

Pannett, A. (1989) *Principles of Hotel and Catering Law, 2nd edn*, Cassell.

Food Hygiene and the Management of Premises

Pedderson, R.B. *et al.* (eds.) (1973) *Increasing Productivity in Food Service*, USA: Cahners Books.

Food Hygiene and the Management of Plant and Equipment

Glew, G. (ed.) (1979) *Advances in Catering Technology*, Applied Science Publishers.

Food Hygiene and Personnel Management

Adair, J. (1968) *Training for Leadership*, Macdonald.

Food Hygiene and Process Management

Eschbach, C. E. (ed.) (1974) *Food service trends*, New York: Cahners Books.
Knight, J. B. and Kotschevar, L. H. (1983) *Quantity Food Production Planning and Management*, CBI Books.

General

Longree, K. and Armbruster, G. (1987) *Quantity Food Sanitation*, USA: Wiley.
Sprenger, R. A. (1988) *Hygiene for Management, 3rd edn*, Highfields, Leeds.

Index